Plateau Indians and t  *700–1850*

Plateau Indians and the Quest for Spiritual Power, 1700–1850

LARRY CEBULA

University of Nebraska Press
Lincoln and London

© 2003 by the Board of Regents of the University of Nebraska

Manufactured in the United States of America

⊗

Library of Congress Cataloging-in-Publication Data

Cebula, Larry, 1961–

Plateau Indians and the quest for spiritual power, 1700–1850 / Larry Cebula.

p. cm.

Includes bibliographical references (p.) and index.

ISBN 0-8032-1521-5 (cloth: alk.paper)

ISBN 978-0-8032-2243-4 (paper: alk.paper)

1. Indians of North America—Columbia Plateau—Religion.

2. Indians of North America—Missions—Columbia Plateau.

3. Columbia Plateau—History.   I. Title.

E78.C617 C43 2003

200'.89'970797–dc21

2002032483

To my wife, Renee, and my mother, Marian

Contents

Illustrations

Figures

Maps

Acknowledgments

None of us work alone. In a very real sense, this book is the work of dozens of people who offered me advice, friendship, love, and support. I am most grateful to my wife, Renee. Her love—and her occasional gentle admonishments—have been indispensable. I also want to thank my children. Mac, Rachael, and Sam often brought me out of the office and reminded me what is really important in life.

James Axtell's comments on each draft have been encouraging, incisive, and exhaustive. His own scholarship has served as a model of deep research, careful thought, and graceful writing. James Ronda had wonderful comments and corrections for many of the chapters. Carroll Sheriff and James Whittenberg insisted that I explain my methods to those who do not practice ethnohistory. Their advice improved the quality of this work.

My colleagues at Missouri Southern State College have been more than supportive. Tom Simpson, Virginia Laas, James Geier, Paul Teverow, Bill Tannenbaum, Paul Kaldjian, Steve Wagner, Penny Honeycutt, Cindi Spencer, and Robert Markman in particular offered friendship, advice, and sometimes cold beer. I also want to thank my department chair, Richard Miller, and the administration for helpfully pointing out that they would in fact fire me if I did not finish this project. This proved motivating.

Many of my friends and colleagues at Eastern Washington University deserve special thanks. J. William T. Youngs has been a friend and mentor for so long that I can hardly recall a scholarly life without him. Claude Nichols helped spark my interest in western history in the first place. Archivist Charlie Mutschler retrieved many hundreds of books and manuscripts for me over the years and offered much encouragement. John Alan Ross brought his terrific knowledge of traditional Plateau life to a close reading of the first chapter. Bruce Hallmark served as a patient and critical sounding board for many of my ideas and shared his research on disease epidemics with me.

Virginia Adsit offered all sorts of administrative support. I especially want to thank Mike Green and Dick Donley, who taught me the fine points of historical analysis and the rudiments of elk hunting. I hope that in these pages I have proven better at the former than I was at the latter.

Plateau Indians and the Quest for Spiritual Power, 1700–1850

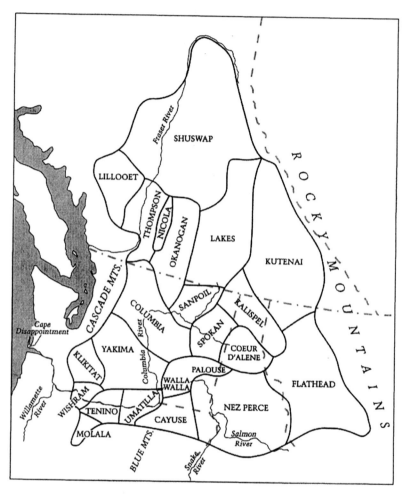

Map 1. Location of Plateau Indian peoples at the time of white contact. Traditionally, Plateau Indian political organization was at the village level, with several villages sometimes coming together to form a band. The ethnic groups shown here became tribes only after the arrival of the horse in the 1700s.

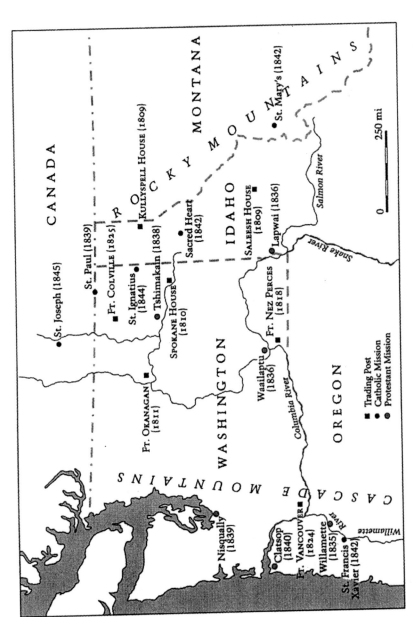

Map 2. Fur trading posts and missions to 1850.

Introduction

Joe Meek knew how to hang an Indian. The recently appointed marshal of Oregon knew as much about the natives as any man in the
territory. As a mountain man, he had lived among Indians for most of
his adult life. Meek traded with Indians, played their games, shared
their prayers, wintered in their lodges, and had taken not one but two
native wives. He had killed Indians as well—sometimes as a member
of a native war party, sometimes in self-defense, and sometimes for
the fun and frivolity of killing. But as the fur trade faded in the 1840s,
Meek abandoned the free life of the mountains and moved to the
Willamette Valley to try his hand at farming. When the burgeoning
American settlement there needed a law officer, Meek was only too
glad to exchange his plow for a badge. As he climbed the gallows that
June day in 1850, Meek was turning his back on his old way of life
and returning to the fold of American civilization.[1]

The Indians knew they would hang. The five Cayuse men who
stood on the gallows had also taken a position on American civilization. Three years earlier, some of them had planted a tomahawk firmly
in the skull of an emissary of the American way of life, the missionary
Marcus Whitman. His wife, Narcissa, and twelve others were murdered as well. Meek tightened the nooses around the men's necks and
checked again the leather cords that bound their hands behind their
backs. The Cayuses had come to Oregon City hoping to tell their stories and to return home, perhaps after presenting the Americans with
some gifts to cover the graves of the dead missionaries. Yet they were
not surprised when the whites instead arrested them and sentenced
them to hang. At the trial they had vainly protested their innocence,
then asked at least to be shot instead of hanged. They "said that they
wouldn't mind being shot," one witness recorded, "but to die by the
rope was to die as a dog and not as a man."[2]

A Jesuit priest, Father Francis Veyret, hovered behind the men,
reciting the Prayer for the Dying. After their trial had ended eight
days earlier, the Indians agreed to take the sacraments of baptism and

confirmation from the priest. And so it was that Tiloukaikt, Tomahas, Ishishkaiskais, Clokamas, and Kiamasumpkin became Andrew,
Peter, John, Paul, and James.[3] As Meek fastened the leather hoods
over the men's heads, Kiamasumpkin begged Meek to kill him with
a knife, but the marshal ignored the request. For the most part, the
Cayuses remained calm—perhaps drawing comfort from the fact that
their relatives had been allowed to depart Oregon City, and that peace
was restored between the Cayuses and the Americans. A few days before, Tiloukaikt had been asked why, if he was innocent, he had put
himself in the hands of the Americans to be tried for Whitman's death?
"Did not you missionaries tell us that Christ died to save his people?"
the chief shot back. "So die we, to save our people."[4] Before the hood
went over his own head, Tomahas expressed the same sentiment in
a low voice addressed to the assembled crowd. "Wawko sixto wah,
wawko sixto wah," he said: "Now friends, now friends."[5]

About a thousand spectators—most of the white population of the
Willamette Valley—watched the ritualized execution drama unfold.
Meek dressed the part of the wild man returning to civilization, clad
in buckskins, with a tomahawk in his belt. Except for Kiamasumpkin, the Indians played the role of savage stoics and waited silently.
The priest said his prayer. Then Meek was supposed to read the sentence from a piece of paper—but the unlettered mountain man instead
merely said, "The Lord have mercy on you," and slashed the drop rope
with his tomahawk.

Tiloukaikt, Tomahas, Ishishkaiskais, Clokamas, and Kiamasumpkin fell toward the earth—and were jerked back. But the construction
of gallows, like many of the civilized arts, was yet in its infancy in the
Oregon Territory. The three-foot drop the platform provided proved
insufficient to break the necks of Tomahas and Clokamas, who strug-
gled and thrashed at the end of their ropes. Meek stepped forward and
savagely kicked Tomahas in the head until he was still. Years later
Meek gave a comic explanation of the event: "I just put my foot on
the knot to tighten it, and he got quiet."[6] The crowd dispersed. The
bodies of the Indian men were carted to the edge of town and buried
all together, hands and feet still bound, leather hoods tied over their
heads. For Oregon, for the Catholic and Protestant missionaries who
had labored among the Northwest tribes, and most of all for the Indians themselves, it was the end of an era.

For the Indians of the Columbia Plateau, the murders of the Whitmans and the hanging of the Cayuse men were a turning point in a
long spiritual journey. Perhaps 150 years before, these natives had first

heard of a different kind of men who had appeared in the East, people with vast spirit power who would remake the native world. Fifty years earlier, the curiously pale and hairy people with their wonderful goods had begun to arrive on the plateau. As the strangers built their forts and trading posts, Indians began to learn about the sources of the white men's manifest spirit power. Fifteen years before the hanging, the Indians had ridden out with joy in their hearts to meet the first Christian missionaries, powerful shamans who would teach the Indians the secrets that would make them as mighty as the whites. Five years earlier, most of the Indians had come to reject the missionary teachings with bitter disappointment. From that point on, the native spiritual journey would carry most Plateau Indians away from the whites, and native religious leaders would promise not assimilation but effective resistance.

This work is a study of that spiritual journey. To the natives of the Columbia Plateau, the arrival of whites was primarily a *spiritual* event. Like many peoples, Plateau Indians looked to their religion to explain what was unfamiliar or confusing. When smallpox struck the native villages, when stories of strange happenings beyond the plateau were told, when people with hair on their faces offered novel goods for beaver skins, the Indians turned to their religion—and their religion often changed as a result. As the status and well-being of many groups eroded during the early contact period, the questions became more urgent and the spiritual changes more momentous. Many Plateau natives came to pin their hopes for renewal on adopting some of the spiritual practices of the whites. But when the missionaries finally arrived, their teachings proved less useful—and less palatable—than anticipated. So the Plateau natives' spiritual journey took a new trajectory, away from white society. In this study I explore how Indians used their religion to understand the intrusion of Euro-American civilization and how that religion was itself changed in the process.

Writing a study like this one is a journey in itself, and one on which I have been guided—and sometimes misled—by monuments erected by previous scholars. These works can be found in the endnotes and bibliography, but a few require special mention. In resurrecting the aboriginal spirit world, as I have tried to do in the first chapter, the descriptive early ethnographies and story collections of pioneering anthropologists like Franz Boas, James Teit, and Archie Phinney were indispensable. By the mid-twentieth century some Plateau Indians were beginning to put their own stories in writing, and I have consulted the works of Allen P. Slickpoo (Nez Perce) and Mourning Dove (Colville) as well. Many of the early fur traders and explorers, such as Lewis and Clark, David Thompson, and Alexander Ross, wrote extensive accounts of Plateau culture, and I have mined these for the colorful descriptions usually lacking in the anthropological tomes.

The second chapter deals with religious change in the protohistoric period. The term *protohistory* usually requires some explaining. Here it means that key interlude that began when the Indians felt the first indirect effects of white contact (about 1700) and ended when the first white people arrived on the plateau to establish permanent posts (in the 1810s). Two generations of Plateau scholars have used Leslie Spier's pioneering 1935 monograph, *The Prophet Dance of the Northwest*, as their lodestar for charting religious change during this period. Spier was the first to describe the Prophet Dance, a protohistoric religious movement that he identified as a traditional part of Plateau culture fueled by new prophecies of the white man's arrival. I accept the existence of a protohistoric religious movement but argue that the causes were more complex than Spier allowed.

Plateau Indians experienced their most sustained, direct contact with white culture during the fur trade era, the mechanics of which are the focus of the third chapter. In recent years historians have done some magnificent work in illuminating the fur trade from the native point of view. But the religious impact of the fur trade, on the plateau as elsewhere, has been largely unexplored.[7] I argue the Indians used the fur trade as a window into white society, incorporating their observations into their own evolving faith. My best sources for this chapter are the published and unpublished writings of the traders.[8]

The fourth chapter examines how Plateau Indians blended the new knowledge and traditional elements into a new faith, the "Columbian Religion." This was a revivalist faith that swept the Plateau on the eve of the mission period. Here again I used the writings of the fur traders, often supplemented by the observations of the first missionaries, who often mistook the Columbian Religion for the Indians' traditional faith.

The bits and pieces of Christian doctrine acquired through the fur trade left many Plateau Indians hungry for more. My final chapter examines the native's response to the arrival of Catholic and Protestant missionaries in the 1830s and 1840s, from initial enthusiasm to violent rejection. This ground has been plowed before, and I do not cut any deep new furrows across the historiographic landscape. There are a host of studies on the Oregon missions, from Clifford Merrill Drury's richly detailed volumes to Jacqueline Petersen's exhibit catalogue *Sacred Encounters*.[9] My only serious quarrel with these works is that they create too much of a dichotomy between the (good)

Catholic and (bad) Protestant missionaries.[10] My thesis is that while Plateau Indians may indeed have preferred the doctrinal flexibility of the Jesuits to the rigid and dour approach of the Protestants, neither set of missionaries made much real progress in converting the Indians before 1850.

The unifying theme of this book is the evolution of an idea—the native belief that the momentous changes under way called for a religious response, and that the faith of the whites held some of the information that the Indians would need. But this did not prove to be the case. The violent rejection of Christianity by the Indians of the plateau ended any hope of peaceful coexistence between the natives and the burgeoning American population. After 1850, Plateau Indians no longer looked to the whites for spiritual answers. A new set of native prophets and leaders arose. These men preached a return to traditional faith and ways and resistance to the American advance. But that, as they say, is another story.

1. *A World of Spirits*

The Old One created the earth, but it was Coyote who made the earth a place where humans might prosper.[1] The Old One shaped the earth from a ball of clay that he set down to float upon the vast oceans.[2] Then he rolled off pieces of the clay into little round balls, from which he fashioned the beings of the ancient world. He shaped the balls into various forms and breathed life into them to create the first animals. The creatures the Old One made were not like the animals we know now. These were the animal-people. Possessed of speech and reason, Bear, Deer, Elk, Beaver, Mosquito, and the other animal-people had great powers. Cunning and often cruel, they wore clothes and lived in lodges the way human people do and made tools and weapons.

Then the Old One made the first human people. They were much like the natives who told these Coyote stories, but they lacked knowledge. They did not have fire and could not cook their food. They had no clothes or shelter because they did not know how to make these things. They had no weapons, and they were hunted by the animal-people who should have been their food instead. Monsters and lightning killed many people as well. These first humans were "the most helpless of all things created."[3]

The Old One saw that without help, all the human people would soon be dead. And so he made Coyote to bring order to the earth. It was Coyote who made things as they are. Coyote traveled back and forth across the plateau making it a fit place for people to live.[4] With trickery and cunning—qualities synonymous with Coyote—he killed the monsters and freed the human people from their bellies. He went to the village of the fire-people and liberated fire, and he taught human people to use it to cook their food and heat their dwellings. Coyote transformed some of the animal-people into harmless game animals and taught men how to hunt them. He planted camas roots and service berries, saying, "Here the people will find them and will be glad."[5] When he came to a village where the people did not know how to have sex, Coyote taught that, too, and the women would not let him leave until he was "thoroughly fatigued."[6]

And it was Coyote who brought salmon to the people of the plateau. Traveling down the Columbia River, Coyote discovered a huge fish weir across the river where two magical sisters were taking all the salmon for themselves. He broke up the weir and transformed the sisters into birds, then he led the salmon upstream to the lands of the various Indian villages. Sometimes he would ask the people to give him a wife. When they granted his request, he would make a good fishing spot for the people. Where he was refused, Coyote created falls and cascades to prevent the salmon from reaching the offending villages.

After a time, Coyote's work was done. The plateau had been made a comfortable home for men and women, and Coyote slunk away into myth and history—in some stories he ascended into the sky.[7] But he did not vanish, he lived on in the sacred and humorous stories of the people who inhabited the land, some of who called themselves the "Coyote People."[8]

The Geography of the Plateau

The people who told these Coyote stories lived on the Columbia Plateau, a distinct geographic region in the interior of northwestern North America. Covering some thirteen thousand square miles in the present Washington, Oregon, Idaho, and British Columbia, this "plateau" is actually a topographic basin, enclosed by the Rocky and Cascade mountain ranges to the east and west and the Great Basin to the south. The mountain ranges wring the moisture from the prevailing winds before they reach the plateau, and the central portions of the region receive fewer than fifteen inches of rainfall a year. Formed by a series of ancient lava flows, the dominant landforms here are low hills with flat tops, covered with bunchgrass and sagebrush. The summers are hot, with temperatures in the nineties, and the winters cold. Great rivers, most notably the Columbia, Fraser, and Snake, cut across the plateau, carving deep canyons. The monotony of the plains is further relieved in those portions of the plateau where the underlying basalt was exposed in a series of cataclysmic floods, creating a distinctively unlovely landscape known as the "channeled scablands."[9]

"Plateau Indians" is an anthropologist's term, a shorthand lumping together of a number of distinct ethnic groups whose beliefs, material culture, and subsistence activities justify the need for a collective noun. Thirty-some ethnic groups are usually grouped under this heading, including the Kutenai, Flathead, Spokan, Coeur d'Alene, Yakima, Cayuse, and Nez Perce Indians. Some of these groups lived on the borders or just outside the boundaries of the geographic region of the plateau, yet the similarities between them are striking. They all depended on salmon from the Columbia and Fraser Rivers for a major part of their diet. All used seasonal movements to exploit food-shifting resources. They were linked by trade, travel, and marriages within the plateau. They shared a common material culture and common religious beliefs and ceremonies. Despite differences in language and ethnicity, the similarities between these groups are great enough to justify considering them as a single culture.[10]

More important, the Plateau Indians themselves recognized their similarities and considered themselves somehow related. The Thompson Indians used the collective term "Coyote's People" for the Plateau groups, and a Walla Walla tale recounts how all the Plateau peoples arose from the parts of giant beaver that Coyote killed and dismembered.[11] The common culture of Plateau Indians was recognized by natives outside the plateau as well, as in the Shoshone term for the Plateau Indians: "salmon eaters."

Estimates of Plateau population before white contact range from fewer than 50,000 to more than 150,000.[12] For most ethnic groups, the first reliable censuses did not take place until the reservation period in the mid-nineteenth century, by which time their numbers had been greatly reduced by a century of wars, famine, and especially epidemic diseases.[13] Working backward from these figures to derive precontact population estimates is a perilous undertaking that necessarily involves a great deal of guesswork. How many times did smallpox strike the plateau before Europeans ever arrived there? How widespread was the disease? What percentage of people died from the disease? To what extent was native fertility able to replace these losses between epidemics? The answers to these questions are unclear, and the cumulative effect is that one plateau population estimate is as good as another.[14]

Human beings probably first arrived on the plateau between ten thousand and fourteen thousand years ago as part of the original peopling of the continent. These first men and women were part of a generalized hunting culture that followed the big game of North America across the continent. The specialized salmon-oriented culture began to develop about two millennia ago, when a long period of high rainfall ended and salmon began to enter the Columbia in huge numbers. By a thousand years ago the Plateau cultures had acquired the material culture they possessed at white contact.[15]

The first impression of any stranger to the Columbia Plateau is the apparent barrenness of the region. "This country looks most unattractive," noted one early visitor, "the hills are bare of vegetation, without a single tree to be seen."[16] Another described the region as "immense plains covered with parched brown grass, swarming with rattlesnakes."[17] A third dismissed the area as "Barren Waste."[18] Meriwether Lewis lamented the scarcity of game animals on the plateau.[19] One early fur trader began a letter to a friend: "I . . . am now in the country of wind and sand and horn and dog flesh."[20]

The plateau is indeed a sparse environment, especially compared to the lush forests of the Pacific Coast or what Lewis called "the fat plains of the Missouri."[21] Plateau Indians did not enjoy the abundant food resources of their coastal neighbors nor the movable buffalo feasts of the Plains. The food resources of the Columbia Plateau offered seasonal feasts, but the people were stalked by periodic famines.[22] There was no single dependable animal food staple, and plant foods could be scarce as well.[23] Roots, berries, salmon, and game animals could be found in great abundance in different places at different times of the year, yet none of these seasonal resources was absolutely dependable. The highlands and mountains that ring the plateau might be sweet with the scent of ripening huckleberries in August, but a late frost could kill the huckleberry blossoms before the fruit ever formed. The camas crop might fluctuate; what had been a patch of camas plants in May might be "parched brown grass" in August. Even the salmon, which composed as much as half the Indian's diet, were available only a few months out of the year.[24] The Columbia River and its tributaries hosted the largest salmon runs on the North American continent. "The quantity of Salmon destroyed here, if put in figures, would exceed the bounds of credibility," exclaimed an observer who watched Walla Walla Indians fishing along the Columbia River at a site known as the Dalles.[25] Another described the shallows of the Walla Walla River as "so full of Salmon that one could hardly cross, without being tripped by them."[26] But these great salmon runs could arrive late or in much smaller numbers than normal.[27]

Winter especially was the lean season, when Plateau Indians tried to supplement their diminishing stores of food with hunting expeditions to the winter hills. When the game animals were depleted or weather conditions did not permit a successful hunt, starvation could soon follow.

Plateau Indians survived in this precarious environment by fashioning a unique culture designed to make the most of what nature had to offer. They adopted a carefully timed seasonal round of movements to exploit each food resource in season. Their system of social organization was simple and flexible, allowing them to work more or less harmoniously in small family bands or large intertribal groupings, as the resources indicated. They practiced a gender system that gave men and women separate and complementary spheres of influence and expertise to further the group's chances for survival. And perhaps most important from their own perspective, they developed a religion that enlisted the aid of powerful supernatural forces.

Harnessing the Spirit World

Plateau Indians had a complex cosmology oriented toward acquiring and using spiritual power. All unusual, impressive, and significant events were explained in terms of spirit power, and native stories are replete with miraculous events caused by the spiritually powerful. Circling Raven, a famed Coeur d'Alene leader, once used his spirit power to bring on a warm Chinook wind to clear a snowbound winter pass in the Rocky Mountains.[28] Sanpoil salmon chiefs could affect the quantity and quality of a salmon run by calling on their power.[29] A chief with strong spirit power was recognized by other groups, even outside the Plateau. In 1823 a Blackfoot hunting party accused the Flathead chief Cut Thumb of having "with your spells and incantations . . . cast sickness into our camp: our children gasp for breath, our very horses are less fleet than was their wont, solely owing to your strong medicines."[30] A shaman with sufficient power could even raise the dead.[31]

Most Plateau peoples believed in a Creator, variously known as the Old One, Ancient One, Father Mystery, or Old Chief.[32] As in many aboriginal North American faiths, he was thought to have created the world but then withdrawn to some distant place; he did not loom large in Plateau consciousness.[33] "This Old Chief they think [of as] Good & asking nothing from them; I never heard that they made any sacrifices or any ceremonies to conciliate his good will," wrote a Hudson's Bay Company trader.[34] The Old One was not worshipped or prayed to and played little part in day-to-day spiritual practices.

More important were the numerous spirits who inhabited the Plateau, of which there were several types. Human beings had spirits, but so did animals, plants, trees, rocks, natural phenomena such as the wind, and monsters. Even some man-made objects, such as sweat lodges, possessed spirits. These spirits were intelligent and self-aware, a kind of nonhuman person. Some were powerful, others weak. Some spirits took little notice of the human inhabitants of the plateau, but others were closely involved in human affairs. In a land of precarious subsistence, individuals' relationships with these spirits determined the quality of their lives and insured their survival. Establishing and maintaining good relationships with the spirit world was the heart of Plateau religion.

The key to good life was to obtain a powerful tutelary spirit as a personal guardian. A guardian spirit was usually acquired in childhood or early adolescence. Animal spirits such as Bear, Elk, and Beaver could serve as guardian spirits, as could such diverse spirits as Wind, Clouds, Sun, Moon, Stars, Lightning, Spring Flood, Mountains, Trees, and Sweat Lodge.[35] Such spirits could be powerful or weak, benevolent or malevolent. Some of the powers that might be gained from a spirit included root digging, hunting, warring, curing, and gambling. Specific spirits were often associated with defined powers. Deer made one a good runner, for example, and Wolf helped its possessor become a great hunter.[36] Some spirits were extremely undesirable. Rattlesnake encouraged its possessor to kill others via sorcery, and Crow rendered a person prone to stealing. Powerful spirits might give different parts of their power to different individuals. Charging Buffalo might make one man brave, while Wounded Buffalo gave another curative powers.[37] The sources of some spirits and the powers they gave could be surprising. One Sanpoil shaman's guardian spirit was a rotting horse he found beside a lake,[38] and a Cayuse warrior gained great prowess from his guardian, Hazelnut.[39]

Guardian spirits might be acquired by chance or through a vision quest. Whenever a young person was alone there was a possibility he or she might meet with a guardian spirit. Lasso Stasso, a Kutenai man, recalled that he acquired his guardian this way: "I had gone into the mountains with my dog. We were walking along, and were passing a stream . . . when I saw a bear swimming in the water. I was going to run away as I was scared, but he told me, 'You stop, I want to talk to you.' He told me he would make me smart. . . . he made me a medicine man. . . . Bear talked to me just this once. He gave me songs and power, but he never came to see me again."[40]

Stasso was fortunate, for rarely was such a desirable guardian spirit acquired by chance. Weak or malevolent spirits, eager to be taken as guardians, waited for exactly such an opportunity to seize a young person. This was especially likely to happen if the young person was lost, scared, or angry. An evil guardian was worse than none at all, since once a malevolent spirit was established it could only be removed at the risk of the child's life.[41] So Indian youths were encouraged to look for guardians by going on a vision quest, a controlled search for a suitable spirit who would assure its recipient of a comfortable life.

Children were prepared at a young age for the vision quest. Physical toughness and spiritual purity were essential, and training for both was rigorous. Sanpoil children were roused at dawn each day, all year long, for a bracing swim in the Columbia River.[42] The purpose was less cleanliness than hardihood; they were being prepared to bear the physical discomfort of the quest. Hot sweat baths and cold plunge baths were also important. Children were encouraged to take emetics to purify the body and to suppress emotions such as anger, sullenness, and jealousy, which might attract an undesirable guardian spirit.[43]

Somewhere between the age of five and ten for boys, seven and ten for girls, Plateau children were ready to seek their guardian spirits. Elders supervised the quest, telling the children what to expect and what to avoid. Theoretically, there was little or no human control possible over what guardian spirit might be obtained on a quest, but in practice certain spirits were actively sought. Someone hoping for Grizzly Bear as a guardian might carry a bundle of items sacred to that spirit, sing power songs associated with it, or draw icons in the dirt meant to portray Grizzly Bear.[44]

Children sought their guardian by isolation and fasting, sometimes going naked as well.[45] Such a quest could last from a few days to more than a week, during which the child sang and prayed for a visitation. The child's suffering was meant to excite the pity of the spirits so that one would consent to become his or her guardian. Seekers might address the spirits aloud: "O you who are the most beautiful, the greatest, the strongest of all the children of the forest, take pity on an unfortunate one who has recourse to you."[46] Seekers were supposed to keep still but not to fall asleep. Some places—mountaintops, notable rock formations, certain trees—were thought to be places of power where a guardian spirit was especially likely to be encountered. The first quest was often unsuccessful; children might be sent out several times before they met success.[47]

Pity was a key concept in the relationship between Indians and the spirit world. In the Plateau ethical system, the powerful were expected to help the powerless.[48] Thus to feel pity for someone was to be obliged to render whatever assistance was possible. It was pity for the suffering of the human people that made the Old One send Coyote to remake the world. It was out of pity that a spirit agreed to become a guardian spirit for some naked, hungry child. Similarly, on the annual subsistence round the leaders of different task groups called on their own spirits and the spirits of the food resource they were seeking, asking the spirits to pity them and aid their quest. "Please, sheep, go your usual way, and follow each other, so that we may eat your flesh and thus increase or lengthen our breath!" The leader of an Okanagon hunting party chanted, "Pity us, and be driven easily down to the place where we shall shoot you!"[49] Such appeals were not easily ignored, and Plateau myths were full of instances where those who failed to pity the less fortunate found themselves punished by powerful spirits.

The first clue that a guardian spirit was approaching was often when the child heard its sacred song. Acquiring this song was perhaps the most important part of the quest, and the seeker tried to listen closely. The Plateau Indians were an oral people to whom spoken words were as immanent and real as physical objects, and to ritually collect the words that made a song was to capture a powerful object indeed. Then the spirit appeared before the child, arrayed in distinctive clothing and with special body paints. These too were noted, for the recipient dressed and painted him- or herself in the same fashion to exercise the power of the guardian. The spirit might appear in the form of a man, only revealing its true identity as it departed.[50]

The guardian spirit spoke, telling the young person that it had taken pity upon him or her and would be his or her guardian. The spirit described the powers that were granted and what to put in the associated sacred bundle or medicine bag. A sacred dance was sometimes taught as well.[51] The spirit usually listed a set of taboos the recipient must obey, at the risk of losing the power. A woman given Salmon as her guardian spirit might be required not to touch live salmon, for example. A man visited by Black Bear might be allowed to hunt such bears but had to promise not to kill the cubs.[52]

After being visited by the guardian spirit, a child returned to the village in a daze. On many parts of the Plateau, the child forgot the whole visitation and only remembered it years later at the winter spirit dances. In other groups children remembered the visit and described it in detail to the supervising shamans or elders, who helped interpret the experience.[53]

Some Indians had more spirit power than others. Those with the most power of all became shamans. A shaman was anyone with a truly exceptional degree of spiritual power. The power of a shaman was not a different kind from that of other people, only greater in degree.[54] Shamanic power came from multiple guardian spirits, or an unusually strong guardian, especially astronomical bodies such as the sun and moon.[55] Shamans had numerous powers: they could see into the future and control the weather, locate lost or stolen objects, and organize seasonal religious ceremonies.[56]

A shaman's most important duty was to cure sickness. Plateau peoples believed that sickness could come about in four ways. The first was by physical trauma, such as a fall from a horse or an arrow wound. Illness could also be caused by intrusion, when a foreign object or spirit was magically inserted into a person's body; a malignant shaman might cause such a sickness. A third cause of sickness was the loss of one's guardian spirit. A spirit could be stolen by a sorcerer, desert its owner because of mistreatment and the neglect of taboos, or simply wander away and become lost. The fourth and most serious cause of sickness was loss of the soul. This was signaled by a loss of consciousness and could soon result in death.[57]

Mild illnesses of the first sort could often be cured with herbal remedies and the sweat lodge, but any more serious sickness required the use of spirit power. Relatives of the afflicted person summoned a shaman to help with a spiritual cure. A curing ceremony often involved singing and the beating of sticks by spectators while the shaman worked on the patient. Shamans chanted, poked and prodded the patient, sometimes bending over to suck the sickness out of a person's body. "Their method of cure [is] harmless enough," wrote a Hudson's Bay Company trader: "Singing beating time on a Pole with a stick, now and then Hallowing also using Antic gestures with a . . . half laugh half serious kind of expression about the mouth . . . calculated to amuse the patient."[58] The process could go on for many days, until the patient either regained health or died. Very often the healing ceremony was effective. "With all this absurdity, many extraordinary cures are performed by these people," admitted a European observer. "[T]heir skill is really astonishing."[59]

Shamans could not only cure illness but cause it. Spirit power was neither good nor bad of its own; it was a tool that could be used for either. Pierre Jean De Smet noted that a Coeur d'Alene Indian "believes he can ask everything of his manitou [guardian spirit], reasonable or unreasonable, good or bad."[60] A shaman with sufficient power to cure illness could also kill—a situation that made shamans both respected and feared. "All classes avoid, as much as possible, giving them offence," noted Alexander Ross of the Sinkaietk shamans, "from a belief that they have the power of throwing, as they express it, their bad medicine at them, whether far or near, present or absent."[61] Among the Colvilles, some shamans had greater influence than the chief.[62]

Gender Roles

Women and men had specific, highly defined roles in Plateau society. Just as a close relationship with the spirit world helped provide the margin of survival in the sometimes harsh environment of the plateau, the strict gender system allowed women and men to work together to make the most of the slender resources of their home. Among the features of the Plateau gender system were a gender-specific system of labor, a political organization that honored the advice and experience of both sexes, rough sexual equality, and a religious system that tapped the spirit power of every individual. By maximizing the productive potential of women and men, this system modified the seasonal booms and busts of the plateau.

In the Plateau world most tasks were either men's work or women's work. This was especially true of subsistence activities. "The Women never engage in Fishing or Hunting," observed one fur trader, "[n]or do the Men ever dig a root for general."[63] Women collected most of the vegetable food, dried the surplus meat and fish, tanned animal skins, made the family's clothing, and provided primary care for the young children. Men fished and hunted, went to war, made their own tools and weapons, cut and worked trees into dugout canoes and other objects, and built the houses. Skilled crafts such as stonework were often performed by men who were too old for the hunt.[64]

As important as the roles assigned to each sex was the social equality that existed between them.[65] Early explorers were often struck by the high status of Plateau women, contrasting it with the situation in other parts of native North America. William Clark noted that the Nez Perce "treat their women with more respect than the nativs on the Missouri."[66] Another visitor speculated that it was a Plateau woman's ability to divorce her husband "which places the two sexes much more on a par than among the tribes west of the mountains."[67]

More likely it was the Plateau pattern of subsistence that promoted sexual equality. Foraging economies like that of the Plateau tend naturally toward egalitarian social relations.[68] On the Plateau this tendency was reinforced by women's disproportionate economic role in providing most of a family's food. A Hudson's Bay Company official noted that Carrier women enjoyed a high social status because "the labour of the women contributes as much to the support of the community as that of the men."[69] Fur trader Ross Cox also deciphered this relationship: "The treatment of the women differs materially among the various tribes. Where food is principally obtained by the exertions of the men . . . the women are condemned to great drudgery. . . . However, where their [women's] exertions in collecting . . . roots contribute to the general support, they assume an air of liberty and independence quite unknown [elsewhere] . . . and in all cases of importance the elderly women equally with the men are consulted."[70]

This sexual equality is seen in the Plateau institution of marriage. Men usually initiated a courtship, and marriages were sometimes arranged by the parents of the prospective partners. But a Plateau woman was always free to turn down a suitor. Among the Spokans, it might be the woman who proposed marriage.[71] Polygyny was known—a chief once observed to fur trader Alexander Henry that "all great men should have a plurality of wives"—but was mostly confined largely to those of the highest social status, chiefs and powerful shamans.[72] An unsatisfactory marriage could usually be terminated by either party.[73] A Protestant missionary noted that divorce "brings no disgrace upon the woman's character, and generally she is soon married to another, and often as advantageously."[74] In the case of separation, a woman kept all the family's food, mats, household goods, and prepared skins; the man left with only his weapons and the clothes on his back.[75] "A passionate woman . . . always could drive the man away," according to one missionary, "for she could always tell him I don't need thee."[76]

Within the family unit, women and men had their separate tasks but women had greater authority. A Colville woman wrote that among her people the woman of the house was "the supreme head of the family, ruling her husband, son, daughter-in-law and grandchildren when they arrived."[77] One fur trader went so far as to claim that favorite wives "have a complete ascendancy over their husbands."[78] Women's household authority is best illustrated by the ownership of food. No matter who had originally obtained it, any food entering the household became the wife's exclusive property, and husbands needed permission to take so much as a piece of dried salmon from the family larder.[79]

In political matters, men had the greater role but women were still important and respected. Chiefs were almost always men—though there are instances of female chiefs. The wife of a chief might act in her husband's place when he was away or in the event of his death. Women commonly spoke before the village councils, and "in their national harangues, they often display great energy of mind, inspire confidence, and frequently give a strong impulse to opinion."[80]

In some groups, highly respected women were recognized as *sku'-malt*, meaning "women of great authority." *Sku'malt* had judicial and advisory functions and helped settle disputes. *Sku'malt* were elected by the council, and the qualifications for the position were similar to those of a chief: intelligence, wisdom, and the right kind of spirit power. *Sku'malt* were among the most respected members of the village and often led the first root-gathering expedition of the spring.[81]

Finally, women and men partook equally of the spirit power of the Plateau. Girls went on spirit quests just as boys did, but could also be visited by guardian spirits while isolated during their menses.[82] Women's powers were often specific to women's tasks—root digging, for example—but this was not always the case. Women sometimes acquired hunting, fishing, or war powers.[83] In the early nineteenth century when an Okanagon hunting party was unable to locate any game, leadership of the party was given to a Thompson woman who had Mountain Sheep as one of her guardians, and she led the party to great success.[84] A woman might even gain enough power from her guardian to be recognized as a shaman. Though female shamans were less common than male shamans, they were no less powerful and fulfilled the same functions.[85]

Menstruating women had special powers. "In this state," Meriwether Lewis observed of the Walla Wallas, "the female is not permitted to eat, nor to touch any article of a culinary nature or manly occupation."[86] Such women were thought to have a superabundance of uncontrolled spirit power that rendered them dangerous. Menstruating women—and more specifically, their menstrual blood—were avoided by men for fear that the men's own powers would be weakened by any contact.[87] It was especially important that menstruating women not touch any hunting or fishing implements.[88] During the salmon run women were prohibited from taking water from streams where fish traps were located or even walking on trails that led to those traps.[89] So dangerous were menstrual women that they were confined to a separate menstrual hut on the outskirts of the village for the duration of their menses. "The men are not permitted to approach this lodge within a certain distance," noted Lewis, "and if they have anything to convey to the occupants of this little hospital they stand at a distance of 50 or 60 paces and throw it towards them as far as they can and retire."[90]

Social Organization

In contrast with the strict gender roles, other aspects of Plateau social organization were simple and flexible. Founded on principles of individual autonomy and consent, the social system allowed Plateau people to create whatever type and level of organization and leadership were necessary for shifting groups and tasks. A winter village elected a camp chief to serve as its leader. A multiethnic fishing camp preserved order with the selection of a salmon chief to supervise the fishing and divvy up the catch. Small hunting or gathering parties selected leaders of known experience and relevant spiritual power for these endeavors. In all cases, Plateau leaders ruled by a consensus of opinion. The looseness and flexibility of Plateau government struck many whites as little more than anarchy. "The power of the chiefs amounts to very little and the people do that which is right in their own eyes," complained the Protestant missionary Asa Smith. "They know nothing of the restraints of law, have no idea of penalty, and apparently no idea of justice."[91] In fact, the system was ideally adapted for the shifting circumstances of Plateau life.

The most basic unit of Plateau social organization was the family. As we have seen, women enjoyed high status in Plateau societies and had a strong influence in most family manners. Social conditioning within the family was based on persuasion rather than force. Children might be chastised for bad behavior but rarely were corporally punished. It was feared that too much physical punishment would destroy the personal autonomy Plateau Indians cherished. They agreed with their neighbors the Shoshones "that it cows and breaks the sperit of the boy to whip him, and that he never recovers his independence of mind after he is grown."[92] An exception to this were the punishments doled out in some villages by the "whipping chief," an old man who sometimes spanked recalcitrant children with a bundle of willow sticks. But this was done not so much to modify the child's behavior as to teach him or her to endure pain.[93]

Above the family stood the village. "All of the villages form so many independent sovereignties," wrote an early fur trader, and village autonomy was among the most basic political principles of the Plateau.[94] Winter villages were collections of anywhere from 10 to 150 people who came together every fall on the banks of one of the region's great rivers. Individuals were in no way bound to their villages; they could and did move from one village to another when it suited them.[95]

Each village was governed by a chief, who acted as a leader, councilor, and judge for his people. The power of chiefs "consists solely in their influence," explained the Jesuit missionary Pierre Jean De Smet; "it is great or little in proportion according to the wisdom, benevolence, and courage that they have displayed."[96] Some chiefs were very persuasive and wielded great authority, but others were far less powerful. Factors influencing a chief's authority included his spirit power, generosity, wisdom, and oratory. A chief might use his eloquence to direct some of the village religious ceremonies. "Every Chief is a parson to his tribe," one fur trader noted, "and . . . holds forth to them in real orthodox style."[97] Sons often followed their fathers as village chiefs, but this was subject to approval by the council.[98]

Social control within the village was limited. "Their laws," observed fur trader Alexander Ross, "admit of no compulsion."[99] Those who acted antisocially were pressured to conform through public criticism and ridicule. A Kutenai who frequently started fights, for example, was told by his chief: "If you want to fight, go over the mountains and count coup" against the Blackfoot.[100] Chronically disruptive persons were driven from the village or abandoned, with the villagers taking advantage of seasonal moves to leave troublemakers behind. A murderer was punished by the victim's kin, and a payment of goods might be negotiated between the parties.[101] People who were dissatisfied with the leadership or members of a particular village were free to leave and join another village or to found one of their own, and population shifted constantly between villages.[102]

Even village government was temporary and seasonal. When a village dispersed in the spring, each small group chose its own leaders according to the task at hand. A hunting party chose as its leader a man of known hunting prowess, probably one whose guardian spirit gave him special hunting power. Women digging camas or collecting berries were guided by a woman whose guardians showed her the location of these things. Men and women could choose to follow established leaders on these tasks or could go on their own.

Every communal subsistence activity had a recognized chief. The Kutenai Deer Chief was typical of these seasonal chiefs. The best and most experienced hunter in each band was chosen for this temporary office. The Deer Chief decided when and where to hunt and supervised the distribution of meat if the hunt was successful. The Kutenai also recognized a Fish Chief and a Duck Chief for these important food sources.[103]

The most important of the seasonal subsistence leaders was the *see-pays*, or Salmon Chief.[104] The Salmon Chief combined civil and religious functions. He decided when the fishing began, parceled out the choice fishing spots, resolved disputes in the camp, and divided the catch among the assembled participants, who would then redistribute the food to their kin. The Salmon Chief organized the First Salmon ceremony, welcoming the returning fish. He also made certain that the numerous taboos governing the salmon fishery were observed. A visitor at Kettle Falls noted that "deep attention" was paid to such taboos.[105] The Salmon Chief ensured that no part of the gutted salmon were returned to the river, for this would show disrespect for the remaining fish. Women were kept well away from the traps, for fear a menstruating woman might offend the salmon. If any of these taboos were violated, or if the salmon were late or sparse, the Salmon Chief called upon his guardian spirit to set things right.[106]

The principle of individual autonomy extended even to warfare. Before the Sinkaietks went to war, they took sweat baths to purify themselves and held a council. After hearing the arguments for and against warfare, "every one judges for himself, and either goes or stays as he thinks proper."[107] As in other endeavors, however, social pressure could be applied to the recalcitrant. The war chief organized a dance, which "answers every purpose of a recruiting service." The whole village was invited to attend the dance, which was "carried on with much spirit and shouting." But it was understood that any man who entered the dance thereby agreed to join the war party and to obey the commands of the war chief.[108]

In some parts of the Plateau, villages were very loosely organized into bands of two or three that would come together for joint subsistence activities or warfare.[109] The band name was taken from the most prominent village, and the band was governed by a council composed of the chiefs and prominent men and women from each village. These bands have been described as embryonic tribes and served as the basis for tribal organization after the arrival of the horse.[110]

Tribal organization did not exist on the Plateau before white contact. Many of the tribal names in use today are actually the names of villages that were applied to similar people by the first white traders on the plateau. Others represent realignments and consolidations growing out of the depopulation of the historic period. But if there were no tribes, that is not to say that no larger ethnic, social, or linguistic groups existed. People speaking the same dialect or extensively intermarried made up a self-aware ethnic unit like the Nez Perce or Spokans. This common ethnicity was reinforced by cooperative use of resources and by frequent visits between villages during the winter ceremonial season, but these groups lacked any shared political structure.[111]

The Seasonal Round

The rhythm of Plateau life was defined by the seasonal round, the carefully timed series of movements by which the Indians traveled from one food resource to the next. The seasonal round was not nomadic wandering. Plateau Indians traveled between known destinations on a yearly cycle, and the same families were usually found at their regular camas patch or fishing site at the same time each year. Indians used their knowledge and experience as well as their spirit power to direct the timing and direction of their seasonal moves.

In March, "the time the buttercups bloom," people prepared to leave their winter villages.[112] Mat houses were disassembled and cached to be reused the next year. The people of the village divided into smaller groups of four or five families and went to find the spring foods that were becoming available on the prairies. Those too old or too ill to follow remained at the site of the winter camp to guard the caches.[113]

Women worked the hardest in the spring. "Their great and principal Employment is digging Roots & gathering berries," wrote a Hudson's Bay Company trader, characterizing the work as "very laborious."[114] Groups of women left camp at dawn each morning to go to the places where edible roots abounded, with their children in tow. Men were forbidden to dig roots or to touch a woman's digging stick. The female leader of each group might call on her guardian spirit to help her locate the best places to dig; Groundhog was one spirit who conferred this power.[115]

The women harvested many species of plant food during the year—camas, bitterroot, wild onion, service berries, huckleberries—over fifty types in all.[116] Camas, by far the most important plant food, grew in great abundance in many parts of the plateau. In 1855 Isaac Ingalls Stevens observed a party of six hundred Nez Perce (with two thousand horses) camped near a camas field "so abundant . . . that it requires simply four days' labor for them to gather sufficient for their year's use."[117] In May 1806 Meriwether Lewis noted that "a great portion" of the Nez Perce "are now distributed in small vilages . . . collecting the quawmash [camas] and cows [cous, another edible root]; the salmon not yet having arrived to call them to the river."[118] Camas was not only a staple but an important status food. William Clark noted that "the nativs are extreemly fond of this root, and present it [to] their visiters as a great treat."[119]

Each woman could dig as much as a bushel of camas a day.[120] The roots were baked in large underground pits and could be eaten immediately or formed into cakes and dried in the sun. These cakes—"of brown color with a texture like new cheese but more glutinous, with a sweet and agreeable taste"—were popular trade items.[121]

As spring moved to summer, Indians began to move back to the rivers, waiting for word of the first arrival of the salmon. Popular fishing sites such as the Dalles or Kettle Falls became huge intertribal gatherings, drawing Indians from hundreds of miles away. The fishing camps were a scene of trade and socializing as well as work. "Gambling, dancing, horse racing, and frolicking, in all its varied forms, are continued without intermission," wrote a white visitor to one such camp.[122]

Men were the busiest at the onset of the fishing season, constructing weirs, scaffolding, and fishing gear. Fish were speared, caught in nets, trapped in weirs, or scooped up in large baskets beneath waterfalls. Plateau Indians consumed an estimated four hundred to eight hundred pounds of salmon per person each year.[123] Not only was dried salmon a food and trade item, the oily fish even served as fuel on the treeless potions of the plateau. The scale of the salmon fishery was enormous: the salmon ascended the river "in one continuous body . . . more resembling a flock of birds than anything else."[124] A visitor to Spokane Falls estimated that she saw a thousand Indians fishing at one time, taking several hundred salmon a day, each weighing between ten and forty pounds.[125]

Once the salmon were pulled from the river, the women took charge, cleaning the fish, splitting them open, and laying them out to dry on wooden racks. Women also made fishnets and collected berries while the salmon were running.[126] The dried fish were cached along the rivers for use during winter.[127]

As autumn approached and the salmon runs tapered off, the fishing camps broke up into smaller groups. Some stayed along the river to pursue the last of the salmon run, but most traveled to the mountains for fall hunting expeditions. Though hunting was the province of the men, women often traveled with the hunting parties to dry the meat and care for the skins. Deer, antelope, mountain sheep, and bear were among the game animals pursued in the fall. Deer were especially important, not only for their meat but for their hides, the primary source of clothing. The Deer Chief directed the hunt and the distribution of the meat.[128] The favored hunting method was the surround, in which a large number of armed hunters formed a tightening circle in the forest, leaving the animals no escape. Deer were also caught in traps and snares and driven into box canyons.[129]

By October, the month the Kutenais knew as "Leaves Fall Off," the winter villages were reopened.[130] Winter was the quiet season. Men and women slept, told stories, and gambled. Men made stone weapons and tools and occasionally went hunting. Women made clothing and domestic items. The Sanpoils had descriptive names for the winter months December, January, and February: "Time That It Snows," "Time That It Gets Cold," and "Time That It Is White."[131]

Winter was also the ceremonial season, when people confirmed and renewed their all-important connections to the spirit world. From December to February, winter dances were held. The spirits were thought to be closer in the winter, and natives reflected on their relationships with their guardians. This was also the time of the winter dance, by far the most important ceremonial event of the year.[132]

At the winter dance, new recipients of guardian spirit power were recognized and celebrated by the community. Participants danced their spirit dances and sang their spirit songs, people with related spirits dancing together. Recipients were usually prohibited from naming their guardian directly, but it was easy enough to guess what animal a given dancer was imitating. In addition, the spirits were known to be very close at hand during the winter dance, and visions were common.[133] The winter dances also featured shamanic performances, power contests between rival shamans, and much feasting and giving of gifts. The dances usually lasted three or four days.

The winter dances served a number of important functions. They enabled the village to take stock of its collective spirit power and to note who might prove useful in different tasks in the coming year. It was at the winter dance that many individuals first remembered the details of their spirit quest years before and recognized their guardian spirit. In their songs the dancers made known the needs of the community to the spirit world. These songs might contain specific requests, such as for a break in the winter weather. The visits between villages at this important season were important for ritual diplomacy and allowed neighboring groups to work out old disagreements and to plan communal activities for the coming year.[134]

The last of the winter dances were over by January or February, and Plateau natives began to look forward to spring. This was the lean time of year. By March much of the stored camas cakes, dried salmon, and smoked meat was gone. If the salmon run had been shorter than usual or if the winter was long, famine became a real possibility. Indians sought to supplement their dwindling stock of provisions by hunting. But a winter hunt was a doubtful business on the plateau; much depended on the weather and the condition of the snow. Explorer David Thompson noted that although antelopes were present on the plateau "in sufficient numbers" to serve as a food source, the hunting was "precarious": "When the ground is soft with rain . . .

they are easily approached, but sometimes the ground is white with snow and a slight frost, the tread of the hunter is heard, and approach is almost impossible."[135] A thick blanket of soft snow made it easier to track game animals, but plateau weather was unpredictable. A trader at Colville House in 1821 wrote that his hunters had been unsuccessful due to the "mildness of the season," since it was only possible to approach animals in "Boisterous Weather."[136] When the winter hunt failed, hunger was imminent.

The early-nineteenth-century travelers on the plateau seldom failed to mention the shortage of food between February and April. In April 1806, Lewis and Clark's sergeant, Patrick Gass, noted that hungry Plateau Indians "are daily coming down" to the coast, presumably to search for food. "There is no game in that part of the country," they told him, adding that "those remaining on the plains are in a starving condition."[137] Hudson's Bay Company trader George Simpson noted that "towards Spring," Plateau natives were sometimes "reduced to the greatest distress by Starvation, and many perish annually from this cause."[138] Another fur trader passing through Kettle Falls one April met a family of Indians "thin and gaunt," so weakened by starvation that they were "scarcely able to move."[139]

Late winter was the time to turn to famine foods. The black moss that hangs from pine trees was collected and "form[ed] into a kind of black cake,"[140] which one fur trader thought tasted "like soap."[141] The bones of game and salmon eaten earlier in the winter were collected and boiled down for soup stock, and pieces of animal hide and salmon skins were crisped over the fire and eaten.[142] Plateau Indians found that the inner bark of certain species of pine trees could sustain life, and the scarred trees from this practice are still visible in places today.[143] And men and women would call on their spirit power to find food or to hurry the spring.[144] When the first shoots of spring plants began to appear on the south-facing riverbanks, the people prepared to leave their winter villages and begin another seasonal round.

Through centuries of adaptation and innovation, Plateau peoples fashioned a complex culture that enabled them to survive and sometimes prosper on the Columbia Plateau, providing the best possible life in an uncertain environment. The seasonal round enabled the Indians to exploit each food resource in turn. The minimal and flexible system of social organization was tailored to these seasonal movements and allowed natives to function smoothly in groups as small as a single family or as large as a multiethnic fishing village of thousands. The Plateau gender system allowed men and women to direct their energies in different, complementary pursuits, and allowed each sex equal access to the spiritual power needed to make these pursuits successful.

But to the natives themselves, it was their religion that ensured their survival and well-being. By maintaining harmonious relationships with the powerful unseen spirits of the Plateau, Indians could find food, cure disease, change the weather, and see into the future. "They attribute all for themselves," wrote a Hudson's Bay Company trader who tried to understand the native faith, "the spring to make the Roots sprout summer to make the Salmon come & Winter for snow to see the tracks of Animals better."[145] Good relations with the spirit world guaranteed the continued survival of Plateau peoples. "The Indian mode of living is very precarious, and yet they are seldom anxious about the future," noted a perplexed missionary.[146] Plateau Indians lived in a world of spirits, and all their activities depended on spiritual power. All came together in a finely calibrated way of life that lasted for thousands of years.

But that way of life was not static; these were not a people without history. The picture of "traditional" Plateau life we have just limned is but an ethnographic snapshot, a moment artificially frozen in time. Before contact with white people, Plateau Indians had complex and changing histories. Wars were fought, inventions made, beliefs and customs evolved and differed, new stories were told and old ones forgotten. Some of this history can be glimpsed—in the debris caught on an archeologist's screen, in tenuous scraps of oral history, and in maps of native languages and customs, we find hazy outlines of historical change before white influence. But much of it is lost, obscured and forgotten in the tumult of the era that was about to begin.

2. *Change in the Protohistoric Era*

"We . . . [are] about to penetrate a country at least two thousand miles in width, on which the foot of civilized man . . . [has] never trodden." So wrote a contemplative Meriwether Lewis as the rain beat against the buffalo skins of his tent. It was the seventh of April 1805 and the Corps of Discovery was preparing to forsake its comfortable winter camp at Fort Mandan for the unknown reaches of the Northwest interior. Whether they would meet with "good or evil" along the way, Lewis reflected, "was for experiment to determine."[1]

As the first whites to cross this section of the "Stony Mountains" and enter the Columbia Plateau, Meriwether Lewis and William Clark might have reasonably believed that they were about to enter a pristine aboriginal world, a place where the Indians lived as they always had. But the natives of the plateau had already experienced the profoundly disruptive effects of a century of indirect contact with European culture. Horses, epidemic disease, Euro-American trade goods, political realignments, and a steady flow of information had entered the region for nearly a hundred years.

The arrival of the Corps of Discovery in 1805 marked the beginning of the end of the protohistoric era for natives of the Columbia Plateau. This period, "the gap between the time when European influences and effects reached a region and the time when Europeans arrived,"[2] was usually one of wrenching change for native peoples, and has figured large in recent ethnohistorical literature for many regions.[3] Plateau natives embraced their changing world, not only adapting themselves to the influences that reached the plateau, but reaching out for further contact with the world outside. Indians entered a new religious world as well, as news of a strange new kind of person came to their attention. Sometime before the first Europeans entered the plateau, the natives there became aware of the existence of the strangers and prophesied the effects of contact. In the journals of Lewis and Clark and other early visitors to the plateau, we find the outlines of this changing world.[4]

The Equestrian Revolution

On an August day early in the eighteenth century, some Coeur d'Alene Indians saw a remarkable sight. A group of families at a camas digging camp spotted a man approaching, mounted on the back of some strange animal. As the man came closer, they recognized him as a friendly Kalispel and invited him to stop and visit. The Coeur d'Alenes "wondered much" at his mount, a huge animal resembling a moose or elk yet quite unknown. The Kalispel offered to let his friends ride, but though the animal was gentle, only one man was able to stay on its back. After the man and his wondrous animal left, the Coeur d'Alenes sent a trading party to the lands of the Kalispel to acquire some horses for themselves. With these animals the Coeur d'Alenes rode into a new world.[5]

Plateau horses were of Spanish descent. Spanish settlers brought the animals to their New Mexican colonies in the sixteenth century, and by the mid-seventeenth century some southwestern Indians had acquired horses. These supremely useful animals were exchanged northward along aboriginal trade routes, reaching the Shoshones in southern Idaho by 1700. The Cayuses brought the first horses to the plateau about 1710, purchased from their Shoshone neighbors to the south.[6]

Most Plateau Indians were quick to recognize the utility of the horse and adopted its use with enthusiasm. The Cayuses and Nez Perces, whose territory contained some of the best horse country in the Northwest, built up particularly large herds. Lewis and Clark's sergeant, Patrick Gass, marveled at their numbers: "more horses, than I ever before saw in the same space of country."[7] Most Plateau Indians had at least some horses by 1750.

Owning horses changed Plateau life in many ways. Greater mobility expanded the seasonal round. Horses allowed natives to travel greater distances to seek out exceptionally rich sources of food and to bring more food back to the winter village. Interethnic gatherings became larger and more frequent. Fall hunting became a more prominent part of the seasonal round, since mounted hunters could kill more game. For many natives, owning horses meant better nutrition.[8]

Horses also allowed Indians to expand their field of operations beyond the plateau. The greatest attraction to the newly mounted Indians was the rich hunts of the northern Great Plains. Early explorers often commented on the contrast between the "fat plains of the Missouri," where buffalo were numerous, and "diet of horsebeef and roots" (and dried salmon) they stomached on the plateau.[9] Plateau Indians were well aware of the difference, and even before the horse, Nez Perce, Flathead, and Kutenai Indians would sometimes travel over the Rocky Mountains to become nomadic hunters for a year or two, returning to the plateau when the buffalo became scarce or the hunters homesick.[10] Such excursions had a negligible impact on Plateau subsistence, since the hunters could bring little back from the plains beyond a few buffalo robes or some dried meat.

Horses allowed the Nez Perces, Flatheads, Cayuses, and others to incorporate a fall buffalo hunt into the seasonal round. Mounted on horseback, even Indians from the most distant portions of the plateau could reach the buffalo plains in less than a month.[11] Men hunted and women dried the meat and processed the hides and horns. Buffalo hunting expeditions became huge interethnic events, in some ways comparable to the communal fishing camps. In 1824 Alexander Ross reported meeting a buffalo hunting party consisting of forty-two lodges of Flatheads, thirty-six of Kutenais, thirty-four Kalispels, twelve Nez Perces, and four Spokans—over eight hundred people, accompanied by eighteen hundred horses.[12] These trips to the buffalo country were not only economically profitable, they were a grand adventure. "The children would leave as children, but they'd come back as grown ups," explained one Coeur d'Alene elder of the annual journeys.[13]

Horses were not only a means to wealth, the animals themselves became an important source of status for Plateau peoples. As the animals proliferated on the southern plateau, some Indians began to acquire herds of horses far beyond any notion of utility, with some prominent chiefs owning herds of over a thousand animals. As a visible sign of the owner's wealth, these herds reflected the possessor's spirit power as well. The ownership of large numbers of horses gave chiefs a ready source of wealth to draw upon to show the generosity that was expected of Plateau leaders. Horses were also incorporated into the spirit world, becoming an important grave good for prominent individuals.

The equestrian revolution prompted changes in leadership. Especially on the eastern plateau, where the huge annual buffalo hunts required greater organization, formerly autonomous villages and bands began to join into tribes. The tendency toward tribal formation accelerated in the 1750s as mounted Blackfoot war parties began to penetrate the eastern reaches of the plateau.[14] The three traditional bands of the Flatheads had become a unified tribe with a single winter camp by the late eighteenth century and had begun to form larger political alliances of mutual defense with the neighboring Pend d'Oreilles.[15] Similar developments were taking place on the southern plateau. "Our hearts are great within us," pronounced a Walla Walla man after reviewing the changes of the protohistoric period. "We are *now a nation!*"[16]

The introduction of horses had little impact on Plateau gender relations. Women on the Plateau maintained their high status, in sharp contrast to the experience of native women on the Great Plains, who lost status when those tribes became mounted.[17] On the Plains, possession of the horse caused a wholesale cultural revolution, with some peoples abandoning female-dominated subsistence pursuits such as agriculture and gathering plant foods to pursue the buffalo year round. As women's subsistence roles declined, so did their social status, with a corresponding increase in the institution of polygamy. On the Plateau, however, the horse reinforced existing patterns. Camas and other plant foods obtained by women continued to make up perhaps half the diet. The annual buffalo hunts of some groups replaced traditional fall hunts closer to home, substituting one male-produced commodity for another. Owning horses also decreased the transportation burdens of both sexes and improved overall health.[18]

Plateau peoples adopted horses to different extents. Most affected were the eastern and southern groups such as the Flatheads, Coeur d'Alenes, Nez Perces, and Cayuses. The Cayuses in particular benefited by getting horses early and by owning some of the best grazing land in the Northwest. An early fur trader noted that the Cayuses had gained "great influence" from their huge herds of horses and were "fond of domineering" their neighbors.[19] Most Nez Perces adopted the horse with enthusiasm, but a few bands living in the narrow Snake River drainage lacked enough grazing land to pasture horses and instead maintained their traditional way of life.[20] The Kutenais experienced similar differentiation, splitting into buffalo-oriented "Upper Kutenais" and salmon-oriented "Lower Kutenais."[21] The Coeur d'Alenes became so enthralled with the possibilities of horse ownership that they abandoned their heavily forested homeland and moved onto more open prairies, the better to become equestrians.[22] Even among those peoples who did adopt the horse, the relative numbers varied. The Spokans and Flatheads had relatively few horses compared to their southern neighbors because their land was more heavily forested—and because of the depleting effects of Blackfoot raids.[23] A few groups, such as the Sanpoil and Klamath, either spurned horses or were unable to acquire them.[24]

Most Plateau Indians used the horse to pursue traditional activities more efficiently rather than to change their whole way of life. A more efficient seasonal round and a richer material culture were the immediate effects of the equestrian revolution. But horse ownership also had unintended consequences, some of which would alter the Indians' world immensely.

"We Do Not Fear War"

All along their route through the plateau, the Corps of Discovery saw signs of conflict and warfare. The Flatheads told the explorers that many of their men were away on an expedition against the Shoshones, who had stolen some Flathead horses.[25] Other Flatheads were raiding to the northwest.[26] A Nez Perce man "had round his neck the scalp of an Indian, with six thumbs and four fingers of the other Indians he had killed in battle."[27] Further down the Columbia, one of his Nez Perce guides showed Clark a place where his nation and the Shoshones "had a great battle . . . in which maney were killed on both Sides."[28] Both captains noted that the natives of the middle Columbia located their villages on the north side of the river for protection against Shoshone raids.[29]

Plateau Indians had always known warfare and violence. An Okanagon elder recalled: "When people were traveling through someone else's territory and had the advantage to destroy the people they saw, they did."[30] While it was rare for one village or band to unite against another, feuds between different groups were common. Though such violence was on a small scale, it was nonetheless deadly, as the archeological evidence shows.[31] But the scale of violence greatly increased with the advent of the horse.

Indians were quick to realize that the horse was more than a beast of burden: it was also a military asset. Mounted war parties could strike enemies at a greater distance and carry away more booty. In open country a party of horsemen could easily defeat an equal or even larger number of men on foot. Horses were themselves a valuable—and portable—new spoil of war, and raiding for horses became one of the most celebrated means of proving one's bravery in many parts of native America. The shifting of tribal boundaries brought on by the horse brought previously friendly groups into conflict.[32]

Much of the new warfare took place on the eastern and southern peripheries of the plateau. The northern plains had been a scene of conflict since the late seventeenth century, when the newly mounted Shoshones left the Great Basin to pursue a life of raiding and buffalo hunting.[33] Their raids took them all the way to southern Canada, where they fought with the horseless Blackfoot. The Shoshones got the better of the conflict until the Blackfoot began to acquire guns from tribes to the east. By 1750 the Blackfoot had both firearms and horses and began their own campaign of expansion. They drove the Shoshones south and established their dominance of the northern plains.[34]

It was about this time—the 1750s—that Plateau Indians began their first mounted buffalo expeditions into this contested territory. At first the Plateau natives were able to hold their own against the more numerous and better-armed Plains tribes. They accomplished this by traveling in large, intertribal groupings under military discipline, by employing a great many horses so they could travel quickly and flee if necessary, and by staying on the plains only long enough to partially dry their buffalo meat and hides. But the large herds of horses they employed to carry their meat and hides only made the Plateau camps more tempting targets to the Blackfoot, who were perpetually short of horses. The situation grew worse as the Blackfoot and other Plains Indians began to acquire more guns near the close of the eighteenth century.[35] In 1781 a British fur trader noted that the Blackfoot had so much ammunition "they don't know what to do with it" and that they went to war "every year."[36]

By the time of the Lewis and Clark expedition, the situation had become critical for many of the enemies of the Blackfoot. Cameahwait's band of Northern Shoshones were hiding in the mountains from their Blackfoot and Hidatsa enemies, suffering from hunger yet too afraid to venture onto the plains. Patrick Gass thought them "the poorest and most miserable nation I ever beheld."[37] For the easternmost Plateau Indians, the situation was less dire but still serious. The three formerly independent bands of Flatheads joined forces and withdrew to a single camp behind the Rocky Mountains.[38] The Kutenais and Pend d'Oreilles also retreated west.[39] Annual trips to the buffalo plains became armed expeditions under military discipline. "When we go to hunt the bison, we also prepare for war," a Flathead chief called Cartier explained in 1811. He added that his people would be hunting buffalo already except that they lacked ammunition for their few guns. "We do not fear war," he exclaimed, "but we wish to meet our enemies well armed."[40]

Plateau Indians were also feeling pressure from the south. By the 1750s some Shoshone bands had taken to raiding the southern plateau for slaves.[41] Plateau slaves were taken to the Spanish settlements in New Mexico, where they could be redeemed for horses and trade goods.[42] The Cayuses were driven from their traditional hunting grounds in Oregon's Blue Mountains by Shoshone raiding parties.[43]

Not all Plateau warfare was defensive, nor was it all directed outside the Plateau. The Nez Perces frequently raided natives at the Dalles as well as the Okanagon Indians.[44] The Klamath became avid slave raiders, striking not only the California tribes but other Plateau groups as well. "We found that we could make money by war," explained a Klamath subchief, adding, "We rather got to like it anyhow."[45]

The increased violence had several important effects on Plateau society. The need for military cooperation accelerated the political changes brought on by horse ownership, consolidating villages into bands and bands into tribes, especially along the eastern and southern edges of the plateau. Military prowess increasingly became a prerequisite for leadership of all kinds. Many tribes came to recognize the office of war chief. Some Plateau groups put away old quarrels to unite against common enemies.[46] But all these responses were not enough and the security of many Plateau groups remained tenuous. "These Indians, with all their independence, are far from being happy people," judged an early trader: "They live in a constant state of anxiety. Every hostile movement about the frontiers excites alarm."[47] For a solution to this dilemma, Indians began to look beyond the plateau.

Expanding Trade Networks

Northwest Indians were experiencing an expansion in their trading patterns by 1805 and European trade goods were ubiquitous on the plateau. At different villages, Lewis and Clark noted white and blue beads, copper teakettles and brass armbands, metal knives and steel cutlasses, English muskets and Spanish coins, red cloth and European jackets—even "a well baked saylor's bisquit"—all among people whom no white man had ever visited.[48] In 1829 Hudson's Bay Company trader Samuel Black noted that Plateau Indians had "long ago" acquired "European Articles" through trade with European trade posts "about the Rocky Mountains" as well as "from the Natives of the Sea Coast."[49]

The European goods noted by Lewis and Clark were only the most visible evidence of an economic expansion that swept the Plateau in the protohistoric period. The horse opened up new trading possibilities, which expanded not only the scale of native trade but its geographic scope as well. New kinds of goods—especially European trade goods—added fuel to the economic expansion. By the nineteenth century, many Plateau Indians were enmeshed as never before in a continental web of trade that connected them with other native and nonnative groups all over the West.[50]

Natives of the Columbia Plateau had traded with one another long before the arrival of the first horses. Trade took place whenever people from different groups came together. The interethnic fishing camps at Kettle Falls and especially the Dalles were important scenes of trade, as were the rich camas fields in the Yakima Valley.[51] Although all Plateau groups enjoyed a similar resource base, there were sufficient regional variations to make trade within the Plateau worthwhile. A Hudson's Bay Company trader reported that "a barter is carried on with articles as are wanted by the one and can be spared by the other."[52]

The term *trade* tends to distort the native context of many of these exchanges, which were more social than economic. Goods changed hands between native groups in at least three ways: as ritual gifts, in negotiated exchanges, and via gambling. Gifts were exchanged whenever different groups met. Such exchanges were ritualized and ceremonial, with rich gifts gaining for the giver considerable social prestige. Such gifts showed the peaceful intent of each party and created the social space for further contact to proceed.[53]

More closely resembling European notions of trade were the exchanges that took place between individuals, often after the chiefs had exchanged gifts. Negotiated exchanges were lacking in ceremony and characterized by haggling and disputes over relative value. The social relationship between the individuals determined the terms of trade. Relatives or close friends might present one another with gifts, with little or no open bartering. In dealing with relative strangers, on the other hand, one would haggle and negotiate, seeking the best deal possible. A Flathead Indian explained that when he traded his dried buffalo meat and robes to the Nez Perces for camas roots, he "bartered . . . for as much as he could get."[54]

Gambling was also a major means by which goods traded hands. The most popular gambling game was a stick game, called by the Okanagons *tsill-all-a-come*, that was played by teams of people using two small wood or bone dice. It was a sleight-of-hand game, in which one team tried to guess the location of the die while a player from the other team shifted it between his hands "with the quickness of lightning."[55] Spirit singing was an important part of the game, as players called on their guardians to bring them victory. To Plateau Indians, *tsill-all-a-come* was by no means a game of chance, since it was a person's spirit power that determined the outcome. So pervasive was gambling that some anthropologists believe that it was the primary means of exchange on the Plateau.[56] The richer material culture of the protohistoric period probably led to an increase in gambling.[57]

These forms of exchange were widespread on the Plateau, but they were local. Goods were usually traded between adjacent groups, passing through many hands to travel any distance. Trade outside the Plateau was largely confined to the coast, where the great difference in resources and navigability of the Columbia River gave rise to a brisk trade.[58] Exchanges with the natives of the Great Plains or Great Basin were sporadic and rare.[59]

Plateau Indians used the horse to greatly expand the geographic scope of their trade relations. Natives venturing onto the plains to hunt buffalo found that some of their possessions—especially salmon pemmican and the fine Plateau horses—were much desired by the Plains peoples. In turn, Plateau Indians coveted the parfleches, buffalo robes, and feathered headdresses of the Plains tribes.[60] So great was the desire of both parties to trade that the normally hostile Flatheads and Blackfoot would arrange temporary truces that they might trade with one another.[61] Several Nez Perces told Lewis and Clark that they had traveled to the Hidatsa villages in North Dakota.[62] In 1805 fur trader François Larocque noted a regular trade between the Flatheads and the Crows of Wyoming.[63] Flatheads and Nez Perces also participated in the greatest of native trade fairs—the Shoshone rendezvous held annually in southwestern Wyoming, six hundred miles from the plateau. Here they met Indians from all over the West, including Ute traders who offered knives, hawks bells, mules, saddles, and other goods from the Spanish settlements in New Mexico.[64] Goods acquired from the plains trade were exchanged throughout the plateau.[65]

Plateau Indians also used their horses to pursue trade to the south. The Walla Walla, Cayuse, and Yakima Indians opened a long-distance trade route to California in the late eighteenth century.[66] Plateau horses, plains buffalo robes and parfleches, dried salmon, and dentalium shells were carried south along the eastern edge of the Cascade Mountains into central California. There they were bartered for slaves, lily seeds, bows, and beads.[67] Plateau Indians had the reputation for raiding as well as trading on these California expeditions, and much of the human and material booty they brought back was again exchanged at the great market of the Dalles, which was emerging as one of the major interregional trading sites in North America.[68]

As Plateau natives became part of a continental trading system, new kinds of goods entered the Plateau economy. Steel knives, bits of copper and brass, and woolen cloth became a part of their material culture. The most important source of European trade items was the Pacific Coast, where natives and Europeans engaged in a thriving trade in the skins of the sea otter.[69] Chinooks showed Lewis and Clark their long familiarity with English and American traders "by repeating many words of English, as musquit, powder, shot, nife, file, damned rascal, sun of a bitch, &c."[70] Coastal natives in turn traded copper goods, iron knives, hatchets, files, blankets, clothes, bits of wool and cotton cloth, and other items for Plateau dried salmon, beargrass, camas, and buffalo robes. "Thus articles which are vended by the whites at the entrance of this river, find their way to the most distant nations enhabiting its waters," wrote Lewis.[71] The desirability of European goods expanded the traditional trade between Plateau and coast. Indeed, Lewis thought these goods were "the soul of this trade."[72]

The arrival of the first European trade goods provoked great interest on the Plateau but had a limited material impact. Kutenai tradition recalls how everyone was amazed by "the thing that could hold water that you could see through," the first glass bottle to reach the tribe from the plains trade.[73] Many of the trade goods acquired by Plateau Indians were employed for aesthetic or spiritual purposes rather than practical ones. Most of the sheet copper and copper kettles, for example, were either cut up and made into copper beads or were used as grave goods.[74] The wool and cotton cloth Lewis and Clark observed on the plateau had mostly been cut into strips and used to decorate clothes and hair.

The trade expansion enriched the lives of many Plateau Indians with new goods, new foods, and new horizons. The Plateau became the link between two vast trading systems: the Missouri–Great Plains system to the east and the coastal system to the west. The Columbia River became the highway of this commerce. But these exchanges brought the Plateau Indians more than they bargained for.

"All Were Dead"

At the junction of the Columbia and Willamette Rivers, William Clark noted the ruins of a "very large Village." When he asked the natives what had become of the people who lived there, they brought forth an old woman who told the explorer a harrowing story. Pointing to the smallpox scars on her cheeks, she "made Signs that they all died with the disorder which marked her face," and that she had nearly died herself while still a girl. Clark judged from the woman's age that the disease had swept through the area about thirty years previously.[75] His partner, Meriwether Lewis, noted that smallpox "may well account for the number of remains of vilages which we find deserted in this quarter."[76]

Native trade networks served as disease vectors, introducing new kinds of sickness to native societies.[77] Like other native Americans, Plateau Indians had no immunity to European illnesses such as smallpox, cholera, measles, influenza, malaria, typhoid, diphtheria, and a host of other exotic pathogens. When such diseases were introduced into previously isolated populations, the result was devastating "virgin soil" epidemics that killed huge numbers of people.[78]

Smallpox was the first Old World pathogen to strike the Plateau, arriving in the 1770s and again around 1800.[79] Plateau Indians probably caught smallpox on a trading expedition to the plains, though Spanish sailors along the coast and even the Russian settlements in Alaska have also been suggested as sources for the epidemic.[80] Wherever it came from, smallpox struck the plateau with stunning ferocity. A Kutenai description of the period, collected about 1900, testifies to the horror of the disease:

The people were living there, and at once they had an epidemic. They died. All died. Then they went about. They told one another the news. Among all the Kutenai there was sickness. They arrived at one town, and told the news to one another. It was everywhere the same. At one town they did not see anybody. They were all dead. Only one person was left. . . .

He was alone. He thought: "Well, let me go around this world to see if there is anyplace where there is any one." . . . When he arrived by the water where the people used to be, there was nobody; and when he went about, he saw only dead ones . . . dead bodies were all piled up, inside the tents. . . . He was crying as he went along. He thought: "I am the only one left in this country, for the dogs are also dead."

When he came to the farthest village, he went about, and he saw some footprints of people. . . . He knew someone was saved. . . . He went along . . . and saw above there two black bears eating berries. He thought: "I'll go and shoot them. . . . Then I'll see if any one is left. After I have dried the meat, I'll look for them. I have seen footprints of people. They might be hungry men or women. They shall eat."

He arrived, and saw that they were not bears but women. He saw one older one, and the other one a girl. He thought: "I am glad to see people. Let me take that woman to be my wife." Then he went and took hold of the girl. The girl spoke and said to her mother: "Mother, I see a man." Her mother looked. . . . She saw a man taking her daughter. Then the woman and the girl and the youth cried, because they saw all the Kutenai were dead. When they saw each other, they all cried together.

The older woman said: "Don't take my daughter. She is still small. Take me. You shall be my husband. Later on, when my daughter is large, she shall be your wife. Then you shall have children."

Then the youth married the older woman. It was not long before the woman said: "Now I see that my daughter is grown up. Now she may be your wife. It is good if you have children. Her body is strong now. Then the youth took the girl for his wife. Then the Kutenai increased from these.[81]

There are several things to note about this story. The epidemic was swift: "at once . . . all died." When smallpox is first contracted, it remains dormant in its human host for about two weeks, during which period the victim is not infectious and remains unaware of the disease. But once the disease breaks out, death can follow quickly, sometimes within twenty-four hours.[82] The Multnomahs recalled how "strong men became ill and died in one day" when smallpox first struck their village.[83] The speed of the epidemic added to its horror.

Then there is the fierce but uneven mortality of the epidemic. Though there was sickness "among all the Kutenais," at some villages survivors went about and "told the news to one another," while at other villages "all were dead." Smallpox is a crowd disease, and close contact is required for effective transmission. The main vector for its transmission is airborne particles from the breath of a person in the third and fourth weeks of the disease.[84] The virus would easily spread through a crowded winter lodge or pit house, but would have been far less contagious among the dispersed spring root-gathering camps or fall hunting camps. Several of the surviving accounts of smallpox on the plateau link especially high mortality to a winter occurrence of the disease.[85] Puss and scabs from smallpox victims are not effective means of transmission, but soiled bedding is quite infectious.[86]

As a result, smallpox spreads like wildfire—striking with a deadly ferocity in some villages, but passing other areas by entirely. Such was the case on the plateau. A people called the Tunaha, an eastern band of the Kutenai, were all but extinguished in the 1770s, with the few survivors seeking refuge with the Flatheads.[87] The Flatheads and the Okanagon Indians were especially hard hit by the first epidemic.[88] For many Plateau groups, mortality appears to have been about 30 percent—typical for a population with no previous exposure to the disease.[89] Natives on the northernmost plateau seem to have been spared entirely. They have no tradition of protohistoric epidemics, nor did early explorers record any pockmarked survivors.[90]

There was a terrible psychic toll on epidemic survivors, who "all cried together." Smallpox is a particularly horrible way to die. *Variola major*, the epidemic strain of smallpox, can strike in at least nine different ways, from hyper acute "fulminating" smallpox (which causes death in twenty-four to thirty-six hours) to "discrete" forms that rarely kill. The most common form by far is the "malignant confluent." The first signs of malignant confluent smallpox are a headache and backache followed by vomiting and abdominal pain. After a few days these are followed by a worsening rash, delirium tremens, and an inability to swallow. By the eighth day many of the swelling pox sores have burst, releasing a horrible stench that, in the words of a modern clinician, "cannot adequately be described." Loss of muscle tone so distorts the victim's face that he or she is "hardly . . . recognized by his relatives." The agony is terrible throughout, and death can come anywhere from the eighth to fifteenth day. With proper care, 20–30 percent of fulminating smallpox victims will recover, though bearing scars over much of their bodies.[91] A Flathead tradition speaks to the different forms of smallpox that struck that tribe: "Those developing red pustules died within a few days, but those who were plagued by the black pustules died almost instantly."[92]

The first reaction of those in afflicted villages was to run away. The Nez Perces recalled how some of their ancestors fled when the epidemic struck and "thus avoided the contagion."[93] A group of Kutenais tried to outrun the epidemic only to watch some of their numbers die along the way—a graphic illustration of how this tactic could serve to further spread the disease.[94]

As deaths mounted, native belief systems were challenged by a sickness that did not respond to traditional medicine. Shamanic treatments of chanting, sucking, and plant medicines utterly failed against the new disease. Shamans probably died in greater numbers than their countrymen, both from increased exposure to the disease and because smallpox is most often fatal to young children and adults over forty—and shamans were "generally past the meridian of life."[95] Others attempted to treat their sickness with hot steam baths in the sweat lodge followed by cold plunges in the river.[96] Though this treatment was highly effective for arthritis and other diseases with which the Indians were familiar, in the case of smallpox it only hastened death.[97]

Community life must have come to a standstill while smallpox raged in the villages. No hunts were organized or fish traps built or camas roots dug while people were dying all around. No food was dried and put away for the coming lean season. So many sick people could hardly be moved even when the local food resource of the season had run out and it was time to travel, leaving healthy relatives with the choice of continuing the seasonal round themselves or staying with their dying relations. Communal dances and trading parties were out of the question.

Religious beliefs and social customs were challenged by the epidemics. Failure to cure the new disease must have weakened the power of the surviving shamans, whose ability to cure and cause sickness was the basis of their power.[98] The large numbers of dead all but overwhelmed Plateau burial rituals. "Grandmother tried to bury people," one elderly informant recalled, "but there were too many."[99] Graves from this era show many signs of hasty construction and careless internment.[100] This must have been upsetting to Plateau people, who believed that burial rituals had to be held in a precise manner if the dead were to ascend to the afterlife rather than become ghosts.[101] The disproportionate mortality of the old was an especially severe loss, for it was the elders who retained the oral literature and knowledge of special ceremonies and specialized skills.[102] There may also have been a breakdown in normal moral constraints after the epidemic. This is hinted at in the Kutenai epidemic tale, wherein the protagonist marries both mother and daughter—an act that would be considered incest in normal times.[103]

Almost as quickly as they came, the epidemics lifted. The susceptibles all died or recovered and the smallpox virus passed from the plateau for another generation. The survivors of the epidemics—and two-thirds of Plateau Indians did survive—set out to rebuild their lives. People from depleted villages and bands sought each other out and joined together to form new social units. Shamans regained their authority as the epidemic receded, for the old cures retained their effectiveness against the old diseases. Holes in a group's collective knowledge were repaired by invention and borrowing. The seasonal round was resumed, and fishing and digging places that might have been crowded in the past were less so. Horses were never more useful to Plateau Indians than now as they worked to rebuild their shattered societies. And rebuild them they did. Though the Clatsops on the coast told Lewis and Clark that smallpox had "distroyed their nation," the Clatsops survived.[104]

Populations might even have recovered between the epidemics and the arrival of the first whites on the Columbia Plateau. Such recovery can be surprisingly quick: an otherwise healthy society experiencing a modest annual population increase of 1 percent can replace a loss of 40 percent of its population in thirty-five years, and with a 2–3 percent growth rate, in as little as ten years.[105] The speed of recovery depends on native fertility, which is usually thought to have been somewhat low on the plateau.[106] But other than the two epidemics, there was little sickness on the protohistoric plateau. An early fur trader observed "few diseases among the Indians," who were "in general very healthy" and lived "to a good old age 50 to 60 and older."[107] Plateau peoples experienced at least a modest population recovery between the epidemics and their first contact with Europeans.

The Information Revolution

Plateau peoples also underwent a revolution in knowledge during the protohistoric period. Expanded trade networks reduced village isolation and increased the geographical horizons of many natives. Lewis and Clark's journals provide many examples of this expanded geographical knowledge. The northern Shoshones described the courses of the Snake and Salmon Rivers, the Great Basin, and the route to New Mexico via the Yellowstone country.[108] The Nez Perces advised against trying to cross the still-snowy Bitterroot Mountains in the spring of 1806 and instead sketched a route through southern Idaho that would later become the Oregon Trail.[109] But the most impressive geography lesson might have come from the Chinooks, whose detailed instructions for travel to the Rocky Mountains point to frequent native travel across the length of the Columbia Plateau: "The Indians inform us that the Snows lyes knee deep in the Columbian Plains dureing the winter, and in those plains we could not git as much wood as would cook our provisions untill the driftwood comes down in the Spring . . . and even were we happily over those plains and in the woodey countrey at the foot of the rockey mountains, we could not possibly pass that emence bearier of mountains on which the snow lyes in winter to the debth of 20 feet; in short the Indians tell us they [are] impasable untill about the 1s[t] of June, at which time even then is an abundance of snow [and] but a Scanty Subsistence may be had for the horses."[110]

This expanded geography was part of a larger knowledge revolution that transformed the Plateau in the eighteenth century. Unfamiliar European trade goods provoked questions—What sort of people made these? What are they like? Where do they live?—and stories of the white man were traded along with his manufactures. It was probably this exchange of stories that set off the wave of prophecies regarding the approaching white men that swept the Plateau in the late eighteenth century.[111] Indeed, one of the really striking things about the "first contacts" made by Lewis and Clark is how the Indians did not seem very surprised to meet them. Curiosity seekers often crowded around the expedition to watch them set up camp, and most Indians expressed a strong interest in the expedition's possessions and intentions.[112] But what is missing in the journals is the open-mouthed wonderment at the sight of strange white people that is so typical of truly first contacts elsewhere. When David Thompson explored the more remote northern plateau, for example, he reported that "the natives were at a loss what to make of us . . . [one man] felt my feet and legs to be sure that I was something like themselves, but did not appear sure that I was so."[113] At another village "the Chief . . . rode down to examine us, he appeared very much agitated, the foam coming out of his mouth; wheeling his horse backwards and forwards, and calling aloud, who are you, what are you."[114] Lewis and Clark never met with receptions like those.

Perhaps disappointed at the relative lack of surprise, the captains sometimes resorted to gimmicks to elicit the reaction they expected. Lewis was forever producing his air gun and gleefully recording in his journal what "great medicine" the Indians thought the device. Lewis recounted how at a Nez Perce camp "we amused ourselves with shewing them the power of magnetism, the spye glass, compass, watch, air-gun and other sundry articles equally novel and incomprehensible to them," only to discover that the Nez Perce had already learned of these objects through native trade networks with the plains.[115] Clark grew so exasperated by his matter-of-fact introduction to a "sulkey" Willamette Valley tribe that he secretly threw a piece of cannon fuse into the fire to impress the laconic natives with his power.[116]

What accounts for the almost blasé native reaction to what should have been such an amazing event? The wide distribution of European trade goods provides a partial answer. Historians who have studied first contacts in other parts of North America have argued that it was not so much the Europeans themselves that the natives found amazing, but the cloth and metal and gunpowder that accompanied them.[117] But to the Indians of the plateau, these more-or-less familiar objects required no supernatural explanation. Significantly, Thompson noted that the Indians who so wondered at him had no European trade goods.[118]

Some Plateau natives had not only heard about Europeans well before Lewis and Clark, they had met some. Trading excursions outside the plateau had produced any number of natives who could describe in detail the appearance, customs, and powers of Europeans.[119] Early explorers often encountered such knowledgeable natives. Different Plateau Indians claimed to members of the Lewis and Clark expedition to have traded at the British posts in Alberta, the Spanish settlements in New Mexico, and with seagoing traders along the Northwest coast.[120] Plateau natives traded at the California missions in the late eighteenth century, and some Flatheads may have joined in raids against the distant New Mexican settlements.[121]

Returned slaves were another source of knowledge. Plateau Indians taken in slave raids were sometimes traded far from their homes. At a Hidatsa village in the Dakotas, Lewis and Clark noted several Flathead prisoners.[122] A Nez Perce woman was captured in a slave raid and exchanged east until she became the wife of a French fur trader. Returning to her people years later, she was named Watkuese, for "returned one."[123] At a Spokan village in 1812, an elderly woman explained that she had lived in a white settlement where she had seen plows as well as churches, "which she described by imitating the tolling of a bell by a rope, etc."[124] The fur trader who recorded her account speculated that she had been in the Spanish settlements in New Mexico.

Shipwrecked sailors living near the coast were another possible source of Plateau familiarity with Europeans. At Fort Clatsop, Lewis and Clark met the mixed-blood son of Jack Ramsey, an English sailor who had lived on the coast for a number of years.[125] Later explorers reported meeting an elderly mixed-blood man called "Old Soto" near the Dalles, whom other Indians described as the son of one of half a dozen Spanish sailors who had lived among them.[126] Lewis and Clark did not themselves mention Old Soto, but their map of the area shows a "Shotos village," probably a reference to the same man.[127] Half a dozen Spanish sailors living for a considerable time at the great trading post of the Dalles would have diffused a lot of knowledge concerning Europeans. And among the Walla Walla Indians one expedition member reported a "half white child," proof, he thought, that white traders had already visited these people.[128] Significantly, it was at the same village that Gass noted: "We were a very interesting sight to the surrounding crowd, as nine-tenths of them had never before seen a white man"—implying that 10 percent of the Walla Wallas *had* met Europeans before.[129]

Indian travelers from beyond the plateau were another source of information. Antoine Le Page Du Pratz, a French settler in Louisiana, described the curious adventures of Moncacht-apé, a Yazoo Indian who, "to satisfy his curiosity," walked first to the Atlantic and then to the Pacific Ocean. The journeys must have taken place in the early years of the eighteenth century. The secondhand details of Moncacht-apé's western journey are unclear (and the story might even be apocryphal), but it appears that he ascended the Missouri River to the Rocky Mountains and went down the Columbia to the sea—preceding Lewis and Clark by a hundred years.[130]

Evidence of other Indian visitors to the plateau is found in the maps of Peter Fidler, a Hudson's Bay Company trader operating on the Canadian Plains in the first decade of the nineteenth century. Ac-ko-mok-ki, a Blackfoot chief, drew Fidler a map in 1801 that showed the continental divide with the Snake and Columbia Rivers flowing west to the Pacific Ocean. The villages of various Plateau Indians were also shown—indicating regular visits between the Plateau and the Plains.[131]

In the last decade of the eighteenth century, Iroquois fur hunters began arriving on the plateau. The Iroquois were freelance trappers who pushed west in search of new fur, often in advance of the European traders. Hundreds of Iroquois and eastern Algonquians were present in Saskatchewan and Alberta by 1802, but many seem to have come west much earlier.[132] In 1799 Alexander Mackenzie noted a whole village of transplanted Iroquois on the upper Saskatchewan River near the present-day Saskatchewan and Alberta border. He noted they were from a "Romish" village near Montreal (Caughnawaga) and had moved west to enjoy "the modes of life of their forefathers," which they preferred to "the improvements of civilization."[133] David Thompson, the first European on the upper Columbia, encountered these Iroquois wherever he traveled on the plateau, and seemed to think it unremarkable that they had gotten there ahead of him.[134] Thompson used the information he gained from these Iroquois explorers to prepare parts of his maps of the northern Rockies.[135]

These Iroquois brought two new types of information to the Plateau. One was their syncretized Catholicism. Alexander Ross noted that the western Iroquois in the employ of the Hudson's Bay Company were "brought up to religion" and sang "hymns oftener than paddling songs."[136] The western Iroquois retained at least the basic sacraments of the Catholic faith and sometimes shared these with local peoples.[137] Second was their knowledge of the fur trade and the effects of contact. Heirs to almost three centuries of experience in dealing with European culture, the Iroquois knew well the promises and perils of the coming encounter with Europeans. The influences of this new information had made itself felt by the time of Lewis and Clark.

The Plateau Indians who stepped from their teepees and mat houses to greet Lewis and Clark knew far more about Europeans than any European knew of them. Indians knew where Europeans could be found in the broad expanses of the West and knew how to get there. They knew about the special kinds of goods the Europeans had and the capabilities of wool cloth, metal implements, and firearms. They knew that there were different kinds of Europeans—Americans, British, and Spanish—and knew the trade policies of each. They understood the outlines of the fur trade, what it was the Europeans wanted, and how furs might be exchanged for goods.

Plateau Indians also knew that more Europeans were coming and had some idea what this meant for their way of life. In a turbulent time when many native peoples were themselves on the move, it might not have seemed especially remarkable that Europeans were moving too. The Spanish mission frontier was advancing in California in the eighteenth century, and Plateau Indians were drawn there to trade for European goods. The British fur companies were pushing across the Canadian Shield, attracting the attention of Indians of the northern plateau, who made efforts to reach them to trade. Frequent trading expeditions to the upper Missouri by Nez Perces and others must have brought news of the expanding American empire to the east. And the very active fur trade along the Pacific Coast attracted the attention of Plateau Indians, who enjoyed a steady influx of trade goods from this source. Every year the Europeans drew closer and the knowledge of them became more definite. Plateau Indians incorporated this unsettling information into their existing knowledge base in a religious revival known as the Prophet Dance.

The Prophet Dance

The imminence of the coming changes was brought home forcefully in the summer of 1800, when the sky ominously went dark all over the plateau.[138] A powerful volcano in the Cascade range erupted, cloaking the sun and showering the plateau with ash for days. A narrative from the Spokan Indians recalls the terror of the event: "One summer morning the entire population were startled by the rumbling and shaking of the earth. . . . the sun became obscured . . . and darkness added its horrors to the scene. . . . terror-stricken inhabitants fled to the hills for safety. The shaking of the earth continued for two days, when a faint rain of ashes began to fall, and so heavy was the fall of them that there was little difference between day and night. The fall of ashes continued for several weeks. The game abandoned the country . . . and desolation spread."[139]

Ashes fell several inches deep over most of the plateau. To people who explained all unusual events by reference to spirit power, the eruption was a powerful religious portent, indicating great unease in the spirit world. The Sanpoils prayed to the "dry snow," calling it

"Chief" and "Mystery" and asking it why it had come.[140] The Kute-nais thought that the darkness and accompanying ashes indicated the sun had burned up, signifying the "end of all things."[141]

Indians responded to this cataclysmic event with a movement an-thropologists label the Prophet Dance, a new religious ritual that promised to restore the human relationship with the spirit world while preparing people for the disruptive events to come. The year of the eruption was probably not the first time Indians danced a prophet dance. Some native traditions link the rise of the dance to the first smallpox epidemics a generation earlier, or to other natural portents such as meteor showers, the aurora borealis, earthquakes, and even the appearance of a two-headed goose.[142] But it is clear that the 1800 eruption sparked the most intensive and widespread prophetic activity.

There were many prophets and prophecies, but the form and the message were much the same.[143] Prophets were usually men and women who had "died" and come back to life. Since any form of unconsciousness other than sleep constituted a temporary "death" in the Plateau scheme of things, such returns from the dead may not have been uncommon.[144] This would especially have been the case with recovery from smallpox, which often renders its victims unconscious.[145]

After returning from death, the prophet would announce that he or she had received a vision or had journeyed to the land of the dead. The prophet had communicated with the Old One or Great Spirit and learned a new dance and song the people were to perform. Natural por-tents revealed that the end of the world was approaching, declared the prophet. Some prophets predicted that the dead would return when the world ended.[146] Europeans, a "different kind of man from any you have yet seen," according to the Spokan prophet, were coming from the east.[147] In some prophecies the Europeans were associated with future material wealth for the natives; in others they were to bring disease and disorder.[148] The Old One wanted the people to live according to traditional moral precepts—not to fight, lie, or steal and to obey the taboos. The dance was adopted by the prophet's village, sometimes with such enthusiasm that normal subsistence activities were abandoned and the people suffered from hunger.[149]

The Prophet Dance seems to have been present over most or all of the Plateau in the late protohistoric period.[150] The means of trans-mission between different groups is unclear. Prophets are described as "preaching" and trying to convert people to the new doctrine of im-minent destruction. Since some nineteenth-century Indian prophets traveled between villages to gather converts, it might have been the same in the previous century.[151]

Dancing was the characteristic feature of the movement. "It is not to be a dance of merriment, but a dance of worship," the Sanpoil prophet told his people.[152] A Modoc woman recalled that the dances were "no fun," but rather something people felt compelled to do because "they believe pretty strong."[153] The dances took place in the daytime and continued for as long as the enthusiasm could be maintained, sometimes for weeks or even months, according to tradition. While the people were dancing and singing, the prophet preached, exhorting them not to lie, steal, molest women, or commit other sins. Prophet dances occurred more often in summer than winter and were always suspended when it came time for the traditional winter dance.[154]

The Prophet Dance was an interesting mix of innovation and traditional religious forms. The dance itself was new—before the Prophet Dance, there were no summertime religious dances—as were elements of the prophecy, particularly the coming of the white men. But many of the forms of the dance resembled traditional practices. The vision experience of the prophets was very like the vision quest, especially in the granting of a sacred song and dance to the visionary. That the world would eventually come to an end was an old belief, but it was news that this was to happen so soon. Prophecy itself was the traditional means of knowing the future, and shamans had long been called upon to predict such things as the arrival of the salmon and the success of a proposed war party. The moral renewal called for by the prophets was a return to the traditional mores of Plateau peoples, not a set of new or unfamiliar rules. And the dance itself drew on the most sacred tradition of the Plateau, the communal winter dances that formed the core of shared religious life. These traditional elements caused anthropologist Leslie Spier, who first described the phenomenon, to argue that the Prophet Dance was a purely traditional form, an "integral part" of Plateau culture.[155]

The dance would continue for a time—perhaps a few weeks, sometimes as long as several months—until people lost interest. People would grow hungry or begin to doubt the prophecy as the world failed to come to an end and the dance was abandoned. People "forgot about" the new ritual and resumed their normal lives. But the prophecies were not forgotten, and the coming of white men and the approaching end of the native world became a part of Plateau belief.

The cause of the Prophet Dance has long been a matter of some controversy among anthropologists. Volcanism was the immediate cause, but few anthropologists have been willing to leave it at that. Leslie Spier thought the dance was of native origin, unrelated to protohistoric stress.[156] Yet it seems too great a coincidence that the Prophet Dance arose in the sometimes calamitous protohistoric period or that prophecies of the coming of the white man were bound together with predictions of the end of the world. Anthropologists since Spier have generally described the Prophet Dance as a new development, a response to deprivation in the form of epidemic disease. The epidemics presented an "insurmountable challenge" and "created a deep spiritual unease," according to the most recent such formulation, and the natives responded with a system of "internal cleansing and renewal."[157]

But there are problems with linking the Prophet Dance so closely to the smallpox epidemic. The first is the matter of timing. Many native accounts of the Prophet Dance associate the prophecy with a fall of "dry snow"—volcanic ash—from the 1800 eruption in the Cascade Mountains.[158] This is almost a generation after the first and most devastating smallpox epidemic ripped through the plateau. On the other hand, this is precisely when the second smallpox epidemic, with a mortality rate of around 10 percent, swept the plateau, so perhaps the two are reconcilable.[159]

A second problem with attributing the rise of the Prophet Dance to the smallpox epidemics is that the Indians themselves rarely did so. Anthropologist Deward Walker found "clear evidence" of a link between epidemics and prophetic activity in three instances.[160] But as we have seen, native accounts more commonly attribute the rise of the Prophet Dance to natural portents.[161] Even the Kutenai, whose memory of smallpox was so detailed, did not link their Prophet Dance to the epidemic.[162] Epidemics may well have set the stage for the Prophet Dance by weakening faith in traditional religion and especially in the powers of the shamans, thereby creating a vacuum of religious leadership. But smallpox could as easily have led to a revival of traditional religion. Ross Cox wrote that "those who escaped, or survived the deadly contagion, strictly conformed themselves to their own code of moral laws" thereafter.[163] Disease alone is not enough to explain the late protohistoric Prophet Dance. The dance had an additional cause—the information revolution.

The looming arrival of the whites and the profoundly disruptive effects they would have on native society were well known on the Plateau by 1800. Yet native accounts almost uniformly insist that it was through prophecies that the Indians first learned of the white man.[164] A Spokan chief named Silimxnotylmilakobok made the point explicitly to explorer Charles Wilkes in the 1840s, saying that before the 1800 prophecy, "we had no knowledge of the white man." But, as Wilkes himself noted, this could hardly be true, since Iroquois trappers had already been living in the area for some years when the prophecy occurred.[165]

In this apparent paradox lies a second, previously unrecognized cause of the Prophet Dance—the information revolution. Plateau people did not first learn of Europeans through late-eighteenth-century prophecies but by more mundane channels. The first news of the existence of Europeans must have come to the Plateau soon after the acquisition of the horse in the early eighteenth century. As contacts between Plateau peoples and Indians from other culture areas increased in mid-century, so too did the stock of knowledge concerning the whites. Face-to-face contacts between Plateau Indians and French, British, American, and Spanish traders at locations beyond the plateau were widespread by the 1780s and 1790s, the same period when the first Iroquois trappers settled on the plateau. By this time, Plateau Indians not only knew of the existence of Europeans, they knew a great deal about what the advance of Europeans across the continent meant to the native peoples they encountered. They knew that the whites would bring great wealth, some of which the Indians could share through the fur trade. They knew also that regular contact with whites would disrupt their way of life.

The function of the Prophet Dance was to integrate this disturbing new knowledge into the existing Plateau cosmology, while at the same time revitalizing the connections with the spirit world so that Plateau natives would be able to survive in their new world. Prophecy, the traditional means of knowing the future, validated the news of Europeans that traveled along the trade networks. Deeply conservative as all oral traditions are, it took the shock of the 1800 eruptions to trigger the innovations of the Prophet Dance. Once this frightening knowledge was absorbed, Plateau natives set about preparing themselves by the same means they always used to survive: their connections with the spirit world. Thus the prophetic exhortations to dance and sing and to live in a moral manner, activities that were known to improve the relationship between human beings and the spirit world.

Contrary to most earlier interpretations, Europeans were not themselves seen as messengers from the spirit world. Leslie Spier drew on one native story to introduce the idea that Indians took Lewis and Clark, David Thompson, and other explorers to be emissaries sent by the Great Spirit and that they were greeted by natives performing the Prophet Dance. This idea has been almost universally accepted by subsequent scholars, including those who disagreed with Spier's analysis of the dance's origins.[166] Christopher Miller took the idea a step farther by accepting an 1840s account in which the Spokan prophet predicts that Europeans "will bring with them a book and will teach you everything, and after that the world will fall to pieces."[167]

The trouble with these interpretations is that there is little in the accounts of the first explorers on the plateau to suggest that they were seen as anything more than important visitors. Spier based his interpretation on the many accounts of Indians dancing to greet white visitors in the first decade of contact. The crux of Spier's argument was his claim that Indians danced *only* for white visitors in this period and that a welcoming dance was not a traditional part of Plateau culture. Spier's statements seemed reasonable at the time they were made, but they have been disproved by later research. Plateau natives did indeed have a traditional welcoming dance, which the Nez Perces call the *telikliin*, or processional song.[168] When explorer David Thompson described Plateau dances in his journal, he wrote that one of them was a dance of greeting.[169] Alexander Ross noted that "dancing and singing" were "the usual symbols of peace and friendship."[170] Early fur trade journals also include descriptions of Indians dancing for one another in greeting.[171] In the case of Lewis and Clark, at least, it seems that the explorers spent at least as much time dancing and making music for the Indians as the Indians did for them. Plateau Indians regarded these first whites on the plateau not as spirits or messengers from the spirit world, but as men like themselves, though important and powerful.

Plateau Indians of the protohistoric period entered into a new world, unknown to their forefathers. Some of the changes were disastrous. Smallpox swept away perhaps a third of the people, leaving some villages desolate and destroying others altogether. The level of violence increased markedly, both on the peripheries of the plateau and within its boundaries. Unsettling news arrived with increasing frequency, news that a new kind of person was on the move and would soon arrive on the plateau, with consequences both good and bad. Ominous portents, especially the great fall of volcanic ash in 1800, caused deep misgivings.

Yet there was much that was good in the protohistoric era. Horses not only eased the seasonal round and improved communications, they opened up a new world of possibilities beyond the plateau. New trade goods enriched both the material and spiritual culture of natives. The information revolution provided Indians with a wealth of new knowledge about the people and events outside their borders. Plateau society recovered from the smallpox epidemics, and flourishing trade networks and alliances were reestablished. The two bouts with smallpox left behind many survivors—a population of disease-experienced individuals who helped protect the plateau from subsequent smallpox epidemics. For those who survived, the eighteenth century was almost a golden era, when Plateau societies reached their apogee on the eve of white contact. Indians were active participants in the process of protohistoric change, seeking out knowledge of Europeans and sources of their trade goods and adopting those goods and customs only selectively, in ways that met native needs.

The protohistoric era was also a time of prophets. Plateau Indians used their religion to understand the turbulent events of the protohistoric era and to prepare for what was to come. Prophecy, the traditional means of knowing the future, validated the new information and helped integrate it into existing knowledge. Communal singing and dancing, the traditional way of renewing relations with the spirit world, were used in new ways to overcome the spiritual crisis that protohistoric events induced.

As the prophecies faded, Plateau Indians were left with a new religious belief. White men would come and bring with them greater challenges and opportunities than any that had come before. The arrival of the Europeans might mean the end of the world or a new era of prosperity. Indians were prepared for either event.

3.   *First Encounters, 1800–1825*

In 1834 American explorer John K. Townsend encountered thirteen Cayuse, Nez Perce, and Chinook Indians at the fur trading post of Fort Hall. The Indians had left their homes on the Columbia Plateau to accompany a trapping expedition to the Rocky Mountains. Townsend studied these natives closely, since they were the first of their peoples he had met. One Saturday evening he went to the Indians' lodge to study what he called their "devotions." The scene he witnessed was extraordinary. "I think," he wrote, "I never was more gratified by any exhibition in my life."[1]

The natives first observed fifteen minutes of silent prayer. Then their chief delivered a sermon in "a solemn and impressive tone," asking his people to worship the "Great Spirit who made the light and the darkness, the fire and the water." If the Indians prayed to the Great Spirit with "one tongue," the chief said, he would listen to their prayers. The Indians then kneeled for the prayers. The chief's prayer was fervent, delivered with "his hands clasped upon his breast, and his eyes cast upwards with a beseeching look towards heaven." After each sentence the assembled Indians responded with a few words chanted in unison. After the twenty-minute prayer, the still-kneeling chief led his congregation in a song. "The song was a simple expression of a few sounds," Townsend marveled, "no intelligible words being uttered. It resembled the words, *Ho-hâ-ho-hâ-ho-hâ-hâ-â*, commencing in a low tone, and gradually swelling to a full, round, and beautifully modulated chorus. During the song, the clasped hands of the worshippers were moved rapidly across the breast, and their bodies swing with great energy to the time of the music. The chief ended the song . . . by a kind of swelling groan, which was echoed in chorus." As the ceremony drew to a close, the natives observed a moment of silence, then "disappeared in the darkness with a step noiseless as that of a spectre."[2]

The ceremony Townsend witnessed was part of a new faith that swept the Plateau in the early 1830s—the Columbian Religion.[3] A syncretic blend of traditional beliefs and selected elements of Christianity, the Columbian Religion arose during the fur trade. The era of the fur trade (1809–40) was one of tumult and opportunity for Plateau Indians. The natives shaped the trade to their advantage, acquiring the few trade goods they desired without substantial disruption to their traditional ways. The cloth, knives, metal pots, guns, and other Euro-American goods improved the quality of life for Plateau Indians. Under the influence of the traders, Plateau natives made peace with one another—and turned their newly acquired guns on their aggressive neighbors outside the plateau. Plateau hunting parties ventured onto the Great Plains with new confidence, and tribes along the southern plateau retook traditional hunting grounds they had lost to the Shoshones during the protohistoric period.

Yet the introduction of the fur trade was by no means an unmitigated blessing. The fur trade brought the plateau fully into the Old World disease pool.[4] Where the protohistoric period had been marked by epidemics every generation, the fur trade would bring new diseases to the plateau every few years. Influenza, cholera, and other sicknesses entered the plateau, while malaria nearly wiped out the nearby natives of the lower Columbia. Despite the new trade goods and political relations, Plateau Indians felt their status slipping by the mid-1820s.

To the beleaguered Indians of the plateau, the fur trade offered hope. But it was not the goods of the traders that the Indians most desired, nor a military alliance: it was spirit power, which the traders seemed to have in abundance. The odd appearance of the Euro-Americans, the strange goods they possessed, and especially their apparent immunity to the new diseases—all spoke a strong and mysterious new kind of spiritual power. And Plateau natives knew it was connections with the spirit world that protected a person from illness. As Indians tried to trace the sources of the strangers' power, it became clear that they had a very different system of religious beliefs and practices than any the Indians had known. Perhaps if the Indians could acquire some of the white man's spirit power, they could arrest the long slide of their populations.

To Plateau Indians, the primary value of the fur trade had nothing to do with goods or alliances or modes of reciprocity. The fur trade was first and foremost a window into white society. Natives used the close associations of the fur trade to ask questions, make observations, and learn more about the beliefs of the fur traders. The scattered pieces of Christian ceremonies and doctrines picked up at the trading posts were assembled into a new faith. Indians believed the Columbian

Religion, a heady mix of the old and new, would give them access to the spiritual power of the Euro-Americans, a power that would protect them from disease, improve their material condition, and forge a new and stronger connection to the spirit world.

First Encounters

The Columbian Religion began with the first encounters. Euro-Americans began to arrive on the Columbia Plateau at the turn of the nineteenth century. Alexander Mackenzie skirted the northern edge of the plateau in 1793, descending the river that bears his name. Lewis and Clark crossed the more densely populated southern plateau in 1805 and 1806 along the Snake and Columbia Rivers. David Thompson traversed the northern Rockies to establish trading posts on the upper Columbia in 1807, reaching the sea in 1811. In that same year representatives of John Jacob Astor's Pacific Fur Company approached the plateau both by land and sea, also establishing trading posts. These posts served as the base camps for further exploration, and by 1820 many native villages on the plateau had hosted Euro-American visitors.

As the explorers arrived on the Columbia, Indians began to map the spiritual terrain of the strangers. The first white men on the Columbia Plateau were regarded neither as spirits nor ambassadors from the supernatural world. Plateau Indians had long known of white people's existence and their arrival was entirely expected. But the odd appearance of the visitors, along with their rich collection of Euro-American manufactures, convinced many Indians that the whites possessed strong spirit power. Natives used their first encounters with Euro-Americans to explore the nature and limits of the white man's spiritual power.

The first native reaction to the presence of white men was to closely observe the strangers. A Thompson Indian tradition tells how the villagers "hurried down" to the riverbank "with the news of the approach" of Simon Fraser's party in 1808.[5] At another point Fraser encountered a camp of twelve hundred "Swhanemugh" Indians, apparently a northern Plateau band, who had heard of his journey and were waiting to meet him. Fraser noted that these Indians "had been waiting a long time for our arrival and were now starving."[6] William Clark recorded how "the Indians Came down all the Courses of this river on each Side on horses to view us as we were descending" the Columbia River in 1805.[7] At some points along the river the plains "appeared covered with Spectators."[8] In 1811 Alexander Ross and his party were accompanied by "a great concourse of Indians" as they ascended the Columbia.[9]

The most striking thing about the white people was their appearance. The long beards, paler skins (even when suntanned), and strange clothing of the visitors all provoked wonder. "Everything about them was strange" to the Thompsons, who gave the men in Fraser's party individual names based on their unusual clothing.[10] Fraser himself they called "Sun" because of a gold medal he wore. When the Nez Perces first saw Lewis and Clark, the thick beards of the explorers made the natives wonder if "they were really men."[11] At Kettle Falls a woman asked Ross Cox to remove his shirt so she could see if his skin was actually white and made a "close examination" of the "supernatural" red hair of his Scots traveling companion.[12] The Wenatchis were especially interested in the bearded men of David Thompson's party in 1811. A Wenatchi man approached Thompson with "strong curiosity," feeling the explorer's feet and legs "to be sure I was something like themselves."[13]

Reassured that the white men were indeed "something like themselves," native curiosity turned to the Euro-American manufactures of the explorers. The more common trade goods—pots, knives, cloth, and so on—were well known before the first whites arrived. What interested the natives was the expectation that the arrival of the whites would make these goods available in larger quantities. The chief of a Sanpoil village welcomed Thompson with "a long speech in a loud singing voice . . . hoping we would bring to them Guns, Ammunition, Axes, knives, Awls, and not to forget Steels and Flints with many other articles."[14] The Wenatchis celebrated the arrival of the traders by "smoking, dancing, and singing, the whole night, and at every pause a loud shout and vociferous exclamation was uttered, denoting that they were happy now. The whites had visited their land, and poverty and misery would no longer be known amongst them."[15]

With friendly relations established, some Indians thought to test the spirit power of the white men. The most spiritually powerful members of the Plateau community were shamans, so Indians tested the shamanic powers of the strangers by asking them to heal sick individuals. Many traders and explorers were willing to make the attempt and some proved successful. The "Swhanemughs" (perhaps Shuswaps) presented Fraser with some sick children and the explorer made a great show of anointing each on the head with a mixture of laudanum and water.[16] The Walla Wallas brought Lewis and Clark "several disordered persons . . . for whome they requested some medical aid."[17] After William Clark treated a Nez Perce man's crippled knee with a liniment, "the fellow Soon after recovered and have [has] never Seased [ceased] to extol the virtue of our medicines."[18] The willingness of many whites to practice medicine was further evidence of their spirit power.

The curing abilities of the whites were not unlimited. Near the junction of the Yakima and Columbia Rivers some Indians came to Alexander Ross with a sad request: "Two dead children were presented to us by their parents, in order that we might restore them to life again," Ross recounted, "and a horse was offered us as the reward."[19] Ross gave the couple "a small present" to assuage their grief and told them to bury the children. He noted that the hills in this region were dotted with Indian graves, markers of a disease-ravaged land.[20] Some natives tested the white men's credulity as well as their power. Joseph Whitehouse of the Lewis and Clark expedition noted that the Nez Perces danced "verry well," adding: "They tell us that some of their horses will dance, but I have not Seen them yet."[21]

Other factors confirmed the native estimate of the strangers' spirit power. When a party of Piegans attempted to pursue David Thompson over the Rocky Mountains, they found their way blocked by "three grizled Bears," which they believed Thompson had placed there to end their pursuit.[22] White people also seemed to possess immunity to shamanic attacks, which impressed the Indians. Alexander Ross noted that shamans were sometimes offended at the white people's lack of respect. "On such occasions," he wrote, "the other Indians, seeing us act with so much unconcern in matters which they considered so hazardous to ourselves, would stare at our ignorance . . . expecting every moment to see us fall down dead!"[23] Prophecy was another shamanic function that some natives invested in the whites. "They believe that this world will have an end, as it had a beginning," Ross noted of the Indians. "Frequently they have asked us when it would take place—the *its-owl-eigh*, or end of the world."[24]

Plateau Indians came away from their first encounters convinced that many whites had considerable spirit power and thus could be useful friends or dangerous enemies. The explorers sensed this attitude and thought it would be short-lived. Simon Fraser thought the hospitality of the natives of the northern plateau resulted from "an idea that we are superior beings, not to be overcome." He concluded that "the less familiar we are with one another the better for us."[25] But when contact between natives and whites was regularized by the fur trade, it only increased the Indians' estimate of white spirit power.

Establishing the Fur Trade

Plateau Indians had long traded in furs. What Euro-American traders would later call "small furs"—martin, fisher, mink, and similar small mammals—were snared and dressed by women and the skins used as ornaments or talismans.[26] Deerskins were the staple of Plateau clothing. Dressed bear robes made warm winter wraps and blankets; after the equestrian revolution, buffalo robes served the same purposes. Valued as gifts and trade goods, furs exchanged hands at the communal fishing camps or as gifts between tribes.[27]

In the eighteenth century, Plateau Indians began to learn about the approach of white people and of the associated fur trade. Articles of white manufacture reached the plateau through expanding native trade networks, along with the information that such articles might be obtained from the whites in exchange for beaver furs. This lesson was reinforced by the arrival of Iroquois fur hunters toward the close of the century, some of whom trapped plateau beaver and carried the furs to white trading posts across the Rocky Mountains. The Kutenais attempted to enter the trade by performing the same journey in 1795, but they were apparently unable to cross the territory of the hostile Blackfoot.[28]

Plateau Indians entered the Euro-American fur trade in earnest when the first English and American trading posts were established on the plateau at the beginning of the nineteenth century. By 1810 beaver populations were thoroughly depleted in many areas east of the Rocky Mountains, prompting traders to push on to the Columbia Plateau.[29] The North West Company crossed the Canadian Rockies and founded Kootenay House and Salish House in 1809 and Spokane House in 1811. John Jacob Astor's Pacific Fur Company used both overland and oceangoing transport to found Fort Astoria, Fort Okanagon, and Fort Spokane in 1811. In 1818 the North West Company founded Fort Nez Perces at the junction of the Columbia and Snake Rivers. The North West Company underwent a forced merger with the rival Hudson's Bay Company (HBC) in 1821, after which the HBC was the main trading concern on the plateau, though Plateau Indians also traded with Americans they met on the Great Plains and Great Basin and at American posts such as Fort Henry on the upper Missouri.[30]

Euro-American traders arrived on the plateau with definite ideas on how the fur trade would develop. The traders would display their wares and exhort the Indians to trap beaver. The Indians, they believed, would soon become attached to and even dependent upon the Euro-American manufactures and would become ever more zealous beaver hunters in their desire to acquire more goods. Alexander Ross contemplated the expected process as he stood in a Walla Walla village in 1813. Though the Walla Wallas had few "European articles," Ross was confident they would soon be addicted to such goods: "The more they get of our manufacture the more unhappy they will be, as the possession of one article naturally creates a desire for another, so that they are never satisfied."[31]

There was much in the initial contacts to support the trader's projections. Indians all over the plateau expressed their enthusiasm to trade in terms that revealed prior knowledge of the fur trade. In 1809 David Thompson found the Flathead and "Skeetshoo" Indians at Kullyspell House eager to trade, especially for guns. He told them that "they must not pass days and nights in gambling, but be industrious in hunting and working of Beaver and other furrs, all which they promised."[32] The Walla Walla chief Yellepit in 1811 declared that his people were in a "helpless state" and entreated Thompson to "bring us Arms, Arrow shods of iron, axes, knives, and many other things which you have and which we want very much."[33] In 1814 a party of Walla Walla and Cayuse Indians traveled down the Columbia to Fort George to ask that a trading post be established on their lands, where they said "the beaver were very numerous."[34]

In the first years of the fur trade, Plateau Indians did indeed appear enamored of white goods and willing to change their ways of living to acquire more. Trading with the Sinkaietk in 1812, Alexander Ross noted: "they cannot resist the temptation of European articles, and will give everything they possess for the toys and trifles of the whites."[35] A few years later Ross Cox noted that the Sanpoils were "tantalized by seeing . . . various articles" their neighbors had obtained in trade.[36] In the winter of 1812–13 the Flatheads and Kutenais made "excellent winter hunts, and returned in the spring loaded with beaver."[37] Some Indians altered their seasonal round to acquire furs. In October 1811 Thompson and his men were caught in an unexpected snowstorm on the upper Columbia when they met a Spokan family engaged in "Working Beaver." When Thompson asked if the snow was "more than usual" for the time of year, the native man replied that he had no idea, since "he had never [before] left the Village at this season." The Spokan man further explained that many of his village were also out hunting beaver for the traders.[38]

It was the policy of the fur traders to create dependency as a spur to native productivity. "Every inducement should be held out to the Indians to renew their industrious habits," wrote Hudson's Bay Company governor George Simpson to the manager of Colville

House in 1820. "Intimate that they will be rewarded in proportion to the amount of Furs they bring us, but if their hunts are neglected, they cannot expect to have their wants supplied."[39] By "proper management" and "judicious treatment," the Indians of the Columbia Plateau would soon "shake off their indolent habits" in favor of "habits of industry," Simpson thought.[40]

Yet by the 1820s it was becoming apparent that few Plateau Indians were willing to devote themselves to hunting beaver in the way the traders had hoped. In 1827 Hudson's Bay Company trader Samuel Black despaired at the Indians' "indifference" to most Euro-American goods. Plateau Indians wanted only guns, ammunition, and kettles, he noted, and even these were considered insufficient "for the toil of going for beaver."[41] At Fort Nez Perces, chief factor Simon McGillivray lamented "what apathy there is among these Indians in going in quest of Beaver." He noted that though the Indians had talked of hunting for months, "no one is got off yet."[42] Another HBC employee complained that the Kettle Falls natives only went into the mountains in the fall to "pick up a few Skins" to trade for the "trifling articles of British Manufacture they require but those are very few indeed; as they are perfectly independent of us for any necessary."[43] Many Plateau natives did hunt and trade beaver; Colville House alone traded more than two thousand beaver skins a year in the 1820s and 1830s.[44] But the returns were always less than the traders had hoped for.

There are a number of reasons why the Plateau Indians did not become efficient fur hunters. First were the cultural barriers. Beavers were of little interest to Plateau natives before contact.[45] Hunting small furs like beaver was classed as women's work in most Plateau societies, and native men proved unwilling to engage in a life the Nez Perce thought "fit only for women and slaves."[46] Another barrier was that for Plateau men hunting was a communal affair, whereas trapping beaver was a solitary or family enterprise.[47] Beaver hunting also conflicted with the seasonal round. The best and most valuable beaver pelts were those taken during the fall and winter, but these were the seasons for hunting buffalo and for winter dances, activities that took precedence for many Indians.[48] "Hardly anything is traded during the winter, nor do the Indians hunt beaver," wrote the chief trader at Fort Nez Perces in 1831.[49]

More significantly, Plateau Indians found they had little need for most Euro-American manufactures. "The natives of this district are brave and independent," noted the chief trader at Spokane House in 1822, "their wants are few and easily supplied."[50] George Simpson remarked that the trade would be "wonderfully increased" if the Indians would hunt beaver with more vigor, but admitted: "They do not have much occasion for our supplies and therefore take little pains in that way."[51] Native indifference to most trade goods is confirmed by archeological investigations, which show few Euro-American manufactures in early historic villages.[52]

This comparative indifference to Euro-American trade goods is explained by the means of subsistence of Plateau Indians. Euro-American manufactures contributed little to the business of making a living on the plateau. The major subsistence activities—fishing and root digging—were best accomplished by native techniques and technology. Nothing in the traders' storehouses captured salmon more efficiently than the wooden weirs and traps already in use, and the fire-hardened digging sticks of the Plateau women were ideally suited to gathering the roots that were the major staple of Plateau life. When asked to list the major obstacles to trade in the Northwest, a Hudson's Bay Company employee cited the "abundance of nutritious roots" and "abundance of Salmon" which, "though they would not satisfy a European stomach, makes them perfectly Indipindant of us."[53] The Indians around Spokane House "live constantly on what Nature bestows," according to the factor there.[54] Even firearms were of limited utility, too hazardous for use in the communal "surround" style of hunting, where natives drove animals to the center of a circle and shot at them from all sides.[55] "Arms they merely require for show of defence as they rarely hunt," one HBC officer noted in 1824.[56] Added another, "as they are not animal hunters Guns are of little or no use to them in procuring food."[57] A visitor to the Spokans in 1841 observed that the Indians used the bow and arrows (with steel points) for most of their hunting, reserving their guns for larger animals.[58]

Even if Plateau Indians had been more enthusiastic trappers, beavers were not abundant on the plateau. Much of the plateau is arid, and the great rivers that bisect it are subject to too much seasonal rise and fall to support beavers. The animals were found on some of the smaller rivers and streams, but these small dispersed populations were quickly trapped out.[59] In 1806 John Ordway noted "plenty" of beaver in the lower Touchet River where it drained into the Columbia.[60] In 1812, the year the first trading post was established in the region, there were still "a good many Beaver & Otter" nearby.[61] But by 1817 there were "scarcely any" beaver in the area.[62] In 1811 David Thompson met an Iroquois trapper along the Pend d'Oreille River who boasted of having taken 850 beaver in that vicinity. Thompson reflected that though the beaver were "very numerous . . . another year of trapping will in a manner exterminate them."[63]

Exterminated they were. In 1812 it was reported that the Spokan country "did not abound in furs," and by 1821 the chief trader at Spokane House wrote: "there are few or no beaver in this part of the country now."[64] By this time many North West Company partners considered the southern plateau exhausted of furs and advocated moving operations northward.[65] By 1827 even the upper Columbia beavers were said to be "on the verge of extermination," while an 1831–32 trapping expedition in Idaho and western Montana found the beaver badly depleted almost everywhere.[66] An 1841 exploring expedition found that beavers had "all but disappeared" from the Yakama territory and were "scarce" in Nez Perce lands.[67] An 1846 expedition in the North Cascades noted that despite "indications of their once having been abundant," there were "few beaver" to be found. "Here as elsewhere," the leader noted, "the trap has evidently done its work."[68]

Alternatives to Trade

Fortunately for the Plateau Indians, there were easier ways to acquire trade goods than chasing the vanishing beavers. These alternatives to the fur trade enabled natives to acquire the goods they wanted with minimal disruptions to their traditional way of life. The first alternative to the fur trade was to provide other necessities to the Euro-Americans. Food and horses were the major nonfur trade items, but whites also parted with manufactured goods in return for clothing, saddles, reins, snowshoes, grease, pemmican, parfleches, leather lodges, native clothing (especially moccasins), and more.[69] The remoteness of the Columbia department and consequent expense of transportation made the traders especially reliant on this "country produce." Hudson's Bay Company trader John Work complained that less than two-thirds of his goods were exchanged for beaver. "The rest is consumed in the trade of what is denominated Country Produce, provisions, and other expenses." Work recognized that the natives were using this trade as an alternative to hunting beaver and recommended curtailing such expenditures so the natives would be "obliged to exert themselves more hunting beaver to procure their wants."[70]

Food was the most common item other than fur traded by the Indians. Traders on the west side of the Rocky Mountains missed out on the rich diet of buffalo pemmican and native corn enjoyed by their comrades on the plains. Rather, dried salmon became the unloved staple of the trading posts—described by one wag as "the New Caledonian staff of life."[71] Another trader complained that the fish had "little more substance than a piece of rotten wood."[72] "God help him that passes many years on such poor stuff," added another.[73] A clerk at Thompsons River described the salmon diet as "quite *Medicinal*," observing how "this very morning one of my men in attending on the calls of nature evacuated to a distance of six feet."[74] Dried salmon had long been a regular trade in the Plateau economy and now the fur companies became major buyers, exchanging trade goods for thousands of the fish each year.[75] Indians found that providing the posts with salmon was easier than hunting beaver and involved less disruption of their seasonal round. At Fort Okanagon in 1826, Alexander Kennedy wryly noted that though his men were "fortunate enough to have 12 or 1300 salmon" purchased, "the name of a Beaver is scarcely heard among the natives."[76]

Horses were another native commodity much in demand by the fur traders, both to ride and to dine upon. The English botanist David Douglas described the "general fare" of travelers on the Columbia as "horse-flesh cooked by boiling, and sometimes roasted on the point of a stick before the fire."[77] Fort Nez Perces, located in the horse-rich Cayuse country, was the main trading center for horses, where 250 a year were purchased from the Cayuses, Nez Perces, and other natives.[78] George Simpson complained that the residents of that post consumed over 700 horses between 1821 and 1824.[79] At Spokane House so many horses made their way to the dinner table that the local supply was diminished, which "consequently enhanced the prices so that now we cannot afford to eat horseflesh," the clerk complained.[80] At Fort Colville trade goods valued at 1,500 beaver skins were traded for horses in a single year.[81] Indians with horses to spare never needed to look for beaver.[82]

Trade goods could also be acquired in payment for labor performed for traders. Native men and women found occasional employment as agricultural laborers, cooks, letter carriers, portagers, guides, interpreters, and watchmen at unused trading posts.[83] The remoteness of the plateau and the expense of maintaining white employees made native labor essential to the trade. "Indeed if it were not for the assistance we get from the Indians at minor jobs around this place, such as cutting firewood, attending on the livestock, carrying water," wrote chief trader Francis Heron at Fort Colville in 1830, "some of the principle work must be neglected, owing to the few hands we have got to get through so much labour as has to be done."[84]

Simple gratuities were another source of trade goods entering the Plateau economy. Such gifts were necessary to establish and maintain good social and trading relations. In the native context, gifts were often presented casually, with a modest deprecation of their value.

"Let me give this to you," one Nez Perce might say to another, "it is just not anything."[85] Traders were less gracious and often regarded the practice as a shakedown, but most came to understand that gifts were necessary to a profitable trade. "A bad custom prevails," complained one trader, "of giving out Cloathings & other Gratuities before trading begins." Yet he admitted: "It is only after they have all from us, that they commence trading."[86]

Tobacco was the standard gratuity, and the enthusiasm of Plateau Indians for the traders' tobacco became the stuff of legend. "The white men made us love tobacco almost as much as we love our children, and now we are starving for it," the Spokan chief Illim-Spokanee declared in 1814.[87] In 1825 George Simpson noted that "tobacco is becoming almost a necessary of life" on the Plateau, and in 1836 the missionary Samuel Parker claimed that "if an Indian is suffering with hunger and nakedness, his first request is for tobacco."[88] Iron knives, cotton or woolen cloth shirts, clothing, blankets, gunpowder, and ammunition were other common gratuities.[89]

To the native way of thinking, the great wealth of the traders and their presence on Indian land put the whites under a reciprocal obligation to be generous with their goods—an obligation of which the whites often had to be reminded. Traders interpreted these reminders as begging. The chief factor at Spokane House complained that the Spokans were "always begging" for tobacco, food, and ammunition, "and if we are slow in complying with their requests, they demand it as a right." The Spokans expected an "Open House" at the post, with "gratis tobacco." "They think us much beholden to them for allowing us to remain on their lands," he continued. Gifts became "a tribute which they look upon as a right."[90]

At Fort Nez Perces the factor observed that the Indians often visited without any furs to trade and "cannot brook a refusal" when gifts were requested. "Indian women are as troublesome as the men as regards begging," wrote another trader, "and at times we cannot be off from them without giving a few Beads and Rings."[91] But gift giving could cut both ways. When the Nez Perces' factor reminded a Walla Walla chief that he had smoked company tobacco all winter without ever giving a gift in return, the chief presented the trader with a "fine horse."[92]

Some traders steadfastly refused to show the generosity required to establish and maintain good relations with the natives. When traders charged too much for their goods, ignored the pressing needs of the Indians, or failed to provide expected gifts, the natives took it upon themselves to remind the white people that not only their business but their very lives depended on continued Indian good will. Plateau Indians rarely used violence or pillaged the goods of stingy traders. But the threat of pillaging—or worse—proved an effective tool to manage the traders.[93] Natives found it to their advantage to keep some traders in a constant state of anxiety.

The threat of pillaging might occur whenever Indians outnumbered whites. "As soon as these Indians find themselves numerous, they will always endeavor to impose and intimidate," fretted a Hudson's Bay trader.[94] When Alexander Ross led a small party of traders to the great Yakima Valley camas camp, the natives there tormented him, stealing his horses and threatening to kill him. A liberal distribution of gifts calmed the Indians and secured the return of the horses.[95]

When a North West Company party traveling down the Columbia River in 1816 attempted to pass by an encampment of Cayuses and Nez Perces without stopping to share tobacco (as was the custom), the Indians waved the traders ashore. Seeing their gestures ignored, the natives fired several shots at the boat until it put ashore. The Indians hauled the canoe and its passengers "up the beach high and dry" and detained the traders "till they had smoked themselves drunk" from the traders' tobacco. When the Indians returned the craft to the water, they warned the Nor'Westers "never to attempt passing their camp again without first putting on shore and giving them a smoke."[96] Fur traders took the lesson. In 1825 a Hudson's Bay Company trader complained that travel on the Columbia was rendered "very slow" by the necessity of stopping at every Indian lodge along the way to share a smoke.[97]

Sometimes the threat of violence was not sufficient. In the 1830s the Cayuse and Nez Perce chiefs Tauitau and Apashwakaiket demanded that Fort Nez Perces factor Pierre Pambrun "promise to reduce the price of goods and give more for ponies."[98] When the trader refused, the Indians tied up Pambrun and his interpreter and gave them a sound thrashing. If he did not reform his ways, the natives warned Pambrun, they would come back and hang him. Pambrun thereafter adjusted his prices more to the Indians' liking.[99]

Incidents like these kept every trader on his guard; a strain of anxiety runs through the writing of most plateau traders.[100] "We are well aware that in this country our lives are constantly exposed," commented one trader, "and in regulating our treatment of Indians neither too much severity nor leniency will answer."[101] Another fretted over the constant "diabolical combinations" of the natives.[102] In describing the fortifications at Fort Nez Perces, Samuel Black described the post as "the best place for defence against an Indian attack on this side of the mountains," and noted that such security was "required as at times there are two thousand [natives] about the place."[103]

Once the threat of pillaging had done its work and goods were extracted from the traders, good relations were usually restored. In 1826 John Work and his Hudson's Bay Company brigade found themselves surrounded by an armed circle of disgruntled Nez Perces. They demanded tobacco to smoke, "that their hearts would be good" toward the traders. An experienced hand in the fur trade, Work noted that the quarrel was merely a "pretext" for blackmailing tobacco from him. Yet after looking over the armed ranks of his potential opponents, he found it "advisable to comply with their request . . . as we had much to lose and little to gain" in a fight. The Nez Perces smoked the tobacco and dispersed, their leader "haranguing" his fellows to trade more beaver skins with Work.[104]

Finally, trade goods could be acquired through actual pillaging and theft. Plateau Indians sometimes relieved unwary traders of unsecured goods, especially when friendly trade relations had yet to be established. HBC trader John McLean described how the Carrier Indians were "the greatest thieves in the world when the whites first settled among them," capable of stealing a trader's belt without his realizing or of cutting away the top portions of a sleeping white man's blanket.[105] White traders inevitably condemned such behavior as theft, but to Indians these were instances of negative reciprocity and forceful reminders to the traders that they must be more forthcoming with their goods if they were to establish good relations.

Actual pillaging was less common than the threat of it, but it sometimes occurred. In 1835 a party of Americans who had failed to establish any trading relations with the natives were surrounded by a band of Walla Walla Indians, "severely" beaten, and left with only a horse and gun apiece.[106] Most traders came to realize that their safety necessitated establishing at least balanced reciprocity with the natives. The American trader Joshua Pilcher stated of his relations with the Flatheads and other peoples that trade "is a pretty good protection to itself, when once fairly opened and prudently conducted."[107] Once regular trade was established with the blanket-cutting Carriers, for example, theft became less prevalent. "No Indians can be more honest in paying their debts" than the Carriers, testified one trader.[108]

If trade relations between Indians and whites grew more peaceful and regular in the 1830s and 1840s, it was because the fur companies came to accept, however grudgingly, the native terms of trade. In 1841 an American watched the employees of the Hudson's Bay Company sorting newly arrived goods at Fort Vancouver. They divided the goods into three categories. First were "articles of gratuity" designated to be given to the Indians as gifts, such as tobacco and knives. Second were articles to trade for furs. These included blankets, cloth, guns, powder, and shot. In theory, guns were to be exchanged only for beaver skins, though in practice they were often traded for horses as well. The final group of trade goods consisted of "articles to pay for services" as well as provisions and included beads, handkerchiefs, ribbons, and shirts.[109] Nothing could better illustrate the traders' grudging acceptance of native concepts of exchange than this ritual sorting of the goods.

The modest quantities of trade goods that entered Plateau society were used in ways that enhanced rather than altered the natives' traditional way of life. Foreign manufactures were most valued when they filled the role of native items. Brightly colored trade beads were used for ornament along with the dentalium shells and porcupine quills that decorated Plateau clothing. Wool blankets served alongside buffalo robes, and copper kettles and woven cooking baskets were used in the same lodges. The American trader Wilson Price Hunt observed the mix of new and traditional goods in a Cayuse camp in 1813: "In their homes they have kettles and copper pots. . . . They have some axes, too, and a skillfully wrought stone hammer that they use to pound roots, cherries, and other fruits, as well as fish. Pointed pieces of elkhorn serve in lieu of wedges to split wood. . . . Their water containers are also made of willow, and in these they cook their meat by putting red-hot stones from the fire into them. However, copper kettles are preferred, three or four of them usually hanging in their tepees."[110]

Increased trade would soon bring other items to the Cayuses, such as woolens, firearms, mirrors, and face paint. Yet the Cayuses and other Plateau peoples did not become any more dependent on white goods as time went on. In 1825 Alexander Kennedy complained that "notwithstanding the long time that white people has been among them," Plateau peoples had not learned "to feel the want of foreign articles . . . nor are their wants in any way increased."[111] Traditional skills helped maintain Indian independence. In 1861, more than fifty years after the advent of the fur trade, the Kutenais were reported to be "fully occupied in making bows and arrows, lines and hooks."[112] As late as the 1880s a Similkameen Indian who could not afford an iron ax was able to quickly fashion one of stone, "the same he said as his father had used."[113] Well into the twentieth century, Plateau life continued to be defined by the seasonal round and dominated by traditional goods and technologies.

Traditional trade between native groups continued in the era of the fur trade. The Kutenais, living in one of the more beaver-rich areas of the plateau, maintained an extensive trade network. They crossed the Rockies each year to acquire buffalo hides to exchange with their more sedentary plateau neighbors. The Kutenais also produced mats of woven tule reeds, which they traded at Kettle Falls during the salmon season. From Kettle Falls the mats were redistributed throughout the plateau. Iron oxide deposits in the Rocky Mountains gave the Kutenais a ready source of vermilion or red pigment, which they also exchanged with other groups. In return for these hides, mats, and pigments, the Kutenai received pounded salmon, horses, dentalium shells, and Euro-American trade goods.[114]

Native women benefited equally with native men from the trade. Steel implements and metal pots eased some of the work in preparing food and dressing hides. Because subsistence was not disrupted, Plateau women maintained high status during the fur trade.[115] Native women were also involved with the fur traders in marriage or less formal unions.[116] It was the policy of the trading companies to encourage unions between traders and native women as a means of gaining influence with their relations. George Simpson described such "country marriages" as "a most important chain of connection to the Natives."[117] Alexander Ross estimated that there were perhaps fifty such unions in the Northwest in 1825.[118] Native wives "never fail to influence" their relatives and fostered a "close alliance" between traders and Indians, he noted. "The vigilance of these women has often been an instrument of safety of the forts, when the most diabolical combinations were set on foot by the natives," Ross added.[119]

With a foot in both cultures, these country wives were also able to manipulate the traders in ways that helped their families and their people. George Simpson, who so forcefully advocated trader-native unions, also worried over fur traders who "neglect their business" and "allow themselves to be influenced by the Sapient councils of their *Squaws*." "The Honble Committee," he wrote, "would scarcely believe that their business is frequently a matter of secondary consideration compared to the little family affairs and domestic arrangements, that their people and Craft are employed in transporting Women & Children with their baggage Pols Pans Kettles & Bags of Moss."[120]

Overall, the fur trade had a limited impact on the material culture of Plateau Indians. But they were affected in other ways. Access to firearms and ammunition increased the security of the natives of the southern and eastern borders of the plateau. The Cayuses used the weapons they acquired to retake their old hunting grounds in the

Blue Mountains and to capture slaves from the gun-poor Shoshones.[121] The Flatheads, Nez Perce, and other eastern groups were able to venture onto the plains with a greater sense of security now that they could match the Blackfoot gun for gun. The level of violence between Plateau groups diminished as well, as fur traders exerted their influence to discourage fighting from interrupting trade.[122] And along with the exchange of goods in the fur trade there was an exchange of ideas.

A Window into White Society

To Plateau Indians, fur trading posts had attractions beyond acquiring trade goods. The forts became general gathering places, sources of entertainment, and places of succor in times of winter famine. Most of all, the posts—and the fur trade in general—were windows into white society. "We must live with them and they with us," wrote Alexander Ross, "we must carry on a free intercourse with them and familiarize them by that intercourse."[123] As natives examined white beliefs, culture, and material goods through the lens of the fur trade, it became evident that white people did indeed possess great spirit power.

The surest proof of the traders' spirit power was their great wealth. To Plateau Indians, material wealth was evidence of a successful relationship with the spirit world. A skillful deer hunter or strong digger of roots was guided by a powerful guardian spirit. A man or woman who acquired great riches in gambling was able to do so because of the gambling power given by his or her spirit. The source of all wealth was a spiritual source. So when Indians saw the huge number of goods in the traders' storehouses, this was certain evidence of the strangers' spirit power. Into the twentieth century the Sanpoil believed that "the white man, with his remarkable material culture, must have strong guardians [spirits] even though he does not admit it."[124]

More important than the number of trade goods the Euro-Americans owned was the novel and powerful technology that had produced them. The metal implements, wool cloth, gunpowder, paint, and beads of the whites were clearly produced by a technology unknown to the natives. Mobile hunter-gatherers with a limited material culture like the peoples of the Plateau regarded technology not as a collection of material objects but as the underlying knowledge used to obtain or produce such objects.[125] On the Plateau, the most valuable technical knowledge came from the spirit world. Guardian spirits helped Indians to build sweat lodges or shape bows by informing their hosts of the best places to find materials and the best ways to build. The unfamiliar technology of the Euro-Americans implied a different source of spirit power. "They think it is *great medicine* which comprehends every thing which is to them incomprehensible," observed Meriwether Lewis as he demonstrated his air gun to some assembled Indians.[126]

The apparent spirit power of the traders was confirmed by their abilities as healers. Not all traders were willing to set themselves up as shamans. Samuel Black at Fort Nez Perces reported in 1829 that the Indians there "have Confidence in the Whites Medesines but more in their own Doctors which we do not wish to remove . . . for they often attribute all their misfortunes to the influence or Sorcery of their Doctors."[127] But traders were frequently appealed to for medical help by the Plateau Indians, and most traders were willing to offer what help they could. A trader with the Carrier Indians on the northern plateau reported that the Indians had "a great deal of confidence in my medical skill" and that "my reputation as a disciple of Aesculapius became firmly established."[128] So extensive was the practice that by 1837 George Simpson clamed that every fur trading post "is in fact an Indian hospital" where free medical care was provided.[129]

In Plateau beliefs the power to heal illness was accompanied by the power to cause it, and here again the traders seemed powerful. Some traders, using native beliefs to their advantage, threatened Indians with sickness. When trader Duncan McDougall feared that the Chinook Indians were plotting against him, he showed an assembly of chiefs a vial that he declared contained smallpox. McDougall told the Indians that although the traders were "weak in number," he himself was "strong in medicine" and would release the smallpox should the Chinooks cause any trouble. Thereafter McDougall was known to the natives as "the great smallpox chief."[130] These threats were taken seriously by at least some Plateau Indians. In the 1830s a band of Nez Perce Indians pleaded with the chief factor at Fort Walla Walla not to inform John McLoughlin of a transgression for fear that McLoughlin would "send some great plague among them."[131]

To be sure, it was clear that not all whites had strong spirit power. Traders got lost, failed to cure the sick, were surprised by events, and sometimes sickened and died. But overall they were seen to have a strong and unfamiliar kind of power. "After the Man of heaven, you are next in dignity," a Carrier chief told the trader at Fort Kamloops.[132] "Their chiefs still have considerable authority," noted another HBC employee, "but much of the homage they claimed and received in former times is now transferred to the white chiefs, or traders, whom they esteem the greatest men in the universe."[133] In 1831 Francis

Heron described how an Indian "fell into a trance" in Heron's presence. When the Indian recovered, he explained to Heron that "he had been struck with a remorse of conscience for his crimes at seeing me, because he thought I might like the Great Master of Life, have the power of seeing into the heart."[134]

Confronted by these spiritually powerful beings, Plateau Indians inquired about the sources of their power. As it became known that white men's religious notions were different from those of the natives, the questions became more specific, focusing on exactly what it was the white men believed. Ross Cox described an 1814 conversation with what he called a "hermaphrodite chief" of a small village south of Kettle Falls.[135] "He inquired particularly about our form of government, laws, customs, marriages, our ideas of a future life, &c.," Cox related "The attempts I made to explain to him some of the abstruse doctrines of our religion were rather bungling; but he appeared much pleased whenever he ascertained that he comprehended what I wished to convey; and, at the conclusion of our discourse, said he would be glad to converse with some of the wise men we call priests on these matters, and more particularly on the subject of a future state."[136]

The Faith of the Fur Traders

Just what were the religious beliefs of the fur traders, which prompted such native curiosity? Historians have long assumed that white traders had little religious inclination or knowledge, so the religious impact of the fur trade must have been nil. Fur trade society has been viewed from the perspective of the first missionaries, who found much to criticize. American missionary William Gray condemned the Hudson's Bay Company posts as a "squawtocracy of skin traders."[137] Anglican minister Herbert Beaver decried Fort Vancouver as a "deplorable scene of vice and ignorance" with "no legal marriage, no regular baptism, no accustomed rites of burial." The men, he wrote, were not practicing their faith, while their native wives were "totally ignorant of the duties of religion."[138] But if Plateau Indians were engaging in an extended religious dialogue with the white traders in their midst, we need to move beyond stereotypes and discover what these men really believed.

In fact, many of the employees of the fur companies were deeply religious. This is equally true of the Anglophone bourgeoisie who managed the trade and the French-Canadian *engagés* who worked for them.[139] David Thompson, the first Nor'wester to enter the plateau, was devoutly religious. He often ended his journal entries with "thank Good Providence," and read passages from the Bible to his employees in "a most extraordinarily pronounced French."[140] Alexander Ross called the Bible his "only consolation" during the long winters on the plateau and claimed the life of a trader offered opportunity "to instruct your family . . . to enjoy the pleasures of religion to better advantage, to serve your God to more perfection, and be a far better Christian than were your lot cast in the midst of the temptations of a busy world."[141] A Hudson's Bay Company trader recalled how he and other traders would interrupt their winter "yarns" about fur trade adventures with "an animated discussion on theology."[142] The Bible was the centerpiece of many post libraries, which often featured other religious and inspirational works as well.[143] The Anglican missionary John West was pleased to find the Scriptures, Books of Common Prayer, and other religious works at many of the Hudson's Bay Company posts he visited on his way to the Red River settlement in the 1820s.[144]

Nor was religious faith the exclusive province of the bourgeoisie. The French Canadian *engagés* who labored in the fur trade had their own faith, Catholicism, to which they added a few white folk and Indian beliefs. Though they seldom had the opportunity to attend a Catholic service or take part in the sacraments, and though many lived in unions with native women that had not been sanctioned by the church, these men considered themselves Catholics and their first request on settling down in one location was for a Catholic priest and the establishment of a church.[145] An 1823 Hudson's Bay Company regulation complied with employee demand by specifying that "sermons or moral lectures in French" were to be provided for the Canadians, "expressed in easy and familiar language suited to their notions and apprehensions."[146] At Fort George, John McLoughlin employed one man as a Catholic catechist to teach the rudiments of that faith to the native wives and mixed-blood children of his *engagés*.[147] (The Hudson's Bay Company also tried to provide for the secular education of the children of its employees by sending spelling books to all its posts.[148])

The same 1823 regulation that provided "moral lectures" also mandated that religious services were to be held on Sundays at the trading posts to promote "the more effectual civilization of and moral improvement" of employees, their families, and the Indians: "Every Sunday when circumstances permit, divine Services be publickly read with becoming solemnity, either once or twice a day, to be regulated by the number of people and other circumstances, at which every man woman and child resident must attend, together with such of the Indians who may be at hand, as it may be found proper to admit."[149]

These Sunday services were sporadic at most posts, depending on the disposition of the trader in charge. Regular services began at Fort Vancouver on the lower Columbia in 1826 and continued regularly throughout the 1830s and 1840s. At Fort Nez Perces, on the other hand, there were few religious observances, or at least few noted in the company records.[150] When services did occur, Indians were regular attendees. "They listen with great attention to our remarks on these subjects and since we have commenced reading prayers in public on Sundays at the Establishment they attend regularly and conduct themselves with great decorum," George Simpson noted at Fort Vancouver in 1828.[151]

Another possible source of Christian ideas was the Iroquois trappers who accompanied and sometimes preceded the traders. The Iroquois were Catholics whose syncretized faith combined Christian and indigenous elements. The numbers of Iroquois on the plateau increased in the 1820s and 1830s. Especially influential was the arrival of the Caughnawaga chief Big Ignace and his twenty-some followers in 1816. Ignace's people settled among the Flatheads, who were glad to get well-armed reinforcements against the Blackfoot. The Iroquois taught the Flatheads at least some of the outward forms of Catholicism, including the sign of the cross, morning and evening prayers, baptism, marking graves with a cross, and the Sabbath day—which the Iroquois marked by raising a flag, as they had seen white traders do.[152] The Flatheads in turn shared some of their new beliefs with other Plateau peoples, notably the Nez Perces.[153]

The religious dialogue between traders and Indian proceeded by fits and starts during the first fifteen years of the fur trade. The beliefs of the traders were a matter of curiosity to some Indians but hardly a matter of necessity. The Indians' quest for the sources of white spirit power began in earnest in 1824, when death returned to the Plateau.

Increasing Mortality

"The returns have fallen off this Season about 300 skins," George Simpson noted in his journal in 1825. "This seems to have arisen from a Mortality that took place in the course of the Winter among the Cai-uses [Cayuses] which prevented them from hunting."[154] The fur trade brought the Indians into a new epidemiological world. Ships arrived at the Hudson's Bay Company's Fort Vancouver from Europe,

China, the eastern United States, the Sandwich Islands, and South America, bringing unseen cargoes of microbes along with their other goods. Potentially infectious traders set out up the Columbia River to fan out across the plateau, where many had daily close contact with the Indians. At the same time, Plateau natives were traveling beyond their homelands more frequently, bringing back new illnesses along with buffalo robes and trade goods. After a generation of demographic recovery from the smallpox epidemics of the eighteenth century, Indians once more began to sicken and die in large numbers. The religious dialogue between Indians and whites gained urgency as a result.

The unspecified "mortality" mentioned by Simpson was probably the smallpox that roared up the Columbia River in the winter of 1824–25.[155] The epidemic swept across the plateau, hitting Indians the hardest where they had most frequent contact with whites. The Yakamas "died by the hundreds," according to their tradition. "They became so terror-stricken that they left their sick to die along the trail, nor would they stop to bury their dead."[156] Perhaps as many as half the natives from the coast to Kettle Falls were killed in the epidemic.[157]

In 1829 "a disease of a very fatal character" struck the densely populated Northwest coast.[158] Called the "intermittent fever" by whites, it was probably an unusually virulent strain of malaria.[159] Along the lower Columbia River, native villages "were literally strewed with the dead and dying" and "birds preying on the uncovered carcasses."[160] Survivors fled from their villages in fear. This dispersal tactic might have been helpful for avoiding diseases such as smallpox that pass from one human being to another, but it did little to protect the Indians from the unrecognized vector of malaria, the *anopheles malcilipennis* mosquito. Unlike smallpox, which usually visited only once per generation when enough new disease-inexperienced individuals were born, malaria recurred every summer, driving coastal populations into a steep decline.[161] The epidemic reached its peak in 1830, but recurred in 1831 and 1832.[162] In November 1830 Fort Vancouver was besieged by panic-stricken natives who set up camp outside the fort, "giving as a reason that if they died they knew we would Bury them," as chief factor John McLoughlin explained.[163] He added that because many of the white employees of the Hudson's Bay Company were also sick with malaria, "we were obliged to drive the Indians away instead of affording them the assistance they implored of us."[164]

Whites and Indians were both susceptible to malaria, but whites generally recovered while Indians usually did not. A horrifying 85 to 90 percent of the natives of the Northwest coast and lower Columbia

River died in the 1820s and 1830s.[165] Some tribes, like the Cascades and Chinooks, all but disappeared. For the next few years travelers on the lower Columbia never failed to mention the large number of Indian ghost towns along the banks. In 1835 the American fur trader Nathaniel Wyeth stood on the shores of the formerly populous Wapato Island on the lower Columbia. "A mortality has carried off to a man its inhabitants," he sadly noted, "and there is nothing to attest that they ever existed except their decaying houses, their graves and their unburied bones, of which there are heaps."[166] For the few native survivors on the lower Columbia, social ties were shattered and there seemed little to live for. The same year that Wyeth made his mournful observation, a party of Americans in the Willamette Valley came upon an elderly Indian woman attempting to strangle her own grandchild. When the old woman was prevented from killing the child, she grew "very angry" and asked who would care for the child now that its parents were dead. "It is good to kill it," the woman insisted.[167]

The Columbia Plateau, too arid to support large numbers of anopheles mosquitoes, was spared the malaria epidemic. Yet Plateau Indians were well aware of the fearful mortality of their longtime trading partners on the lower Columbia. They also seemed to understand that the presence of the fur traders was somehow a contributing factor. At Fort Nez Perces many Indians avoided coming in to trade or to socialize in the summer and fall of 1831, explaining that they were afraid of falling ill.[168] Memories of the recent smallpox epidemic undoubtedly heightened native anxiety.

Smallpox and malaria were the most dramatic but by no means the only contagious "mortalities" introduced by the fur trade. Permanent trade posts regularly brought new sicknesses to the Plateau. While less dramatic than smallpox, the cumulative effects of illnesses such as influenza, typhus, and cholera were nearly as damaging. Winter, always a lean time on the Plateau, was when Indians were most vulnerable. Food stocks were low and overall health diminished. And it was during winter that Indians congregated most closely together.[169]

"Winter illnesses" became a new and deadly part of the seasonal round for many Indians. "Many of the Indians about the place are sick," noted the chief factor at Fort Colville in December 1830. Although he attributed the sickness to the crowded conditions of the winter camp, increased exposure to Old World diseases must have been part of the equation. As winter wore on, the health of the Colville natives continued to deteriorate. "The sickness amongst the Indians seems to be gaining ground, for constant demands are made upon me for medicine," he wrote a week later. By the fifth of January "many of the Indians . . . continue sickly, and two have already died." Ten days later, "an Indian child has died . . . and many others are in a low state."[170] The combination of new epidemic and endemic illness drove Plateau populations into a steep decline in the mid-1820s and 1830s. Somewhere between 20 and 50 percent of the Nez Perces, for example, died from 1824 to 1837.[171]

A Religious Dialogue

The return of epidemic illness gave a new impetus to the native search for the source of Euro-American spirit power. When George Simpson toured the HBC's plateau posts in the spring of 1825, months after the most recent smallpox epidemic, he was besieged by Indians seeking religious instruction. At Fort Okanagon he had a "long interview" with a Thompson chief who "enquired particularly if they might soon expect a 'Messenger from the Master of Life' on their lands (Meaning a Missionary)."[172] A few days later a delegation of headmen from the Spokan, Kutenai, and Flathead peoples "joined in a most earnest request that a Missionary or religious instructor should be placed among them."[173] The next day Simpson met with two Nez Perce chiefs who had traveled over two hundred miles with religious inquiries. "My fame has spread far and Wide and my speeches are handed from Camp to Camp throughout the country," Simpson marveled. "Some of them have it that I am one of the 'Master of Life's Sons' sent to see 'if their hearts are good' and others that I am his 'War Chief' with Bad Medicine if their hearts are bad."[174]

One of Simpson's goals on his tour of the interior was to recruit Indian youths to attend the HBC's school at Red River in Manitoba. The Indian parents were initially horrified by the suggestion that they part with their sons, asking if the Indians "were looked upon as dogs— willing to give up their children." But when they learned the boys would be receiving religious instruction, they told Simpson he could have "hundreds of children in an hours time."[175] Simpson chose two boys, sons of prominent chiefs, whom he christened Spokane Garry and Kootenay Pelly. As the boys prepared to leave their homes, the recent mortality weighed heavily on the parents' minds. "You see, we have given you our children, not our servants, or our slaves, but our own," said the father of one of the boys. "We have given you our hearts—our children are our hearts—but bring them back again to us before they become white men. We wish to see them once more Indians, and after that you can make them white men if you like. But let them not get sick or die. If they get sick, we shall get sick; if they die, we shall die. Take them, they are now yours."[176] In 1830 another five boys went to Red River.

Plateau Indians were not willing to wait for the return of the children or arrival of white missionaries to gain some of the desperately needed Euro-American spirit power. Instead they observed the religious ceremonies of the trading posts and requested instruction with renewed intensity. By the late 1820s and early 1830s, traders at various posts were discussing religion with curious natives. These dialogues had little effect on the theology of the fur traders, whose scattered observations on native faith show that they considered it a mere tissue of superstition.[177] "Being ignorant of whence they originally come, they take a superstitious, ridiculous story of their forefathers being placed in such and such a situation by their Sinchelep/Little Wolf," groused a trader who had apparently spent an evening listening to Coyote stories at Fort Colville.[178] At Fort Nez Perces the chief factor wondered at the native explanation of the seasons: "They attribute all for themselves[,] the spring to make the Roots sprout[,] summer to make the Salmon come & Winter for snow to see the tracks of Animals better."[179] But if white traders thought native faith "ridiculous," the natives took the faith of the fur traders far more seriously.

Wishram tradition recalls how some of their people traveled to Fort Vancouver to study the white men's religion, trips that were the beginning of "understanding about Sunday."[180] The traders at Fort Vancouver gave the Wishrams a piece of cardboard and instructions to punch holes in it to keep track of the days. They also taught the Wishrams "to dress up on Fridays and confess their sins." The Wishrams understood these practices as a cure for the disease episodes—"this religion was a belief in God to help sick people." It seemed to work. "After that [the new beliefs] came," the Wishrams remembered, "the sick people stopped dying." The success of the new faith encouraged other natives to adopt its practice, and it spread "up the Columbia River way back east."[181] Similarly, the Clakamas remember a native prophet named "Father Woods," an "old preacher" who brought his people religious doctrines he had learned from the Hudson's Bay Company in the 1820s or 1830s. Father Woods "surprised the old people" with his new doctrines, which included Sunday services and certain Christian holy days such as Christmas. Father Woods wore special "vestments" when he preached and used flags and bells in his services. The Clakamas remember his teachings as being "almost like the Catholics" who arrived in the 1840s.[182]

Fort Nez Perces, at the confluence of the Snake and Columbia Rivers, was another place whites and natives joined in a religious dialogue. "Indians in general are very . . . inquisitive & fond of stories from far and other places & old times," a factor at Fort Nez Perces noted in 1829. "They are seeking light sitting in darkness."[183] In 1831 the chief factor at the fort wrote: "We have instructed [Indians] in the forms of religion."[184] As the epidemic of 1831 ravaged the lower Columbia, Walla Walla, Nez Perce, Cayuse, and Palouse Indians came to the fort for a "devotional dance" each Sunday. Similar native dances took place that summer and the next at Spokane House and Fort Colville as well.[185] Sometimes the Indians asked the factor for tobacco as a reward for their dancing and inquired if the dance had been pleasing to the factor.[186] The native reasoning was that since the traders had "instructed them in the forms of religion we must pay them for it," according to one trader.[187] Yet Indians were willing to pay for such knowledge as well. After one Sunday dance an excited Nez Perce man gave a "good horse" to the chief factor. "He asks nothing for His horse except information about the forms of religion," noted the amazed trader.[188]

A few years later a different chief trader, Pierre Pambrun, told the American adventurer Captain Bonneville that he had given the Indians a "code of laws"—apparently moral laws—to follow and had introduced "the Christian religion, in the Roman Catholic form." Bonneville noted that the Indians had "altered and modified" what Pambrun taught them "to suit their peculiar habits of thought, and motives of action," while retaining "the principal points of faith, and its entire precepts of morality."[189] Pambrun's son recalled how every winter his father taught some Indians a translation of the Lord's Prayer. "This was quite novel to the Indians who took quite an interest and soon learned the prayer," the junior Pambrun recounted, "then the Apostle's Creed was taught the same way."[190] On Sundays the natives collected at the fort and the chief chanted Christian prayers while the Indians danced in cadence.[191]

Factor Francis Heron at Fort Colville was another trader who promoted Christianity. Heron was so enthusiastic in this role as preacher that a modern historian accuses him of having "a messiah complex."[192] In 1831 Heron boasted how he had delivered a sermon "the purport of which was to inculcate religion, morality and industry, to all which they promised a faithful observance."[193] Specifically, Heron taught the natives to pray in the morning and evening to "the Great Master of Life," to say grace at mealtimes, and the concepts of heaven and hell. Soon he was describing the surrounding natives as "religiously disposed," noting that "beaver skins are frequently sent to me to pray for them and for which they will on no consideration take payment."[194] To a friend Heron wrote, "From the little instruction I have given them on religious matters, they have become perfect saints . . . they are the very best Indians I have ever seen."[195]

Heron's teachings fell on ready ears. In January 1831 the Indians at Fort Colville "formally renounced, in full council, their ancient superstitious doctrines, such as conjuration, medicine, etc. And acknowledged and professed themselves to be, and ever to continue, true and faithful Christians," Heron exulted.[196] That same year a group of fur traders at Kettle Falls was approached by an excited Indian man who held a book of some kind in one hand. As the man approached, he grew "more and more animated pointing with passionate gestures alternately to the sun and Book."[197] Apparently no interpreter was present, but the trader believed the man was asking for information regarding religion.

When the Protestant missionary Samuel Parker toured the plateau in 1835 and 1836, he found the natives everywhere were eager to learn more about the Christian faith. Parker claimed that the traders took advantage of this searching, selling the Indians "packs of cards at high prices, calling them the Bible," and threatening them with the wrath of God "on almost any occasion when their wishes have been resisted."[198] But the Hudson's Bay Company had more for the Indians than packs of cards. It had some of their sons attending school at Red River, and in the early 1830s these boys began to return.

4. *The Columbian Religion, 1825–1840*

Prodigal Sons

While most Plateau Indians were acquiring Christian doctrine in dribs and drabs, at least seven young men were fully immersed at the Hudson's Bay Company school in Red River. Red River was a settlement of a few thousand people sprawling along one hundred miles at the junction of the Assiniboine and Red Rivers in present-day Manitoba. The settlers there were a mix of French Canadians, Scots, and English fur traders along with their native wives and métis children. As we have seen, Spokane Garry and Kootenay Pelly arrived at the school in 1826. In the winter of 1829 the two went home for a few months and returned to Red River in 1830 with five more native boys. As with Garry and Pelly, the boys were given "English" names by combining the name of their tribes with those of prominent Hudson's Bay Company officers. Thus the boys were dubbed Kootenay Collins, Spokan Berens, Cayuse Halket, Nez Perce Pitt, and Nez Perce Ellice.[1]

The curriculum at Red River was harsh, designed to "civilize" first and convert second. John West, the Anglican missionary who established the school, wrote that a broad English-style education would be necessary for the native children before "their characters will be changed under the mild influence of the Christian religion."[2] Each day began with a prayer and the mornings were given to schoolwork. The Indian boys learned to read and write and pondered the rudiments of mathematics, European history, and geography. Lessons from the Bible and catechisms from the Book of Common Prayer were supplemented with hymns.[3] In the afternoon students proceeded outside, where they mastered the intricacies of the hoe, planting vegetables, and growing grain. Breaches of discipline were punished with severe whippings.[4] Native dress was discarded for Euro-American-style clothing, hair was cropped short, and the students were required to speak English.[5] English was a practical as well as an ideological necessity, since at first the boys spoke "dialects so unalike, that their only intercourse was by signs."[6]

The young men began returning to their people in the early 1830s. Garry and Pelly began instructing their people even before they arrived. In 1828 at Fort Kamloops, George Simpson harangued some Shuswaps "never to be guilty of theft, murder, or of any inhuman deed towards the Whites"—a lesson he reinforced by reading passages from two letters written by the boys.[7] Garry and Pelly came home for a visit in 1829 and returned to Red River the following spring. Even in the few months they were with their people, Garry and Pelly made a "very great" impression "in relation to what they had learned," according to fur trade observers.[8] Garry returned for good in 1831. Collins, Halket, Ellice, and Pitt came back in 1833. Pelly and Berens never saw their homes again. Pelly died at Red River in 1831 after a fall from a horse, Berens three years later after a long illness.[9]

Armed with their King James Bibles and Books of Common Prayer, wearing the clothes and haircuts of white men, and speaking and reading English, the young men from Red River bore every outward appearance of having acquired some of the spirit power of the whites. They created a sensation wherever they went. According to Red River missionary David Jones, when Garry and Pelly came home for their 1829 visit, "the Indians on the Upper part of the Columbia paid utmost attention to the information conveyed to them" by the boys "and readily received whatever instructions or doctrines they thought proper to inculcate."[10] All the Red River boys tried to build on this initial enthusiasm in the weeks and months that followed their returns, with varying success.

Cayuse Halket returned to his people on the Umatilla River in 1833. He was perhaps thirteen years old. Halket held Sunday services "of the Church of England form of Worship" and taught Christian doctrine and English hymns.[11] At first his preaching roused great interest and "exerted good influence in favor of religion," according to a missionary who succeeded him.[12] Yet Halket's career as a religious teacher was to be short lived, for the boy seems to have lost his place in Cayuse society while he was away. His father, the chief Willatmotkin, had died just before Halket's return, and as the half-Europeanized teenager tried to minister to his tribe he discovered that he was unable "to reconcile himself to their mode of life."[13] Halket went back to Red River, where he died in 1837. "You see the return we get from sending the Young Cayouse Chief to be educated at Red River," chided Hudson Bay superintendent John McLoughlin, "now that he is dead, his Relations . . . give it out that we killed him."[14]

Pitt and Ellice returned to the Nez Perces in 1833. Pitt, the only Red River student who was not the son of a powerful chief, seems to have had little impact on the beliefs of his people. He died in 1839. Ellice was more influential, teaching his people a simple form of Anglican beliefs and becoming a chief in his own right. He discarded "Ellice" in favor of a Nez Perce name: Twvish Sismnen, or "Sparkling Horn."[15] When the first Protestant missionaries arrived a few years later, Sparkling Horn served them as a headman and interpreter. Kootenay Collins also returned in 1833, but died before he could have a significant impact on the beliefs of his people.[16]

Spokane Garry was by far the most active and influential of the Red River scholars, perhaps because he spent longer at Red River than any of the others, perhaps because he was the first to return. He came home for good in 1831 and set about teaching the Spokans what he had learned. Garry spent his first winter "preaching, teaching & expounding the Scripture to them also singing *Hymns*."[17] He built a tule mat church and school along the Spokane River. Garry had acquired a bell (perhaps a handbell) that he used to call his people to prayer. Some Spokans had probably already learned some of Garry's teachings at Fort Colville or other HBC posts. Garry taught "brotherly love, peaceful behavior and humility," along with morning and evening prayers (followed by "Amen"), a "simple ceremony of worship," and the Lord's Prayer.[18] His teachings were well received by the Spokans, "who were so anxious to hear him that they brought presents of various kinds, and indeed they seem to have maintained him in Indian abundance."[19]

Yet what Garry taught was not necessarily orthodox Anglicanism. Almost immediately upon his return, Garry took two wives, one from the Sanpoil people and another from the Umatillas.[20] While many powerful Plateau men practiced polygamy, it was contrary to Anglican doctrine. "Having received his knowledge away from his Tribe, he has in several instances imposed on their credulity by his superior knowledge," noted one Protestant missionary in 1837, six years after Garry had begun preaching.[21] Whatever Garry's doctrines, his teachings at first met with great acceptance and influenced not only the Spokans but the Coeur d'Alenes, Flatheads, Nez Perces, and other Plateau peoples.[22]

The Columbian Religion

Plateau Indians incorporated the gradually gained knowledge of Christianity into their own faith. The result was a syncretic blend of

Christian and native beliefs and practices that one trader called the "Columbian Religion."[23] Its "groundwork seemed to be Christianity, accompanied by some of the heathen ceremonies of the natives," according to the trader.[24]

This new faith spread rapidly across the Plateau after 1831. Transmission was fueled by an ancient tradition of exchanging religious ideas, especially during the winter season. The usual pattern was for the northern Plateau tribes, who relied more on hunting and practiced greater seasonal mobility, to borrow traditions from the southern Plateau, where the richer runs of salmon made for a more settled life. In 1812 David Thompson observed of the Flatheads, "their continual removal from place to place leaves them little or no Time to think of religious ceremonies. They wholly depend for these on the Village Tribes on the Columbia, who living an idle life have leisure for forming ceremonies, which being sanctioned in public Dances, are made known from Tribe to Tribe."[25] In 1829 a Hudson's Bay Company trader noted that the Indians "are fond of visiting and of making singing and dancing parties which are mostly of a religious nature."[26]

The kinship networks and trading partnerships that were of such importance on the Plateau also proved ideal for the transmission of new ideas. A tradition of exogamy, especially among high-status individuals, insured that many Plateau Indians had kin outside their own village. Regular visits were one method of reinforcing those ties of kinship. Giving gifts and working together in food-gathering activities also cemented kinship relations. Epidemics further increased intermarriage between ethnic groups, as the pool of available marriage partners in each village was reduced. Men of high status with multiple wives—such as Spokane Garry—were in a perfect position to transmit new ideas between groups.[27]

The most powerful element in the Columbian Religion was its emphasis on a single ruling deity. Plateau Indians had not traditionally recognized a ruling deity, and if they believed in a Creator at all, he was seen as distant and uninvolved in human affairs. As late as the 1820s, travelers on the Plateau reported no clear native conception of the Almighty. George Simpson stated categorically in 1825 that the Columbian natives had no idea of single supreme god.[28] At Fort Nez Perces in 1821, Samuel Black reported that the Indians had only a vague idea of "some Old Chief some where about the sea."[29] A trader living with the Carriers of the northern plateau claimed that they were "entirely ignorant of a Supreme Being," and that when the Columbian Religion arrived in 1833 the Carriers invented a term for the deity: "Yagasita—the 'Man of Heaven.'"[30] In the Chinook trade jargon this new deity was known as Sah-ha-le-tice, "the Great Chief Above." By the 1830s various terms describing a supreme being—"the Great Spirit," "the Chief Above," "the Great Chief Above"—became more common among the Indians.[31]

Observing the Sabbath was another important Christian element of the Columbian Religion. "Sunday is invariably kept sacred among these tribes," Captain Bonneville observed of the Cayuses in 1834: "they will not raise their camp on that day . . . neither will they hunt, nor fish, nor trade, nor perform any kind of labor."[32] Plateau Indians had a tradition of sacred days, so it was not too much of a stretch to add the Sunday observances of the traders to their own practices. On Sundays the fur company employees put aside their work, donned their best clothes, and sometimes held a religious service.[33] A Nez Perce explained how his people had noticed in the 1820s that "on certain days" the traders "were shaved & dressed different than usual & were engaged in horse racing and gambling."[34]

To observe the Sabbath, Indians first had to learn to count their days as the white men did, by units of seven. Traditionally, Plateau Indians counted time by groups of ten: ten days, ten full moons, ten snows (years). "Ask an Indian his age," Alexander Ross noted, "he immediately casts his eyes on his hands, calculates his age by his fingers, and answers by holding so many of them up to view, each finger standing for ten years."[35] To get the Indians to adopt Euro-American conceptions of time and thus better to organize the fur trade, traders gave the Indians pieces of cardboard punched with holes to keep track of the days.[36] In 1831 a party of Indians visited Fort Colville in part to get "their calendar for the Sunday examined and corrected."[37] In 1832 Captain Bonneville described the Nez Perces's "rude calendar of the feasts and festivals of the Romish church."[38] By the 1830s this observance of Sunday as a holy day was widespread. In 1834 a Walla Walla chief showed missionary Jason Lee "some old papers with scraps of writing on them, and a calendar showing the day of the month with Sunday distinctly marked."[39] In the 1860s an observer noted Indians using strings of beads to keep track of the day and month.[40]

The Nez Perces were particularly resolute in their observance of the Sabbath, refusing to change "their camp on Sundays tho: in distress of provisions," according to Captain Bonneville.[41] They gave Bonneville a dramatic proof of the strength of their new faith in October 1832. Bonneville and a party of five Nez Perce families were sharing a "miserable" winter camp along the Salmon River in Idaho. Food was scarce. "Now and then there was a scanty meal of fish or wild-fowl, occasionally an antelope; but frequently the cravings of hunger had to be appeased with roots, or the flesh of wolves and muskrats," Bonneville remembered. Finally he decided to send out a hunting party and asked his Nez Perce companions if they would like to come along. The hungry Indians answered that it was Sunday—"a sacred day with them, and the Great Spirit would be angry should they devote it to hunting." The white hunters left without them. "Simply to call these people religious," Bonneville concluded, "would convey but a faint idea of the deep hue of piety and devotion which pervades their whole conduct."[42] Not that every white person was impressed by such piety. "They appeared to keep a Sabbath," wrote one trader, "for there is a day on which they do not hunt or gamble, But sit moping all day and look like fools."[43]

Sunday services usually began with a call to order from "a sort of sub-chief," who directed the people to gather together, either in a special lodge or the open air.[44] Indians gathered in rows, much like a white congregation, to listen to the chief's address. In 1835 missionary Samuel Parker was invited to address such a gathering of Nez Perces. Parker described how five hundred Nez Perces erected their lodges so as to create a 20-by-120-foot "sanctuary of God" in the center, and that the Indians kneeled in rows facing the chiefs, leaving an aisle down the center of the congregation. The missionary was astounded that the natives knew how "to erect so convenient and so decent a place of worship."[45]

Yet the Indian manner of honoring the Sabbath was not the same as it was for contemporary Americans. After the prayer service it was time for communal dancing—the most prominent traditional element of the Columbian Religion. Bonneville described the Nez Perce dance as "a wild fantastic ceremonial, strongly resembling the religious dance of the shaking Quakers; but from its enthusiasm, much more striking and impressive." Nathaniel Wyeth observed that when the Okanagons performed their Sunday dance, "the[y] keep their feet in the same position the whole time merely jumping up to the tune keeping the hands in front of them."[46] In the early 1830s Sunday dancing ceremonies were observed among the Nez Perces, Walla Wallas, Cayuses, Palouses, Colvilles, Flatheads, and other groups.

"With these religious services," noted a visitor to the Cayuses in 1836, the Indians "mingle some of their old Indian ceremonials; such as dancing to the cadence of a song or ballad."[47] Although communal dancing, especially in the winter, was a traditional aspect of native faith, Plateau Indians insisted that the dances that were characteristic of the Columbian Religion had been taught to them by the traders. In

1836 an Indian from the Dalles told Samuel Parker how "a white man gave them a flag, and told them to set it up on a pole, on Sundays, and meet and pray, sing their songs, and dance around the pole bearing the flag; and that they had done so a long time."[48] Parker told the man that Sunday dancing was "very wrong, and would offend God." Later Parker apparently asked a Hudson's Bay Company man why they had taught the Indians that dancing was a part of Christianity and was told that "praying and singing without dancing would not interest the Indians." Since dancing was a usual part of Plateau religious worship, the traders explained, to introduce Christian ceremonies without dancing would only serve "to excite aversion to worship."[49]

After prayers and dancing, Sundays were given over to traditional native entertainment, notably gambling and horse racing. Bonneville wrote that Plateau Indians made Sundays "a peculiar day for recreations of the kind, not deeming them in any wise out of season."[50] This, too, they may have learned from the fur traders, for whom Sunday was a day of both worship and levity.[51]

Prayers were by no means confined to Sundays; they often took place twice a day, usually in the morning and evening. The American Nathaniel Wyeth observed a morning ceremony among the Walla Wallas: "At day dawn the chief called the Inds. to prayers which consist of a short recitation followed by a tune in which all join without words."[52] The Flatheads practiced a similar ceremony. "Every morning some important indian addresses either heaven or his countrymen or both," Wyeth explained, "I believe exhorting the one to good conduct with each other and to the strangers among them and the other to bestow its blessings. . . . [W]hile prayers are being said on weekdays everyone ceases whatever vocation he is about if on horseback he dismounts and holds his horse on the spot until all is done."[53] A visitor to the Cayuses in 1836 noted similar daily prayers led by the chief. "On all occasions, the bystanders listen with profound attention, and at the end of every sentence respond one word in unison; apparently equivalent to an amen."[54]

Many travelers on the plateau in the early 1830s noted similar prayers.[55] One man who camped with a Nez Perce family described how "while eating, the frequent repitition of the words Jehovah and Jesus Christ, in the most reverential manner, led me to suppose they were conversing on a religious topic." The visitor was even occasionally awakened from sleep by the family's prayers and hymns.[56]

One of the most complete descriptions of a Plateau religious service from this period comes from Meredith Gairdner, who watched the Walla Wallas in 1835:

The whole tribe . . . were assembled in their craal, squatted on their hams; the chief and chief men at the head arranged in a circle: these last officiated: towards this circle the rest of the assembly were turned, arranged in ranks, very similar to a European congregation. The service began by the chief's making a short address, in a low tone, which was repeated by a man on his left hand, in short sentences, as they were uttered by the chief. This was followed by a prayer pronounced by the chief standing, the rest kneeling. At certain intervals there was a pause, when all present gave a simultaneous groan. After the prayer there were fifteen hymns, in which the whole congregation joined: these hymns were begun by five or six of the men in the circle, who acted as leaders of the choir: during this hymn, all were kneeling, and kept moving their arms up and down, as if to aid in keeping time. The airs were simple, resembling the monotonous Indian song I have heard them sing while paddling their canoes. Each was somewhat different from the other. All kept good time, and there were no discordant voices. The hymns were succeeded by a prayer, as at first, and the service ended. My ignorance of the language prevented me from observing much of the service; but I was struck with the earnestness and reverence of the whole assembly. All eyes were cast down to the ground. . . . All were dressed in their best clothes, and they had hoisted a union-jack outside their lodge. The whole lasted about three-quarters of an hour.[57]

"It is about five years since these things found their way among the Indians of the Upper Columbia," Gairdner noted.[58] This would put the beginning of the Columbia Religion for the Walla Wallas around 1830.

Beyond the existence of a Great Spirit and the need for regular prayer, the doctrines of the Columbian Religion are unclear. Samuel Parker recorded some of their beliefs in 1835. "They believe in one God, in the immortality of the soul, and in future rewards and punishments," he wrote. The natives worshiped a "Great Spirit" who "may be displeased with them for their bad conduct, and in his displeasure bring calamities upon them." The Indians also feared an "evil spirit" they called "the black chief below" who caused undeserved misfortune. And there was a "future world" where the souls of the departed might be rewarded "with an abundance and enjoyment of those things which they value here" or punished by "all causes of misery here."[59] Pacifism was another value of the Columbian Religion. Bonneville noted that the Pend d'Oreilles had a set of beliefs that, "like [that of] the Nez Perces," "hold that the Great Spirit is displeased with all nations who wantonly engage in war."[60]

Though Indians gained new beliefs from the Columbian Religion, they kept many of their old ones. Bonneville observed that the Pend d'Oreilles, "like most savages," believed in dreams and "the power and efficacy of charms and amulets" and told "marvelous anecdotes" of spiritually powerful members of their tribes, such as one chief who was believed to "wear a charmed life" that rendered him bulletproof.[61] When pneumonia struck a Nez Perce camp in the winter of 1832, many turned to their traditional shamans, though with little success.[62]

The native leaders of this religious movement gained status from the new knowledge they bore, and status was one reason for the spread of the faith. In May 1833 Nathaniel Wyeth cynically observed that "there is a new great man no[w] getting up in the Camp" of the Okanagon Indians. "Like the rest of [the] w[o]rld he covers his designs under the great cloak religion. . . . [P]erhaps 1–5 [one-fifth] the Camp follow him when he gets enough followers he will branch off and become an independent chief."[63] Bonneville claimed that the Columbian Religion spread to the Shoshones when a chief of that tribe observed how the Nez Perces gained status with the white traders by incorporating bits of Christianity into their religious ceremonies. The Shoshones soon began observing Sundays and holidays and practiced the hymns and dances of the Nez Perces.[64] The missionary Asa Bowen Smith noted a few years later that it was the "chiefs & principal men" who were most eager for religious instruction, since by "hearing something new & telling of it . . . they gather many about them & increase their influence & sustain their dignity among the people."[65]

The Journey to St. Louis

Despite the intermixture of traditional beliefs, the Columbian Religion was ultimately an attempt by the Indians to capture some of the spirit power of the white men. Even as the Indians of the plateau adopted the new doctrines of the Columbian Religion, they understood that what they were doing was incomplete, that there was more to white religious practices than observing the Sabbath and praying to the Great Spirit. Indians who practiced the Columbian Religion continued to inquire about the white people's faith and how they could practice it. "Many a time, my little lodge thronged, or rather piled with hearers," recalled Captain Bonneville, "all listening with greedy ears to the wonders which the Great Spirit had revealed to the white man. No other subject gave them half the satisfaction, or commanded half the attention."[66] When a Protestant missionary arrived at Fort Nez Perces in 1836, the Indians made "frequent visits" to ask very specific questions concerning the white man's faith. How should the Indians pray? Should they stand or kneel? What should they say? Should they pray in a group, or as individuals? Was dancing pleasing to the Great Spirit?[67]

Indians discovered that conversations with religiously inclined fur traders and chance encounters with visiting missionaries were not enough to answer all their questions. As Indians made religious inquiries of the traders, they learned that white society had religious specialists, men like the Indian shamans, who directed the religious affairs of their communities. The return of the Red River boys after 1830 and the impressive body of knowledge these young men had gained made some natives all the more eager to meet the white shamans. But the shamans seemed slow to arrive.

In the winter of 1830 Spokane Garry served as a translator for one of Francis Heron's sermons at Fort Colville. The audience was an illustrious one, including chiefs of the Spokans, Nez Perces, Coeur d'Alenes, Kutenais, Pend d'Oreilles, Sanpoils, and Kettle Falls Indians. Garry also gave sermons of his own that winter and the Indians were deeply impressed with what they had heard. One especially attentive listener was Hol-lol-sote-tote, a Nez Perce chief whose negotiating skills caused whites to dub him "Lawyer." Lawyer brought home the news that the doctrines of the Columbian Religion as practiced were incomplete. He had met a Spokan youth who had learned the whole story of the white man's beliefs from the missionaries at Red River.

The Nez Perces considered Lawyer's news. They wanted the spirit power that young Garry seemed to possess and they were jealous of the status the Spokans were gaining from having Garry among them. There were the two Nez Perce boys, Ellice and Pitt, at the Red River school, but they were just boys and might not return for a long while. Or perhaps not at all, given the fearful mortality of late. Meanwhile, terrifying news of a new malady depopulating the lower Columbia reached their ears. The need for spirit power was urgent, there seemed little time to waste. They consulted with their friends the Flatheads and hatched an audacious plan.

In the spring of 1831, seven natives set out for St. Louis. Their plan was to travel to the July rendezvous of the American Fur Company at Green River and accompany some of the American traders back from the rendezvous to St. Louis, where they hoped to find "Christian teachers."[68] They may have known of the Catholic cathedral in St. Louis from which missionaries were sent to other western tribes. The Nez Perces might also have heard that their old friend William Clark resided in St. Louis—whose Nez Perce son was now a young man.[69] It is perhaps significant that Lawyer, who inspired the journey to St.

Louis, was the son of Twisted Hair, who had guided Lewis and Clark across the plateau twenty-five years earlier. In addition, there may have been a strong streak of secular curiosity behind the journey. St. Louis was a place the Nez Perces had heard about for at least twenty years, the point of origin for the American traders they sometimes encountered in the mountains.

None of the seven Nez Perce and Flathead men who departed for St. Louis in the spring of 1831 would complete their mission. Three turned back at Council Bluffs along the Missouri River. Four arrived in St. Louis that autumn. Tipayahlanah, or "Eagle," a Nez Perce chief, and Ka-ou-pu, "Man of the Dawn Light," a young man of mixed Nez Perce and Flathead ancestry, died in St. Louis and were buried in the Catholic church. The two survivors, Hi-yuts-to-henin ("Rabbit Skin Leggings") and Tawis Geejumin ("No Horns on His Head") left St. Louis in the spring of 1832 aboard the American Fur Company steamboat the *Yellowstone*. No Horns on His Head died on board as the ship ascended the Missouri, apparently from some "disease which he had contracted in the civilized district." Rabbit Skin Leggings was able to join a band of his people that was hunting buffalo on the Great Plains but was killed in a battle with the Blackfeet without ever returning to the Nez Perce homeland.[70]

Yet the men had not journeyed in vain. The news that some Indian men had crossed the continent in a quest for Christian teachers spread quickly through the American evangelical community. The result would be a series of changes more wrenching than anything the people of the Plateau had yet experienced.

5. *The Rejection of Christianity, 1836–1850*

The romantic story of a small band of pagan Indians crossing the continent in search of Christian teachings fell like a thunderbolt on the Protestant evangelical community. "The remembrance is distinct of what at the time was regarded as wonderful," wrote one Oregon missionary years after the event.[1] Much of America was in the throes of what historians have termed the Second Great Awakening, an upsurge of popular religious enthusiasm. The story of the Macedonian Appeal—as the Indian request quickly became known—reached an idealistic evangelical community already bent on propagating the faith.

A flood of sermons, tracts, and pamphlets stressed the need for devout men and women to go forth and spread salvation.[2] A popular tract was Gordon Hall's *The Conversion of the World: Or the Claims of Six Hundred Millions and the Ability and the Duty of the Churches Respecting Them*. "It is the duty of the churches to send forth preachers of the gospel in such numbers to furnish the means of instruction and salvation to the whole world," Hall proclaimed. "Every individual by putting his hand to the work, commences a new sort of life."[3] Persons contemplating this "new sort of life" might peruse another evangelical best-seller, *Ought I Become a Missionary to the Heathen?* For most, the pamphlet advised, the answer was yes. "Persons of nearly every variety of disposition, and every grade of intellect, may find stations suited to their capacities." Especially influential in the Protestant community was Jonathan Edward's *Life of David Brainerd*. Brainerd was a dyspeptic, ineffectual missionary who wandered the mid-Atlantic forests in the eighteenth century. Despite his singular lack of the success converting Indians, Brainerd was much admired by evangelicals for the strength of his piety and his spirit of sacrifice.[4] The narratives of Harriet Newell and Harriet Boardman were also popular reading, especially for women preparing to embark on a missionary career.[5] A steady diet of such literature inspired in many Protestants a desire to begin a "new sort of life."

New missionary organizations arose to channel the spirit of evangelization. The largest and most influential was the American Board of Commissioners for Foreign Missions (ABCFM), founded in Bedford, Massachusetts, in 1810.[6] Governed by its Prudential Committee, the interdenominational ABCFM supported and organized the missionary efforts of a variety of Protestant churches. Their goal was nothing less than "the evangelization of the world in the present generation."[7]

For many American missionary organizations, the main thrust of activity was overseas. The ABCFM, for example, first established missions in India, Liberia, South Africa, and Siam. The relative urgency of converting the American Indians was a matter of debate within the missionary community. As early as 1816 the Prudential Committee of the ABCFM noted: "Many friends of missions . . . have thought it strange, that while so much has been doing for the distant heathen of India, so little should have been done for the not less destitute tribes on our continent."[8] But others defended the decision to employ the board's limited resources where they could do the most good, contrasting the dense populations of Asia and Africa with the declining numbers of American Indians. "Could a man know that inevitable ruin was coming down upon a kingdom," asked a missionary on his way to Calcutta in 1812, "would he not haste to the capital, and lift up his warning voice among the multitudes, rather than bend his course to a few depopulated villages?"[9] Other evangelicals argued that it was precisely the dwindling numbers of the Indians that made their conversion a priority. Indians were on a precipice and only the gospel could save them. "*Immediate, vigorous,* and *persevering* efforts are required," thundered the Baptist Missionary Board, "the present is the *crisis.* . . . [S]hould the experiment now being made fail, the fate of this unfortunate race . . . will be sealed."[10] Interest in the Indians grew and the ABCFM sponsored it first domestic mission in 1817 among the Cherokees.

By 1820 the ABCFM was devoting half its human power and resources to American Indian missions.[11] Stations were established among the Cherokees, Choctaws, and Osages. Day schools were built alongside the new churches, and Indian youths were taught English, farming, and rudimentary trades as well as the gospel. After a rocky start the missions prospered. In 1830 the board reported thirty-four mission stations and 150 missionaries, farmers, mechanics, and teachers laboring among the Indians.[12] More important, it numbered 900 Indians as converted and noted that another 1,000 were attending mission schools.[13]

In the spring of 1830 Congress voted to authorize the removal of the Cherokees, Chickasaws, Choctaws, and other tribes to lands west of the Mississippi River. The removal was a disaster not only for the Indians involved but for the hopes of the missionaries who had labored so long for their salvation. The American Board, which had been active in opposing the removal, at first considered resisting the order. In 1831 the Prudential Committee narrowly voted to obey the order and asked its missionaries to develop new stations west of the Mississippi.[14]

At the same time as the Cherokee Removal, the Osage mission was being threatened by approaching settlement and itinerant whiskey traders. The two ruinous events forced the ABCFM and other American missionary organizations to reevaluate their approach to converting the Indians. In the past the policy had been to encourage contacts between Indians and white settlers in order to help "civilize" the Indians. But now it was believed that the missionaries must try to shield Indians from contact with settlers, who brought with them whiskey, licentiousness, and a desire to dispossess the natives of their land.[15] An 1837 Baptist history of their missions to the Indians summed up the prevailing wisdom. Tribes that had been "hemmed in by whites . . . melted away amidst depravity and wickedness," the author concluded, while larger tribes, more distant from white frontier society, became "far advanced in civilization"—even resembling "a new country settled by white people."[16] The ABCFM concurred. "Shall we merely keep up with that tide which is overwhelming [the Indians]," asked the Prudential Committee, "or should we press forward in advance of this tide, and preach Christ to those tribes which are exposed to a less debasing foreign influence?"[17]

But where to find the uncontaminated Indians? As early as the 1820s, some Protestants began to look to the northwestern corner of the continent, broadly known as the Oregon Country. In 1829 the ABCFM dispatched Jonathan Green to survey the Northwest coast for possible mission sites. Green found the coastal Indians already corrupted by the traders and rapidly declining in numbers and the ABCFM looked elsewhere.[18] In 1831 the Prudential Committee voted to try to establish a mission somewhere west of the Mississippi River if a practical site could be found.[19] In the spring of the next year two missionaries were dispatched into the "unlimited wilderness" west of Lake Superior in an inconclusive search for pristine Indians as yet uncorrupted by frontiersmen and whiskey traders.[20]

Such was the state of mind of the missionary community when news of the Nez Perce delegation became public. The surprising visit of the Nez Perces to St. Louis first came to the attention of Protestant

America in the spring of 1833 through an article in the *Christian Advocate and Journal and Zion's Herald*. The article included a letter and a drawing by William Walker, a Protestant mixed-blood Wyandot with a "vivid imagination" who claimed to have met the Nez Perces in St. Louis.[21] There are reasons to doubt the authenticity of Walker's story—his drawing showed an Indian with an artificially flattened head, which was not a practice of any Plateau tribe—but his tale was accepted as true at the time.[22]

Walker reported in the *Advocate* that "some white man" had observed the religious ceremonies of these Indians and told them that "their mode of worshipping the supreme Being was radically wrong" and that the white people "toward the rising of the sun had been put in possession of the true mode of worshipping the great Spirit." The puzzled Indians then held a "national council" and appointed four chiefs to journey to St. Louis to discover the truth. After a three-thousand-mile journey on foot, the Indians met with "their great father" William Clark in St. Louis. Two of the Indians died in St. Louis, Walker reported, and whether the other two made it back was unknown.

Walker's letter was followed by a commentary on the event. "How deeply touching is the circumstance of the four natives traveling on foot 3,000 miles through thick forests and extensive prairies, sincere searchers after truth!" the author enthused. "The story scarcely has a parallel in history. . . . With what intense concern will men of God whose souls are fired with holy zeal for the salvation of their fellow beings, read their history! There are immense plains, mountains, and forests in those regions whence they came, the abodes of numerous savage tribes. But no apostle of Christ has yet had the courage to penetrate into their moral darkness. . . . May we not indulge the hope that the day is not far distant when the missionaries will penetrate into these wilds where the Sabbath bell has never yet tolled since the world began!"[23]

Truthful or not, Walker's version of the journey was retold again and again in the evangelical press of the day—and it did not lose in the telling. An especially colorful version of the tale included a spurious farewell banquet for the Indians hosted by William Clark, where one of the Nez Perces was made to deliver a wrenching lament:

My people sent me to get the "White Man's Book of Heaven." You took me where you allow your women to dance as we do not ours and the book was not there. You took me to where they worship the Great Spirit with candles and the book was not there. You showed me the images of the food spirits and the pictures of the good home beyond, but the book was not among them to tell us the way. I am going back the long and sad trail to my people in the dark land. You make my feet heavy with gifts and my moccasins will grow old in carrying them, yet the book is not among them. When I tell my poor blind people after we have snow, in the big council, that I did not bring the book, no word will be spoken by our old men or by our young braves. One by one they will rise up and go out in silence. My people will die in darkness and they will go a long path to the other hunting grounds. No white man will go with them and no White Man's Book to make the way plain. I have no more words.[24]

Stories of the Macedonian Appeal set off an avalanche of letters, donations, and volunteers to help the savage Flatheads. The *Advocate* published a fiery editorial calling for volunteers: "Hear! Hear! Who will respond to the call from Rocky Mountains? . . . we are for having a mission established there at once . . . All we want is men. Who will go? Who?"[25]

The Missionaries Arrive

Jason Lee would go. The Methodist Missionary Board dispatched Lee in 1833 with instructions to gather white settlers from the frontier regions who were "acquainted with the Indian character and manner of life" and to establish a self-supporting mission colony in the homeland of the Flatheads.[26] Lee executed his instructions faithfully—until he actually met some Nez Perce and Flathead Indians at the Green River Rendezvous in 1834. It was not that the natives were not eager to learn what Lee had to teach; as he journeyed across the Northwest, the Indians he met were almost uniformly eager for Christian knowledge. When he showed the Indians at Green River the Bible and taught some of the commandments, "they listened with the utmost attention, and then replied that it was all good." Another man asked Lee to take his children and "teach them to read and write and be good."[27] But now that Lee was, for the first time in his life, meeting Indians in the flesh instead of in the pages of a missionary tract, he found them deeply unsettling. At Green River a Nez Perce man, Tackensuatis, got drunk and practiced his English by cursing with the American trappers. A fellow tribesman, the Bull's Head, drove a frightened buffalo through the camp while the mountain men laughed and cheered him on. The Indians, Lee concluded, were "slaves to Satan and spirituous liquors."[28] At one stop Lee encountered a group of natives who prayed and sang in their tent. "How encouraging to see these red men thus religiously inclined," Lee rhapsodized—yet that night the same Indians built a bonfire and held a war dance.[29]

Lee's party had shipped much of its equipment by sea to Fort Vancouver. The plan was to scout the plateau for a good mission site, pick up the supplies at the fort, and then return to the plateau, perhaps the following spring, to break ground for the mission. As he crossed the plateau, the Indians met him with excitement and begged him to teach them not only the white man's religion but farming, reading, and writing as well. One Plateau man promised Lee that if he would build a house for the Indians, they "would catch plenty of Beaver for us," showing that at least some Indians were conflating the missionaries with the fur traders. "They seemed desirous," Lee wrote, "That we should settle among *them*."[30]

But somewhere along the way Lee's spirit began to waver, and he never did settle on the plateau. At Fort Vancouver, HBC chief factor John McLoughlin told Lee's party that the Plateau Indians, despite their apparent zeal, were unsuited for enlightenment. "I observed to them that it was too dangerous for them to establish a mission in the Flat-head country," McLoughlin recounted. The fur trader told the missionary that the Willamette Valley in western Oregon, where many white families had already settled, offered "a fine field" for a mission. There Lee and his brethren could "collect them [the Indians] around them [and] teach them first to cultivate the ground."[31] McLoughlin was probably protecting the fur trade from the meddlesome interference of missionaries: he knew full well that the malarial Willamette had been all but depopulated of Indians. And there was little prospect of persuading Plateau peoples to abandon their rich environment for the strange and unhealthy Willamette. Yet Lee required very little persuading to abandon the mission to the Flatheads. "To the Willamette we have concluded to go," he wrote in his diary a few days after arriving at Fort Vancouver.[32] Within a few years he had abandoned all pretense of converting the Indians and turned his energies to business, politics, and real estate speculation. A visitor in 1842 noted that while Lee still talked about erecting a large Indian school, he had "a great deal of business . . . which seems a hindrance to the work of religion."[33] Plateau Indians, disappointed by Lee's decision, traveled to the Willamette to visit his mission in its early years. A Cayuse man even brought his children and left them under Lee's care—where they died within the year.[34]

Samuel Parker would go. Although the Methodists were first on the scene, it was the ABCFM that mounted a larger and more influential missionary effort to the Northwest. In 1834 the ABCFM authorized the Reverend Samuel Parker to journey west and investigate the possibility of establishing a mission "among the Indians near or beyond the

Rocky Mountains."[35] Parker and another missionary, Marcus Whitman, arrived at the Green River Rendezvous in 1835. Some Nez Perces and Flatheads were present, overjoyed to meet more missionaries after their disappointment the year before when Lee passed them by. A Flathead chief told Parker that "he was old, and did not expect to know much more; he was deaf and could not hear, but his heart was made glad, very glad, to see what he had never seen before, a man near to God." Tackensuatis, whose drinking and cursing had so appalled Lee the year before, now proclaimed how "he had heard from white men a little about God, which had gone only to his ears; he wished to know enough to have it go down into his heart, to influence his life, and to teach his people."[36] A few days later another Nez Perce made a wrenching plea: "I have been like a little child, uneasy, feeling about in the dark after something, not knowing what; but now I hope to learn something which will be substantial, and which will help me to teach my people to do right."[37]

Here at last were the pristine Indians of evangelical dreams. Parker made the point explicitly when he reported the results of his expedition. "In politeness and decency," Parker wrote, "they are very unlike the frontier Indians, who have been corrupted and degraded by their acquaintance with ardent spirits and wicked white men."[38] The signs were so promising that the two missionaries decided to separate. Parker traveled on to carry out his survey of the plateau for mission sites, while Whitman returned east to organize a major missionary expedition to arrive the next year. Two Nez Perce men agreed to send their sons, Tackitonitis and Ais, east with Whitman (who renamed them Richard and John) to begin their education and to guide the missionary to their homelands the following year.[39]

In 1836 missionaries began arriving on the plateau to stay. That year Marcus and Narcissa Whitman, Henry and Eliza Spalding, and William H. Gray made their way west to establish missions. Some Nez Perces met up with the party just as they crossed South Pass. The natives were "gratified to see us actually on our way to their country," remarked Eliza Spalding. "All appear very anxious to have us locate in their country, that they may be taught about God."[40] The Spaldings settled in Nez Perce country at a spot the natives called Lapwai, "place of butterflies." The Whitmans established a station with the Cayuses at Waiilatpu, "place of tall ryegrass."

In 1838 the Protestant missionaries were reinforced with new arrivals. Three couples arrived: Elkanah and Mary Walker, Asa and Mary Smith, Cushing and Myra Eels. There was also a young single helper, twenty-three-year-old Cornelius Rogers. The Walkers and

Eelses went to live among the Spokans at Tshimakain, and the Smiths were persuaded by the Nez Perce chief Lawyer to establish a mission at Kamiah.[41]

The Catholic Church also heard the Macedonian Appeal. News of the Nez Perce journey to St. Louis was reprinted in the Catholic press not only in the United States but in Europe as well.[42] As the Catholics told the story, the Nez Perce request was specifically for "blackrobes," meaning Jesuit missionaries. Yet the Catholic Church was slow to respond to the Indians' plea. Catholic resources were stretched thin in the West, especially after the 1829 opening of St. Louis College.[43] As late as 1834, when some retired French Canadian *engagés* and their families in the Willamette Valley petitioned the bishop of Quebec for Catholic missionaries, he denied their entreaty. "I have no priests disposable at Red River," the bishop apologized, promising to travel to Europe to find willing missionaries.[44]

Interest in the Northwest Indians continued to build and soon "a certain atmosphere of holy romance" surrounded the Catholic impression of the Northwest tribes.[45] Like their Protestant rivals, the Catholics were intrigued by the promise of Indians who, in the words of Bishop Rosati, "have not yet been corrupted by intercourse with others."[46] In 1835 a second group of Plateau Indians arrived in St. Louis, again seeking spiritual instructors. This second delegation consisted of Old Ignace, an Iroquois who had long lived among the Flatheads, and his two half-Flathead sons. Ignace impressed the Catholics as "very tall of stature and of grave, modest and refined deportment." He was familiar with Catholicism and went straight to the cathedral to have his sons baptized. There he told the blackrobes that the Flatheads had sent him to St. Louis to request missionaries and that other Plateau groups, including the Spokans, Nez Perces, Cayuses, and Kutenais, wanted missionaries as well. Ignace was told that no Catholic missionaries were currently available but that some would arrive soon.[47]

Old Ignace tried to reach St. Louis again in 1837 to renew his request but was killed by some Sioux along the North Platte. In 1839 a fourth Plateau delegation traveled to St. Louis. This time they were promised that "next spring two Fathers would undertake a journey" to the Flatheads. One Flathead man traveled all the way back to his people in the dead of winter to spread the good tidings.[48]

In 1840 Father Pierre Jean De Smet arrived at the American Fur Company rendezvous on the Green River to make good that promise. De Smet would not found a mission on this trip; he merely wanted to gauge the Indians' readiness for conversion. He was greeted by a group of Flatheads and Pend d'Oreilles, following the shaman Chalax, who had come to escort him the rest of the way. At Pierre's Hole on the edge of Flathead territory De Smet was met by a crowd of 1,600 Indians, not only Flatheads and Pend d'Oreilles but Nez Perces and some friendly Shoshones as well. "From time to time, good white men have given us advice and we have followed it," proclaimed Bear Looking Up, a Flathead chief. "Blackrobe, we will follow the words of your mouth."[49]

Six hundred Flatheads and Pend d'Oreilles took baptism from De Smet, including the principal chiefs of those tribes. Hundreds of others were turned away until De Smet could be more certain of their sincerity. The blackrobe stayed and traveled with the Indians for six weeks in the summer of 1840, preaching four times a day. The Indians' "zeal for prayer and instruction," wrote De Smet, "instead of declining, increased until the day of my departure."[50] A Flathead chief became De Smet's catechist and "in less than ten days the whole nation knew their prayers."[51] Convinced that the Flatheads were ripe for conversion, De Smet prepared to return to St. Louis to organize an expedition to establish a mission the following spring. His last prayer service was met with "weeping and sobs" from the assembled natives. "Blackrobe, may the Great Spirit accompany you in your long journey," said a man named Old Big-Face. "We will continue to offer vows until you return. . . . [W]hen the spring flowers return, we will set out to come and meet you."[52]

De Smet returned the next summer with two more Jesuit fathers, Nicolas Point and Gregory Mengarini, and three lay brothers. The Flatheads had already chosen a spot for the mission and directed the party to the Bitterroot Valley, where they founded St. Mary's Mission. "On the first Sunday of October, feast of the Rosary, we took possession of the promised land," De Smet boasted.[53] Within days representatives from other Plateau tribes began arriving at the mission, asking for a religious establishment of their own. "Father we are truly deserving of your pity," said one Coeur d'Alene. "We wish to serve the Great Spirit, but we do not know how."[54] Another native told De Smet, "I am a Sinpoil [Sanpoil]. . . . I have been sent to hear your words, and learn the prayers you teach the Flatheads."[55] In 1842 the Sacred Heart Mission to the Coeur d'Alenes was established. By 1847 there were a dozen Jesuit missions on the plateau, including stations among the Kutenais, Okanagons, and Pend d'Oreilles.

Missionary Tactics

Introducing the natives to agriculture was the first priority of Catholic and Protestant missionaries alike.[56] Only by abandoning the seasonal round for the sedentary life of a farmer could the natives become Christians. Pierre Jean De Smet explained to the Flatheads "the necessity of settling permanently in a fertile and suitable spot" as soon as he arrived, decrying the Indians' "inclination to a wandering life."[57] Gregory Mengarini denounced the Flatheads' annual buffalo hunts, claiming that "this single factor is enough to render completely useless and without fruit all the efforts of a missionary."[58] Nicolas Point worried about "the hardships imposed on the aged and the very young" by the seasonal round, the chance of partially converted Indians coming into contact with "strangers unsympathetic to religion," and "the Indian's rapid transition from dire poverty to great abundance."[59]

The Protestant approach was much the same. "You cannot evangelize a people always on the wing," Henry Spalding argued.[60] "We must use the plough as well as the Bible," opined Elkanah Walker; "they must be settled before they can be enlightened." Noting the diminishing game available since guns and horses had come to the plateau, Walker believed that only agriculture could save the Indians from extinction.[61] Both groups of missionaries believed that the Indians would have to change their way of life before they could become Christians.

Plateau Indians were curious about agriculture, though skeptical. When the Jesuits showed their carefully preserved collection of vegetable seeds to the Flatheads, the natives laughed, telling the blackrobes that "it was foolish to destroy the grass that fed their horses and to bury seeds that were good to eat."[62] Other Indians made fun of the idea that men should spend their days digging in the ground, a task that Plateau Indians classified as female work. "Are you a woman?" an Okanagon man asked a missionary who was weeding a field.[63] But the missionaries were insistent. "You will earn your bread from the sweat of your brow," Mengarini warned the Flatheads.

On the southern plateau where the Protestants settled, the natives proved more willing to at least experiment with agriculture. The HBC posts on this part of the plateau had been farming for years, often hiring native laborers, so these Indians understood the concept. A few Spokans were already raising potatoes when the missionaries arrived.[64] Some Cayuses began farming under the Whitmans' tutelage in 1838, planting potatoes, corn, and peas.[65] Eighty Nez Perce families established farms the same year.[66] At the Wascopam mission Henry

Perkins planted cabbages and parsnips in 1838, adding corn and potatoes the next year.[67]

Plateau Indians found agriculture less useful than promised. Plateau summers are often dry, and many crops failed without irrigation. Where timber was scarce, the lack of fencing meant that "what is cultivated by the natives is liable to be destroyed by horses & cattle," wrote Asa Smith.[68] Nor did prime farmland abound. "Good land is found only in small tracts here & there on the banks of streams," Smith noted, "not enough in any one place."[69] This meant that if the Indians did come to depend on agriculture, they would have to spread out in individual homesteads scattered across the plateau, making them even more difficult to proselytize. And the white concept of ownership of crops seemed foreign to a people accustomed to helping themselves to the bounties of the earth. In a few days and nights more than fifty bushels of Henry Perkins's potatoes were dug up and spirited away from the Wascopam mission.[70]

Wisely, Plateau Indians adopted agriculture only selectively.[71] After some experimentation, they decided that raising potatoes offered them advantages without disrupting their seasonal round. Potatoes were hardy and survived the dry summers far better than other introduced crops.[72] And potatoes tasted like some of the other starchy tubers, such as camas and wapato, that were staples of the Plateau diet. Nor was harvesting potatoes any different than digging up camas bulbs. Best of all, potatoes required little attention. Indians could plant them in the spring, depart on their seasonal round, and return in the fall or winter to harvest what they needed. Potatoes fit into the traditional way of life. A few Indians did adopt other crops such as corn, melons, and peas—even wheat and cattle.[73] But most planted only those crops that required little tending. Asa Smith noted that although seventy or eighty Nez Perce families farmed plots of land around Lapwai, this only meant that the Indians "encamp at that station & remain a few weeks during the year," with "scarcely any" staying more than a few weeks at a time. "Almost all are away a great part of the summer," Smith wrote, when the Indians went to fish for salmon or to hunt buffalo.[74]

By combining agriculture with the seasonal round, Plateau Indians defeated the intention of the missionaries in introducing agriculture in the first place. "It was our first concern to introduce them, little by little, to a much more sedentary existence," explained Nicolas Point: "This could be done only by substituting the fruits of agriculture for those of the chase, the innocent pleasures of the fireside for those offered by the varied life of the hunter. Above all, religion had to assume an important position in their lives."[75] But agriculture by itself seemed to produce neither a sedentary life nor religious conversion. In 1843 Marcus Whitman was interviewed by the *New York Daily Tribune* during a hurried trip back east. "We did not learn what success this worthy man had in leading the Indians to embrace the Christian faith," the newspaper drolly noted, "but he very modestly remarked that many of them had begun to cultivate the earth and raise cattle."[76] Sedentary living could even interfere with conversion. The year before Whitman's interview, Eliza Spalding fretted over Moses, a formerly promising student at the Lapwai mission. Moses "is not now so much attached to reading as formerly" and was neglecting his lessons, she worried. Instead, Moses planned on "taking some horses to the Willamette" and trading them for cattle.[77]

The Language Barrier

Learning the native languages, another early missionary priority, also proved to be a stumbling block to converting the Indians. When Samuel Parker first surveyed the plateau for the ABCFM in 1835, he warned his brethren that it was "all important" that missionaries be able to address the Indians "in the language wherein they were born." Parker mistrusted the mostly mixed-blood Catholic interpreters who were available for hire. "The missionary must become, as soon as possible, his own interpreter," counseled Parker. And after all, he asked, why shouldn't a committed man or woman of God be able to "learn the Indian language as well as the trader and hunter?"[78]

Parker was a naive optimist. The Columbia Plateau was divided into two very different language groups, the Sahaptin and Salish. Within these broad groups were dozens of individual tongues. The American explorer Charles Wilkes described the "remarkable" diversity of Plateau languages in 1841. "The dialect seemed to change with almost every party of Indians" Wilkes met on the plateau, "and it was frequently necessary for words to pass through three or four different interpreters."[79] A tradition of marrying outside one's own village promoted a widespread multilingualism among the Indians, for whom the Babel of languages presented few problems.

Even fur traders found Northwest Indian languages more difficult than Parker realized. Ross Cox thought the Chinook tongue "the most unpronounceable compound of gutturals ever formed for the communication of human thoughts."[80] When it came to learning the languages, these traders had a vital advantage over the missionaries—their intimate connections with native women, who provided tutoring in native languages and culture. And the information that traders needed to communicate—the price of brass pots, the route across the mountains—was much less complex and abstract than the missionaries' talk of the Holy Trinity, Atonement, and eternal damnation. No wonder the language barrier would emerge as a major source of misunderstanding between the Indians and the missionaries.

Elkanah Walker's frustrating attempt to master the Spokan language may be taken as typical. Walker was a fair linguist and had some knowledge of Greek, Latin, and Hebrew when he arrived at Tshimakain in 1838. He delivered his first sermon through an interpreter and found the experience maddening. "I attempted to say something to them in regard to the death of Christ but could not make them understand anything about it," Walker complained; "our interpreter . . . could not tell his people what was told him."[81] Walker vowed to learn Spokan and employed his interpreter as a tutor. Within a few days he had "learnt several words & to count [to] five."[82] Within a week he was employing Spokan words in his Sunday sermon. "They seemed to come of their own accord," he marveled.[83]

Yet fluency eluded Walker. "I must say I never studied so hard as at the present time," he wrote, yet "it seems to me I shall never learn this language. . . . [I] strained my mind so hard last night that I was almost crazy."[84] After six months Walker reported to the Board of Commissioners that "my progress in the language is quite slow." Walker blamed his language block on the time he spent laboring around the mission instead of studying.[85] After two years at the mission he was complaining that "it is impossible for me to do much at studying the language when I am worn out with labor."[86] But even in the slow time of winter Walker seemed to make little progress. "I should be willing to give all my goods, house & all if I could by it understand the language," Walker sobbed in January 1841, two and one-half years after he began his studies.[87] Eventually Walker was able to deliver simple sermons in Spokan, but never with any fluency. In February 1842, three and one-half years after his arrival, Walker proudly noted that he finally had a Spokan translation of the Lord's Prayer—supplied to him by Spokane Garry.

Walker was one of the most linguistically successful of the Protestant missionaries. Asa Smith at Kamiah called the difficulty of translating the Nez Perce language "insurmountable." "Indeed it appears utterly impossible to translate literally," Smith wrote. "General terms are not to be found. . . . [T]he verb expresses the precise *manner* of the action, as well as the action itself—all that we would express in our language by a verb, together with an adverb or other adjuncts. Hence we are obliged often to say more than we wish to, & more than the Bible itself says."[88] Henry Spalding denounced Nez Perce as "destitute of regularity" and "varied without any rule or reason."[89]

One alternative to mastering the native languages was to preach in the Chinook jargon. This five-hundred-word trade language had spread steadily across the Plateau in conjunction with the fur trade.[90] One missionary dismissed the jargon as "gibberish," a "vile compound," and "such a miserable medium of communication, that very few ideas can be expressed in it."[91] But the ease of learning the Chinook jargon and its wide distribution over both the coastal and plateau areas made its use tempting to more than a few missionaries. Jesuit John Nobli preached in Chinook jargon in 1844 before deciding it was insufficient for his purposes.[92] A visitor to a Protestant mission in 1844 noted that the missionaries preached "in the jargon" since they "did not altogether understand the language used by the natives."[93] Most Plateau missionaries experimented with Chinook jargon early in their missions but eventually all rejected it as inadequate.[94]

Even missionaries who had some success in learning the native languages proper found it difficult to preach in the vernacular. "The number of words and terms in their language is very small so that those who wish to instruct them are compelled to do it by means of illustrations and circumlocutions," Samuel Parker warned. "Whenever a feeling of ignorance upon any subject prevails, we find all endeavors to elicit the true amount of knowledge, are repelled or evaded. Even men of talents, with us, who converse fluently upon most subjects, are often silent when religious topics are introduced." Parker might have been mistaking traditional Indian reticence to contradict someone for a shortcoming of the language. But even more skilled linguists found it difficult to translate certain Christian concepts. "It seems they have no language to express the atonement," Elkanah Walker puzzled.[95] Asa Smith complained: "The number of words in the language is immense & their variations are almost beyond description. Every word is limited & definite in meaning & the great difficulty is to find terms sufficiently general."[96]

In short, it was years before any of the missionaries could manage a passable sermon in the native languages—and most never could.[97] "I cannot do much more than stammer yet in their language," Narcissa Whitman confided in 1838, after two years of living among the Cayuses.[98] Her husband, Marcus, did learn to preach in a native language, but that language was Nez Perce rather than Cayuse. The

Cayuses had close ties to the Nez Perces and most Cayuses understood the Nez Perce language. When interest in Whitman's message ran high, in the first few years of the mission, many Cayuses were willing to listen to Whitman preach in their neighbors' language.[99]

As they realized the difficulty of learning native speech, some tongue-tied Protestants rationalized that it would be a better use of their time to teach the natives English, rather than to devote years to learning languages that were in any case doomed to vanish. "The thought of spending one's life translating for such a little handful of people," moaned Asa Smith, "is truly heart-sickening."[100] Since the ultimate goal of the Protestants was to assimilate the converted natives to white civilization, such a decision was easy to justify on practical grounds. Moreover, in the early days of the missions many Indians seemed as eager to learn English as they were to learn the other secrets of the missionaries. "Judging from the present, this people will probably acquire the English, before we do the Nez-Perces language," Henry Spalding admitted. The Spaldings and Whitmans especially turned their energies to teaching English.[101] After a brief vogue, however, the attractions of learning English waned. In 1839 Smith noted that despite several years of English schooling at Waiilatpu and Lapwai, "not a child can be found who can read a single sentence of English intelligibly."[102] Compounding the problem, the idea that teaching English was the best approach had a "pernicious effect" on the missionaries themselves and "paralyzes all efforts to acquire the native languages," according to Asa Smith.[103]

The Jesuits also understood the need to learn native languages. "You will apply yourselves, as soon as you arrive, to the study of Indian languages," ordered the bishop of Quebec to the departing missionaries in 1838, "and will endeavor to reduce them to regular principles, so as to be able to publish a grammar after some years of residence there."[104] Yet in spite of considerable advantages, the Jesuits found the process nearly as difficult as did the Protestants.

The first Jesuit advantage was a rich linguistic tradition. The highly educated priests were not intimidated by the task of learning a new language. Most of the Jesuits who came to the Oregon Territory had been born and raised in Europe and spoke several languages before they joined the order. The constitutions of the Society of Jesus also encouraged proficiency in the language of those to be converted. Nineteenth-century Jesuit training included not only Latin, Greek, and Hebrew but syntax, rhetoric, and logic as well.[105] More time to devote to the task was an additional advantage: as celibates, the

Jesuits had no families to distract them from learning the language, and they had lay assistants, called *donnés*, to do much of the heavy work of the missions. At St. Mary's Mission there were three such laborers, all skilled in the trades, who helped erect buildings, plant crops, and trade with the Indians. These *donnés* were not hired hands but devout members of the Society of Jesus who had not taken final vows. Their assistance gave the priests an edge over their Protestant rivals, who often complained that they were forced to spend more time establishing their homesteads than studying languages or preaching.

Despite their advantages, many Jesuits also discovered that learning the Plateau languages was no easy task. De Smet complained that it was "very hard to acquire a knowledge" of Indian tongues, and his thumbnail ethnographies of various tribes nearly always described their language as "difficult" or "very difficult." [106] Father Mengarini quickly discovered that the Salish language of the Flatheads was "truly very difficult and complicated." "One might say that brevity of expression is carried to excess," he complained. "For them, one word is really a complete phrase. Often the Salish closely combine two, three, of four words with the singular result that the word composed is shorter than the . . . words which made it." [107] "The language is our greatest difficulty," agreed Joset, "there is no written language, there are no interpreters, there is very little analogy with other tongues." [108]

The Catholics, like the Protestants, found the native languages ill suited to the expression of Christian doctrine. "Religious instruction is very slow," complained De Smet, "retarded especially by the difficulty which the missionaries encounter in the language of the Indians, which is very rich to express whatever is material, but excessively poor in all that relates to the explanation of spiritual things." [109] Joset echoed the same complaint: "The turn of thought is entirely different from ours. They have no abstract ideas, every thing is concrete. . . . [T]he savages know nothing that is not material." [110]

The Indians, for their part, found the Jesuits' mangling of their tongues confusing. "You pronounce like a child learning to talk," a Colville man told Father Joset, "when you speak of religion, we understand you well; but when you change the subject, it is another thing." [111] A source from the early twentieth century hints that the multiplicity of Plateau languages might have been part of the problem. An Okanagon woman recalled that the local priest "had a way of jumbling up words from several Indian languages he had learned so that his words sounded childish." [112]

Given the difficulty of oral communication, many missionaries turned to the use of pictures to illustrate their beliefs. "Experience showed that the natives learned more quickly through their eyes than through their ears," Nicolas Point proclaimed; "while the truths entered their souls through their eyes, the great virtues were infused into their hearts."[113] Point was skilled with charcoal pencil and water colors and soon was busy painting biblical scenes and moral lessons: "Some scenes showed the mysteries; others, the sacraments; some represented the precepts; others, prayers," Point described. "Still others represented the great virtues and the vices." "These pictures," Point boasted, "impress the Indians very vividly."[114]

At the Lapwai mission Eliza Spalding made a series of paintings "representing several important events recorded in scripture." These pictures, she wrote, "we find a great help in communicating instruction to ignorant minds, whose language as yet we understand imperfectly."[115] These images were presented to Indians and circulated along trade routes as valued items. Soon after his arrival at Tshimakain, Elkanah Walker was surprised to find that Chief Big Head was already in possession of a Sunday school book and "a painting of Mrs. S representing the Bible history of Christ."[116]

Paintings and drawings offered the natives the chance to pass on the lessons of Christianity without a missionary present, and when the missions were popular, so were their images. Several of Nicolas Point's paintings of the St. Mary's Mission show Indians clustered around some painting or drawing, pointing out its features and explaining to one another.[117] But this form of religious instruction was also dangerously prone to error, since the natives' interpretations might well differ from the missionaries' intentions. Asa Smith claimed that this was exactly what happened with many of Eliza Spalding's pictures. Denouncing this "very dangerous" method of instruction, Smith claimed the Indians "filled up the picture with their own imaginations & in this way they have acquired a vast amount of error which I find no easy matter to eradicate."[118] An even greater fear, especially to the Protestants, was that the Indians might come to revere not the message the paintings were supposed to impart but the actual physical objects themselves.[119] Smith claimed the natives had fallen into just such idolatry. In 1843 an American traveler met a Nez Perce named Jacob with a "large picture" representing the devil. Jacob would charge the other Indians a fee to watch him pray to the image, then would use some sleight-of-hand trick to make the picture rise in the air, by which he gained "unbounded influence" over the other Indians.[120]

Native Resistance

As great a barrier as the native languages were the existing native religious leaders. The missionaries saw the shamans as the most serious impediment to conversion and worked to discredit and displace them. De Smet called the shamans "the most formidable and dangerous adversaries of religion" and "the ministers of Satan himself."[121] Missionaries all offered medical help, both for humanitarian reasons and to lessen the natives' confidence in their own medical practitioners. When the natives seemed to recover from their illnesses after such treatment, the status and power of the missionaries increased. But when it failed, the missionaries might be blamed as if they had caused the deaths themselves.

In the spring of 1837 the wife of Umtippe, the Cayuse chief who claimed the land beneath the Whitman mission, fell ill and was soon "near dying" from an unspecified illness.[122] She came to the white shaman, Marcus Whitman, for treatment. "For a season they were satisfied with my husband's attention," Narcissa Whitman wrote, but when the woman suffered a relapse she visited a Cayuse shaman who told her that Whitman's medicine was bad. "Umtippe got in a rage about his wife," Whitman reported, "and told my husband . . . that if his wife died that night he should kill him." Umtippe summoned a Walla Walla shaman who treated his wife and accepted a horse and blanket in return. But still the woman remained sick and soon Umtippe was saying darkly that the shaman "was bad and ought to be killed." When Umtippe himself fell sick a few weeks later, he went to the Whitmans for treatment and soon recovered.[123]

Missionaries not only used Western medicine to displace the shamans, they publicly challenged the native healers. After hearing of an Okanagon shaman's ability to suck blood and foreign objects from beneath a patient's skin, Father Joset approached the man. "Suck me!" challenged the blackrobe, extending his bare arm. The surprised shaman smiled meekly. "You are not sick," he answered. "I need not be sick," Joset persisted. "There is blood, and my skin is surely not thicker than an Indian's." The shaman declined the challenge. "To do any such thing I must be angry," the shaman explained, "when calm I can do nothing."[124]

At Tshimakain, Cushing and Myra Eels entered a lodge where a group of female shamans were trying to heal a sick woman. "The woman who was sick was standing about half bent, beating upon a board with a stick . . . sighing and sobbing as if her heart were broken, and sweating profusely," the horrified missionary noted. "Five or six old women were sitting around her, keeping perfect time with all her gestures by drumming upon something with a stone." The missionary couple remonstrated with the women, telling them such medicine was "bad," and the ceremony ceased. "But as soon as we were away," Eels concluded, "they were drumming again."[125]

Even better than defying shamans was converting them. Many missionaries singled out the shamans for special attention, believing that if these individuals could be brought to Christ, the rest of the tribe would easily follow. Louise Singhorn, a Coeur d'Alene Catholic convert, went from one shaman's lodge to the next in her tribe, arguing with each in turn. She eventually persuaded one man, Nataken, to undergo baptism and he was renamed Isidore.[126] In the winter of 1841 Nicolas Point found himself in the unusual position of sharing a horse with a shaman as the two went together to visit a wounded man. At the injured man's lodge, Point "spared no effort" and cured the man. The shaman was so impressed with the blackrobe's medicine that he became an enthusiastic friend of the missionaries.[127]

But successful and lasting conversions of shamans were rare. At Lapwai, Old James, a Nez Perce shaman, stalked out of a prayer meeting and left the village when shamans were denounced. When he returned weeks later, the missionaries gave him special treatment. Eliza Spalding printed out a special card with the Ten Commandments and her convert Timothy read the commandments and "devoted his whole attention" to Old James. The shaman was impressed and asked for a schoolbook like the other native scholars had. "He seems much pleased with his book," Spaulding beamed, "he copies a few lines every day, which he commits to memory." Yet Old James gave no indication of rejecting his traditional beliefs. "Poor old man, his medicine business seems to be his delusion," she concluded.[128]

Elkanah Walker made a similar effort with an influential Spokan shaman he dubbed the "Old Chief." When Walker told the Spokan man how the Bible condemned his practices, the Indian "manifested a good deal of anger" and stalked out of the Walkers' house. A week later Walker noted that he "had some contention with the O.C. but he yielded. . . . I think he improves some in prayer." But a few weeks later the Old Chief hosted a winter dance in his lodge. The shaman, it seemed, was "more strongly attached to his medicine than ever."[129]

Plateau shamans did not take kindly to the new challenges to their authority. "The presence of the priest is . . . odious to them," Pierre Jean De Smet wrote, hence "the incessant war they wage on the ministers of the true faith."[130] At the Coeur d'Alene mission a shaman named Stellam was the bane of the Jesuits' existence. Stellam always played "the role of objector" to any doctrine proposed by the Catholics, according to Nicolas Point. Stellam often contradicted the missionaries as they preached and recalled "the happy times when . . . one could earn a living through gambling alone." He organized traditional shamanic ceremonies to compete with the Catholic services. When confronted directly, he would either fall silent or promise not to do it again.[131] Finally the blackrobes isolated Stellam by converting his wife and closest relatives, who then "united in a assault against him." Stellam finally relented; he threw his medicine bag in a fire, saying, "Now I reject you, to obey only the true God."[132]

Polygamy was another major impediment to conversion. It was common for important Plateau men to take more than one wife. Both missionaries and Indians were quick to focus on polygamy as the one of the greatest divides between white religion and that of the Indians. When Samuel Parker conducted his initial tour of the plateau, most natives welcomed his message, except for one old Cayuse chief. Parker noted that the chief came "several times" to hear Parker expound his doctrine and "disliked what was said about a plurality of wives." The man announced that he would not be giving up any of his own wives, and if that meant "going to the place of burning," so be it.[133]

The missionaries' horror of polygamy only increased with time. "Wives are to them what slaves are to the planters," concluded Mary Walker.[134] But a few of the missionaries realized that polygamy was something more than simple economic or sexual exploitation. Asa Smith described how many Nez Perce bands suffered from a shortage of men due to high casualties in war.[135] A Chelan chief complained to the Jesuit Diomedi that since his tribe had abandoned polygamy, there were fewer children. "Our hunters and fishermen are disappearing," the chief lamented, "and in case of war we will have no more soldiers."[136]

Yet the missionaries denounced polygamy strongly, and in the early days of the missions some Indians were willing to "put away" their second wives.[137] But most polygamous Plateau Indians simply ignored the missionaries on this matter. Nicolas Point boasted how the Jesuits had driven away "gambling and idolatry" but admitted they had little success in banishing polygamy. Though the blackrobes refused baptism to polygamists, still all the Flathead and Coeur d'Alene chiefs practiced "this shameful traffic." "It would be difficult to form an idea of the pain it cost most of them" to give up excess wives, Point explained. And it was not only Plateau men who defended the institution; Point despaired of the native women "who prefer half the heart of a man to the friendship of God."[138]

Henry Spalding was particularly resolute on the matter of polygamy, denouncing it with great zeal and threatening the Nez Perces with dire consequences to their souls if they continued in the practice. Impressed by Spalding's pronouncements, a Nez Perce man came to Spalding one day. Was it true, he wanted to know, that he would have to give up his second wife if he wished to receive baptism? "Absolutely," Spalding told the man. "Polygamy is a sin. You will have to send your second wife away." The man thought for a moment. "You tell her," he said.[139]

Given the Indians' fierce defense of polygamy, some missionaries simply gave up, conceding the point until some future time when they hoped to exert more control over the Indians. Henry Perkins taught the Indians at his Wascopam mission that they were allowed "but one wife to each man," but he did nothing to enforce this edict. "For a time we had to let things be," he admitted, "only stipulating that if a man had one wife, he should take no other during her lifetime."[140]

Catholics versus Protestants

As the initial enthusiasm of the natives faded and the task of conversion proved more difficult than hoped, the Catholic and Protestant missionaries began to look at one another as the source of their problems. Though they tried to show a certain minimum of politeness when they met face to face, there was a deep antipathy between the two camps. Neither considered the other legitimate representatives of Christ and both spent considerable time denouncing the other to the Indians. To the Indians, the constant rivalry only showed that the white shamans were fallible. Sectarian rivalry was itself an important impediment to conversion.

The establishment of the Oregon missions coincided with the most violent anti-Catholic prejudice in Protestant America. There was a dark undercurrent to the Second Great Awakening, a crusade against Catholicism that swept through the evangelical community in the 1820s and 1830s. Members of the "No-Popery" crusade condemned "Romanism" and referred to the Catholic Church as "the Whore of Babylon." A grisly anti-Catholic literature emerged. Readers of *Female Convents: Secrets of Nunneries Disclosed* were enthralled to learn of secret passageways between the nuns' convents and the priests' quarters and murdered babies buried beneath convent floors.

Jesuit Juggling: Forty Popish Frauds Detected and Disclosed told of salacious priests who seduced women in their confessionals.[141] Especially popular was *Fox's Book of Martyrs*, which retold the history of Christianity as a perpetual series of outrages by a corrupt papacy against true believers. As foreign immigrants, many of them Catholic, moved west, American Protestants feared that the pope was allied with European despots to wrest the Mississippi Valley from the United States. Jesuit priests were thought to be the field agents of the scheme. "A minister of the Gospel from Ohio," one Protestant journal warned, "says that the western country swarms with them [Jesuits] under the name of puppet show men, dancing masters, music teachers, peddlers of images and ornaments, barrel organ players, and similar practitioners."[142]

Members of the ABCFM were caught up in the anti-Catholic feelings of the day and considered their Catholic rivals to be little short of satanic. They read anti-Catholic literature and referred to the pope as the "Man of Sin."[143] When Narcissa Whitman visited the Catholic cathedral in St. Louis on her way to Oregon, the service "appeared to me like idolatry." Noting the priest's "embroydered robes . . . of the richest material," she reflected on "the many dellicate fingers that had been employed . . . preparing vestments for such hypocritical characters." Observing the crowd of worshippers, Whitman felt a rush of gratitude "that I am not of the number who willfully shut my eyes to the truth, deceiving and being deceived."[144]

It was a dark day for the Protestants when the first Jesuits—François Norbert Blanchet and Modeste Demers—arrived on the plateau in 1839. "Catholicism is now making its appearance, & the errors of that church are beginning to be defused among this people," Asa Smith fretted. "At this very moment the Catholic priest is at WW [Walla Walla] instructing the people & the Indians are gathering together there to listen to the false doctrines which he inculcates."[145] When the Jesuits arrived at Fort Walla Walla and the chief factor extended an invitation to the nearby Whitmans and Walkers to visit their colleagues, the Protestants "hardly know what to do about accepting it."[146]

The loathing was mutual. Fathers Blanchet and Demers looked down on the Protestants as poorly educated provincials. The Jesuits dismissed their rivals as "self-styled ministers," "Bible colporteurs," and "selfish professors of false doctrines."[147] It was Catholic policy in the Northwest to precede the Protestants where possible and to disrupt the Protestant missions that already existed. In an 1845 letter Bishop Blanchet underscored this policy, writing that it was important to establish missions along the Frasier River "before the Protestant missionaries come and sow error."[148]

The two sides immediately began to disparage one another to the Plateau Indians. Asa Smith claimed that as Blanchet and Norbert passed through the southern plateau in 1839, they "denounced us because we have wives."[149] In the spring of 1841 Elkanah Walker had a long talk with some Spokans who had visited the Catholic mission at St. Mary's. Apparently the Jesuits of St. Mary's had a great deal to say about the Protestants, none of it good.[150] The Protestants went so far as to send trusted Indians to contradict and confound the priests. Asa Smith proudly recounted how his language instructor and convert Lawyer "tried to get the cross" with (get the better of) a priest he met while on a buffalo hunt:

He [Lawyer] heard considerable from the priest & says the priest inquired of him about the mission. . . . According to his account he ridiculed the priest & his doctrines most thoroughly to the interpreter & of course it must have gone to the priest. When they pretended that the cross was God, he said it was only *Kiswi* [nothing], like the ring on his finger. He denied . . . the saving efficacy of baptism & when the priest said it was bad for us to have wives, he in a sarcastic manner asked the interpreter how the priest came into the world? if it was not by means of a father & mother? When the priest pretended that when he got established, he should give the people a *plenty* of food, he said to the interpreter: "I am very glad, my servant, I will come here & do nothing & load my horses with provision & go home again."

Even as he boasted over his pupil's triumph, however, Smith was worried. Though Lawyer had "no faith in the priest," it nonetheless seemed to Smith that Lawyer might yet "fall a prey to Catholicism."[151]

As the Protestant missions seemed to be going nowhere, the missionaries increasingly put the blame on their Catholic rivals. In 1843 Cushing Eels of the Tshimakain mission gave a visitor a "discouraging" account of his progress, blaming the failure on "the opposition arrayed against him by the Catholics."[152] "Romanism stalks abroad on our right hand and on our left and with daring effrontery boasts that she is to prevail and possess the land," Narcissa Whitman gloomily observed in 1842.[153] Her husband, Marcus, apparently lashed out with even greater passion. In 1847 a Cayuse man made a "long speech" to a Catholic priest. Though no interpreter was present, the native was able to get his point across: "The name of Whitman was repeated a number of times, and each time the Cayuse would take hold of the large crucifix that hung from the priest's belt and make the motion of throwing it down, and showing great rage." The priest and others understood the man's actions "as a description of what the Cayuses considered the disposition of Whitman to the Catholic religion."[154]

Predictably, the rivalry between the Protestants and Catholics caused the natives to argue with one another. In 1843 a Walla Walla or Cayuse chief, Tauitau, refused the Reverend Perkins's offer to join in a religious service. "We are Catholics," Tauitau told the Protestant missionary, "and our worship is different from yours." He and his band fell to their knees and demonstrated their prayers. "We are poor," they repeated ten times, followed by an invocation of the Trinity: "Good Father, good son, good spirit." Then Tauitau moved some of his rosary beads about with a brass cross. "This is the way the priest taught us to worship God," Tauitau said. Before Perkins could answer, one of his Protestant Indians shot back that "Tauitau and his band prayed from the head, but we pray from the heart."[155]

In 1842 Father De Smet had proposed to Marcus Whitman that the Protestants and Catholics adopt "one common phraseology" regarding the Holy Trinity so as not to confuse the natives who were hearing the sermons of both. Whitman grew angry and refused. "We were the first in the field," he told De Smet, "& we shall hold our right to make our own words."[156] There were no further attempts to cooperate.

The full enmity that developed between Catholics and Protestants can be seen in a pair of visual learning aids: the Catholic and Protestant ladders. The Catholic ladder was first developed in the Pacific Northwest by Father Blanchet in 1839.[157] The ladder was a mnemonic device, a long piece of paper with a series of pictures portraying the history of the world from Creation to the present. The pictures represented important biblical events such as the Great Flood, the destruction of Sodom and Gomorrah, and the birth, death, and resurrection of Christ. This learning aid was termed a ladder both for its linear shape and because it portrayed the path to heaven. The ladder helped the Indians make sense of the many strange and wonderful stories of the blackrobes. "It was a sweet satisfaction to each of them," Blanchet proclaimed, "to comprehend the origin of created things . . . the point where Adam died; that of the Deluge; when God gave his ten commandments; [and] when Jesus was incarnated, died, and rose to Heaven."[158] The first ladders were sketched by hand, but the demand was such that the fathers could not keep up. In 1842 Pierre Jean De Smet had a batch of the ladders printed in St. Louis. These ladders were popular gifts to the Plateau Indians, who used the sketches to teach Bible stories to one another.[159]

To a Protestant minister, the most notable feature of the Catholic ladder was a branch that departed from the path to heaven about two-thirds of the way up. "Modern Heretics," the branch was labeled, and a list of names included Luther, Calvin, Wesley, and "Mormons." Above the branch was printed a verse from Matthew: "And if he will not hear the church let him be to thee as the heathen and the Publican."[160] The Protestants, naturally, objected to this characterization. Marcus Whitman told a visitor that the ladder "represents all Protestants as the withered ends of several branches of Papacy," and he claimed that "oral instruction of a similar character" usually accompanied the presentation of these ladders. "The possession of one of these manuscripts by an Indian binds him not to hear any more the instructions of the Protestants," Whitman fumed.[161] Spalding claimed that the Catholics told the Indians how "Luther laid down his black gown & cross together and went off in the Road to hell after a wife & never returned & that all American preachers . . . are on the same road to destruction."[162]

The Protestants responded by creating a ladder of their own. The Protestant ladder, designed by Henry and Eliza Spalding, showed two parallel paths. On the right was the path leading to heaven—narrow and austere, with only a few embellishments. In heaven angels flew through a bright blue cloud to place a crown on a soul who had just completed the climb. The left side of the Protestant ladder portrayed the path to hell. Eve offered Adam an apple in the first drawing, and subsequent scenes illustrated the Tower of Babel and a smiling daughter of Herodias accepting the severed head of John the Baptist. At the death of Christ a black robed figure is seen departing from the narrow road of righteousness to take the road to hell. From that point on, the road to hell is illustrated with robed Catholics. A priest kneels at a bloody altar, a corpulent pope is presented "with a sword in one hand and & torch . . . in the other, a king kissing one foot & a bishop the other," as Henry Spalding proudly described the scene. The top half of the road to hell is a history of Catholic atrocities, clearly taken from the classic anti-Catholic tract *Fox's Book of Martyrs*. A young priest emerges from a nunnery and pays an indulgence for the sin of fornication, the pope accepts the severed head of Admiral Coligny at the St. Bartholomew's Day massacre, and another priests burns a stack of Bibles "in New York State." At the head of the ladder the pope appears once again, tumbling down into hell while Satan reaches up to claim him. "The end of the Man of Sin is represented by his falling back into hell at the approach of the Lord Jesus Christ," Spalding chortled.[163]

Unfortunately for them, the Protestant missions never had their ladder printed. Eliza Spalding produced each copy by hand, using ink, lampblack, and berry dyes; thus the Protestant ladder must have circulated less widely in native camps than did the Catholic version. And the Protestant ladder yielded little information about what the Protestants believed. Instead it was almost entirely dedicated to disparaging the Catholics. When the first Protestant ladder was created, Henry Spalding employed it with gusto. "About 9 o'clock we came to a village of some 40 lodges, alighted, rang a bell . . . unrolled the Chart & talked about two hours," Spalding wrote. The next day Spalding "rode hard to reach another village" where he "explained the Chart to them as long as brush could be found for a fire light."[164] Though fewer Protestant ladders were produced, William Gray claimed that the "Indian preachers" whom Spalding equipped with the charts "could attract larger crowds of Indians . . . than those who had the Catholic tree."[165]

The effect of all this sectarian rivalry was predictable—in fact, it had been predicted a generation before. After spending a winter with the Okanagon Indians in 1811, the fur trader Alexander Ross considered the likelihood that Christian missionaries would eventually settle among those people. Ross offered "a few observations" to future missionaries in that part of the world:

The paramount evil which frustrates all the labours of the missionary is that arising from sects of different persuasions interfering with one another, and evil which tends rather to destroy than promote religious feelings among savages. . . . [I]t is no uncommon thing in the wilderness to see the pious and persevering evangelist, after undergoing every hardship to open a new field for his labours among the heathen, followed by some weak zealot of another sect . . . who no sooner reaches the cultivated vineyard of his precursor than he begins the work of demoralization and injustice, by denying the creed and labours of his predecessor, clothes some disaffected chief, and infuses animosity and discord among all parties, in order to get a footing . . . and every additional zealot of a different creed in this field of strife increases the disorder, for all Indians are particularly fond of novelty; consequently, the last creed with them is the best. . . . [The result is that] every moral and religious sentiment is destroyed, and the people are sunk deeper and deeper in the gulf of moral degradation.[166]

By 1840 the Indians were becoming confused by the rivalry between Protestants and Catholics, just as Ross had predicted. "With their methodist ministers, & priests all preaching for themselves the poor Indians get bewildered and they do not know what religion is best," claimed one fur trader.[167] Another visitor to the plateau described the natives as only "nominally Christian" and "about equally divided betwixt the Protestant and Catholic religion."[168]

Another source of friction was the native expectation that the missionaries would provide the Indians with large quantities of trade goods, which the missionaries were unable or unwilling to do. The only previous white settlements on the plateau had been the trading posts, and Indians naturally expected the spiritually powerful missionaries would also have an abundance of goods to share with their new friends. When a Nez Perce man was trying to convince Jason Lee to establish a mission in the man's village, he promised that his people would "catch plenty of beaver" for the missionary.[169] When Henry Spalding asked the Spokans if they wanted a missionary to take up residence in the Spokan country, the Indians replied that "they were glad we took pity on them" and that "they were very poor and their country was poor; and if a white man came to live with them . . . they wanted to look up to him as a father."[170] In 1826 the HBC had closed Spokane House and the Spokans seemed to look on the proposed missionary station as a replacement, a new source of trade goods and free tobacco.[171] The Flathead Indians pleaded for a missionary in much the same terms. "Their chief said they would be glad to have us come and live with them," reported William Gray, "they were glad we took pity on them now; they were so poor, they had nothing."[172] Father Blanchet complained that Plateau Indians "don't cease asking for gifts" and thought it was the Protestants who had spoiled the natives by giving them trousers, cloaks, and shirts.[173] The expectation that the missionaries would fill the role of traders would soon bedevil the missionary effort.

When a Protestant missionary delivered a sermon in which he told the Indians how they must pray, one elder had a ready answer: "Yes, my friend, if you give us plenty of blankets, pantaloons, flour, and meat, and tobacco, and lots of other good things, we will pray to God all the time and always."[174] The missionaries failed to understand Indian ideas of reciprocity and so were often seen as "stingy." "They have manifested a great desire for missionaries but . . . much of this desire has been in the hope of temporal gain," Asa Smith complained. The Indians were willing to help the missionaries "when they receive plenty of blankets, shirts, ammunition &c for it," Smith noted, and when he failed to provide such goods the natives called him "stingy chief."[175] Elkanah Walker echoed Smith's complaint, stating that the

Spokans "think more of obtaining goods from the missionary than of hearing religious instruction."[176] Cushing Eels told some American visitors that "the Indians are glad to have whites settle among them" since they believed that "the more the whites come the more they must receive."[177] When some Nez Perces badgered Asa Smith for presents, he replied that Christ had sent forth his disciples without gifts. "God is stingy," replied one chief.[178]

To the Plateau Indians, the great wealth of the missionaries, the manner in which they flaunted that wealth, the fact that they were living on Indian land, and the way the missionaries seemed to want to establish themselves as chiefs all put the missionaries under an obligation to distribute goods. Narcissa Whitman came the closest to understanding the native point of view when she wrote: "It is difficult for them not to feel but that we are rich & getting richer by the houses we dwell in and the clothes we wear and hang out to dry after washing from week to week."[179] Asa Smith eventually puzzled out the rules of native reciprocity, but interpreted it as hypocrisy. "I understand Indian presents now very well," Smith wrote. "They always give, expecting as much or more in return. . . . [T]hey manage if possible to lay a white man under obligation to them, & if he suffers them to do it, he finds it no easy matter to cancel such an obligation."[180] A bitter Elkanah Walker condemned the Spokans as "eternal beggars." "We see the same dark faces and hear the same language which is the language of the leech give give," Walker complained.[181]

Plateau Indians approached the missionaries as they had the fur traders, expecting that eventually the missionaries would see the necessity of establishing good trade relations. "They are continually harassing us" for ammunition, Asa Smith complained of the Spokans, "they seem to wish to make the stations their trading posts."[182] Some natives made the point explicitly. The Spokans "frequently refer back to the time when there was a rivalry in the [fur] trade," noted Elkanah Walker. As they had with the fur traders, Indians occasionally turned to intimidation to soften the flinty hearts of stingy missionaries. When Henry Perkins refused to give some Wascopam Indians an ax in exchange for six dozen salmon, they threatened to tie him up and whip him.[183]

Even had the missionaries wanted to distribute more goods, the finances of the missions did not allow such extravagance. "We are much embarrassed for want of funds, and the expenses of our mission are at this time very great," David Greene reminded the Oregon missionaries in 1837; "we can only furnish you with items abso-

lutely necessary for your health and usefulness."[184] The fur traders
had established good relations with the Indians at minimal cost by
distributing tobacco as the standard gratuity. But this most of the
Oregon missionaries were unwilling to do. "Tobacco *I will not sell*,"
Marcus Whitman told the importuning Cayuses, who refused to work
for anything else.[185] To the Whitmans, tobacco was associated with
alcohol and gambling, all paths to sin.[186]

Christianity's greatest failing, from the native point of view, was that
it did not protect the Indians from illness. Asa Smith wrote that the
Indians looked to Christianity to free them from "hunger, sickness,
and death in this life, and misery after death."[187] The 1840s brought
increased contact between the plateau and the rest of the world. American immigrants from the east arrived in large numbers, and Plateau
Indians ventured as far as California and the Green River Rendezvous
on trading and raiding expeditions. The result was a new round of
imported illness on the plateau. In 1842 whooping cough arrived, followed by dysentery the next year and measles in 1847. There were
also outbreaks of influenza, typhoid, and typhus. These diseases were
especially fatal to infants and young children. "It was hard with the
native children," wrote E. Perkins at the Wascopam mission, "several
have died and several more are near death."[188]

   Indians turned to the missionaries for help with these new illnesses,
and the missionaries did what they could. But given the state of Western medicine at that time, the treatments were as likely to kill as to
cure. Marcus Whitman, Elkanah Walker, William Gray, and Pierre
Jean De Smet employed bleeding as a treatment for all manner of dis-
comforts. The results could sometimes be fatal, as when Gray bled an
old Spokan chief to death in 1839.[189] Purgatives were another common
cure of the day that were freely dispensed at the missions. Narcissa
Whitman was a believer in Thomism, a species of medical quackery
that prescribed large quantities of cayenne pepper to be taken inter-
nally. Other cures used in the Oregon missions included the use of
niter, sulfur, blisters, leeches, calomel and jalap "to move the bow-
els," morphine, and castor oil.[190]

   Plateau shamans possessed the power to cure or kill. As the missionaries failed to arrest the declining health of the natives, not a few
Indians began to wonder if the missionaries might be killing them on
purpose. Perhaps the white medicines were actually poisons. Protestant missionaries did possess powerful poisons, the natives knew, poisons they used to kill wolves and coyotes and sometimes the Indians'
dogs.[191] Could they be using them to murder the Indians? Dark rumors

of the missionaries killing the Indians to take their land flitted across the Plateau. "The impression is so strongly fixed in the minds of all the people in all quarters that the whites are poisoning them," fretted Elkanah Walker in 1847.[192]

Plateau Indians did not kill shamans merely for failing to cure. Shamans were killed when they used their power to inflict illness.[193] Such malevolent shamans had very specific sets of powers. They often stole the spirit power of individuals they were pretending to cure, thus hastening their death. Bad shamans could employ herbal hate magic—poison—or kill by other means, such as pointing a small magic tube at the intended victim, or walking in that person's footprints while pronouncing maledictions. The most feared and effective form of sorcery was psychic sorcery: a malevolent shaman could make someone sicken and die merely by thinking bad thoughts about the person. If a community had reason to believe that a witch was present, they might detect who it was by examining the personality types of those present. Witches had a distinct personality profile. They were quick to anger, aggressive, selfish, and egocentric. A detected sorcerer could be ritually executed by persons appointed for that purpose.[194] At least twenty such killings occurred between 1837 and 1855 in the southwestern part of the plateau alone.[195] As Indians continued to sicken and die, some began to suspect the missionaries of being the cause.

The Native Uses of Christianity

Even if the missionaries were not actually malevolent shamans, some of their doctrines were proving unpalatable. After a generation of trying to learn more about Christianity, Plateau Indians finally had an open source of knowledge about the white man's religion in the missions. Some of the beliefs, like that of a single omnipotent Great Spirit who could be reached by prayer, were readily assimilated. Other ideas, especially the ban on polygamy, were understood but resisted. Some beliefs, such as the Holy Trinity and Atonement, were simply incomprehensible. Plateau men and women combined the elements of Christianity that made sense to them and met their needs with traditional beliefs and ceremonies. But in the end, there was surprisingly little in Christianity that the natives could use, and what they did use often broke with official Christian doctrine.

Prayers to spirits were an integral part of both traditional faith and the Columbian Religion. In traditional prayers, their "first request is long life, and second is plenty of food," according to an early fur trader with the Colvilles; "in these two things consist the main and principal object of an Indian's petition."[196] Decades later a Catholic missionary complained that despite his teachings, Flathead prayers "consisted in asking to live a long time, to kill plenty of animals and enemies, and to steal the greatest number of horses as possible."[197] Protestants made the same observation of the natives under their tutelage. "Even now when they pray to Jehovah the most they ask for is a temporal blessing," Asa Smith wrote of the Nez Perces; "the most they fear is hunger, sickness & death, that they be assisted in stealing horses &c. & in killing their enemies."[198]

Singing hymns was another acceptable Christian practice. Sacred songs were a large part of traditional religion. Part of the vision quest was learning a song of power, and the Indians were eager to learn the songs of the powerful whites. Many of the new songs had a similar theme to traditional songs—asking the spirits for pity. The missionaries were quick to learn that singing was the part of their religious services the Indians liked best. "I was not aware that singing was a qualification of so much importance to a missionary," wrote an amazed Narcissa Whitman to her family.[199] "It is incredible how the savages like music," marveled Gregory Mengarini of the Flatheads.[200] The Jesuits were quick to pen new songs in the native languages, sometimes employing traditional native tunes to carry the new messages.[201]

Cushing Eels described the Spokans as "passionately fond of music" but noted that they were given to "lewd songs." Eels composed a Christian hymn, based on an existing Indian tune, to replace the more ribald traditional ballads. The Spokan words of the hymn translate: "Thanks thee Jehovah/ We not dead/ We all alive/ We sing we pray." The song was popular with the Spokans and Eels's son claimed that some fur traders "heard Indians singing it on the tops of the Rocky Mountains."[202]

Indians saw no contradiction between singing the songs of the missionaries and continuing to practice their old beliefs. At Tshimakain Elkanah Walker heard a Spokan man warn his sleepy son to stay awake during the sermon or "he would get the medicine man put on him."[203] Walker gloomily concluded that even when the Indians listened to his teachings, "it is so mixed up with their old superstitious ideas that it is like diamonds scattered in the mud."[204]

The clash between native and Christian beliefs could be dramatic. In 1843 Henry Perkins was delivering a service at the Dalles mission when a native man wielding a butcher knife broke into the meeting hall. With one hand he seized a "decrepit old woman" from the audience by her hair and decapitated her in front of the stunned congregation. It developed that the man thought the old woman was an evil shaman and held her responsible for the death of his brother. "Yet these men had been, and still are, represented as *evangelized* in an eminent degree," wrote a skeptical fur trader who witnessed the scene.[205]

The Missions in Decline

Each mission station enjoyed a vogue of popularity and influence with the natives, usually lasting a year or two. After this period of initial enthusiasm, Indians grew less interested in the messages of the missionaries. The process occurred more quickly at some missions and slowly at others, but all followed a similar trajectory. By the mid-1840s most Plateau Indians were drifting away from the missionaries, Catholic and Protestant alike.[206]

The Protestant missions were the first established and the first to feel the loss of interest. The Nez Perces were having second thoughts about the Protestant Lapwai mission by 1839. According to his own Protestant associates, Henry Spalding had been "much in the habit of using the whip or causing it to be used" on stubborn or boisterous Indians.[207] In 1839 when a Nez Perce woman ran away from her abusive American husband, Spalding had the woman lashed seventy times. The Nez Perces were appalled—they believed a woman had the right to divorce her husband if she chose—and wanted to whip the husband for his abuse of his wife. Spalding used his influence and with "great difficulty" persuaded the Nez Perces not to whip the man. Later that year one native man threatened to whip John Gray, one of Spalding's associates, over a minor dispute. When Spalding tried to intervene again, he discovered that his authority was fast eroding. He found himself surrounded by a "multitude" of Indians, some of whom threatened to subject the missionary to a little of his own medicine. Although the threatened beating did not come to pass, Spalding was shaken by the confrontation, admitting for the first time that he felt "discouraged" at the Nez Perces' prospects. "Surely many of them appear like another race of beings from what they did when we first came among them," Spalding reflected.[208] The Spaldings' influence with the Nez Perces rose and fell in the next few years, but the general downward trend was clear. By the winter of 1844 the missionaries noted that the "numbers and interest" of Indians coming to their services and their school was a fraction of what it had been. Eliza Spalding, of course, blamed the influence of American emigrants and the "leaven of Jesuitism."[209]

In 1840 Asa Smith had a frightening confrontation at Kamiah, when two minor Nez Perce chiefs, Insinmalakin and Inmtamlaiakin, demanded payment for the mission lands. The Indians "insulted me with the most abusive language," wrote Smith, "then in the most absolute terms ordered me to leave the place the next day." The incident provoked a division within the tribe. Some Indians urged Smith to stay, but others, he noted, were "indifferent" and offered no support. Smith's native supporters threatened to tie up Insinmalakin and whip him, though "it was evident that none dared to do it." As the Nez Perces argued among themselves, Smith thought they looked "more like demons from the bottomless pit than like human beings." In the end it was decided that Smith could stay for the time being.[210]

The Catholic missions experienced a similar pattern. Many Flatheads were losing interest in the St. Mary's Mission by 1846. The position of the mission, exposed to Blackfoot raids on the northern plains, made it a dangerous place to be. Most Flatheads never settled at the mission permanently but only made it a stop on their seasonal round. After 1843 these stops became less frequent. In 1846, when the Flatheads returned from their buffalo hunt, they openly challenged the blackrobes with displays of prohibited behavior such as gambling. One Flathead disrupted religious services and others practiced shamanism within the mission itself. A Catholic Flathead who watched the scene told Father Mengarini that the Indians now "behaved worse than they did before you came."[211] A new bout of smallpox claimed eighty-six Flatheads that winter and further reduced the status of the blackrobes.

From St. Mary's, native discontent spread to the other Jesuit missions. At some missions the blackrobes were threatened by pistol-wielding natives. The Flatheads "gave up private prayer and vented insult and injury every day upon the missionary," according to one Jesuit. "Our men are discouraged and the evil is becoming contagious," Father Joset warned his superiors. If matters did not soon improve, "nothing remains but to close all the missions, one after another."[212]

As the Indians they had come to proselytize turned distant and then hostile, many missionaries felt bitter disappointment. Increasingly, the missionaries saw the Indians as lazy, proud, arrogant, and most of all ungrateful. "I fear our missionaries are too scornful toward the poor, naked Indians," fretted one visitor after a tour of the missions in 1842.[213] One fur trader claimed that Henry Spalding "had got so that he did nothing but whip Indians and kill dogs."[214]

A strong strain of self-pity ran through the thoughts of the missionaries as the Indians turned away from Christianity. "The trials of a missionary," moaned Henry Spalding, "lie not in the days of hard labor, not in the wants of comforts of life . . . [not even] in witnessing a great amount of wickedness and filth. It lies perhaps in days and nights of sore grief and disappointment, discouragement, occasioned sometimes by the treachery of those whom you have left all to benefit, or in the want of gratitude for great favors received, or rather making those favors an occasion for insulting you."[215]

A second theme in the missionary thought of this period was the eventual extinction of the Indians themselves, an event that seemed both imminent and providential as disease swept the villages of Indians who had turned their backs on salvation. "Few candidates are willing to go among the Indians," ABCFM secretary Jonathan Green noted; they spurned the "fruitless toil in reclaiming small tribes . . . who are wasting away and seem devoted to extinction."[216]

To the indifference of the Indians, the missionaries reacted differently. Some, like the Walkers and Eelses at Tshimakain and most of the Jesuit fathers, comforted themselves with their few converts and continued to try to gain a foothold. Others felt resentment toward the "ungrateful" Indians and began to withdraw from their missionary labors in favor of other pursuits, usually managing the farm associated with their stations. Henry Spalding complained in 1842 about having a house full of "heedless Indians" covered with "mud and filth [and] lice."[217] Soon the Indians were not allowed into the Spaldings' private residence. The Whitmans began limiting their contact with the Indians even earlier. "The greatest trial to a woman's feelings is to have her cooking and eating room always filled with four or five Indians," Narcissa wrote. "They are so filthy they make a great deal of cleaning wherever they go." Fortunately, she reflected, her husband was constructing a new house where they could keep the Indians in a special room for that purpose and "[we] shall not permit them to go into the other part of the house at all."[218]

Some missionaries quit altogether. Asa and Mary Smith left Kamiah in the spring of 1841 and became missionaries in Hawaii. Their lay partner, Cornelius Rogers, quit about the same time. William Gray resigned from the mission in 1842 and settled in the Willamette Valley. The Jesuits abandoned their Flathead mission in 1850, moving the priests and resources to more promising locations. The Spaldings, who had managed to convert a small core of Nez Perces even while alienating the rest, withdrew into themselves, spending more time with their crops and less with the Nez Perces.

Massacre

By the mid-1840s most Plateau Indians had rejected Christianity. The white man's source of spirit power, the object of such curiosity and even urgency since the protohistoric era, had proven a disappointment. Christianity had failed to protect the Indians from disease or provide them with a richer material culture. Indeed, Christianity and Christian missionaries proved deadly for some natives. On the northern plateau the Jesuit fathers were perversely determined to share their spirit power with the hostile Blackfoot Indians who raided the plateau. On the southern plateau the Protestant missionaries openly disdained the Indians, even as they welcomed the white settlers who abused Indians and coveted their land. All over the plateau Indians continued to die from imported diseases.

The missions had failed for numerous reasons: unrealistic expectations, a shortage of material inducements, linguistic conundrums, the missionaries' failure to understand native cultures, ongoing disease epidemics, and increasing white migration. But the main reason the missions failed was that Christianity did not prove to be what the natives had thought it was. The Nez Perces and Flatheads who journeyed to St. Louis after 1829 sought a source of spirit power so strong that it would restore the aboriginal world of their fathers. They sought not eternal reward but blessings in this life. But after Christianity arrived on the Plateau, their situation only grew worse.

Of all the Plateau Indians, it was the Cayuses who were losing population and status most quickly in the 1840s. "The number of this people is evidently diminishing & has been for many years," Asa Smith wrote in 1840. "The excavations in the ground where the people formerly had their lodges indicate that the number of people was much greater than at present," he observed.[219] Not only were many Cayuses dying, but those who survived could feel their status quickly eroding year by year. Although never a large tribe, the Cayuses had once been powerful, using their early acquisition of the horse to dominate the middle Columbia. There the Cayuses enjoyed a lush homeland in the Walla Walla and Grande Ronde Valleys, areas that were perfect for horse breeding and that lay along native trade routes. By the fur trade era, the Cayuses allied themselves with the powerful Nez Perces and dominated their weaker neighbors the Walla Wallas. The Cayuses impressed white observers with their power and arrogant dignity. Early visitors described them as "extremely proud" and "of a haughty and imperious disposition."[220]

The Cayuses suffered from their location in the 1840s, when large numbers of Americans began to cross the Cayuse homeland on a path that would become known as the Oregon Trail. Though the bravery and nobility of the early emigrants is deeply ingrained in our national mythology, many contemporary observers saw otherwise. "Many of these adventurers," one fur trader delicately noted, "are of that class of persons who have always hovered on the frontiers of civilization."[221] Another thought the emigrants as a class "have never been refined by either mental or moral culture."[222] Francis Parkman was less charitable as he personally viewed the 1846 emigrants. Though a few were "very sober-looking," he thought, others were "some of the vilest outcasts in the country."[223] Few had any experience in dealing with Indians or any vested interest in maintaining peaceful relations with the tribes whose land they were crossing.

"When they get beyond the range of Law and Civilization, a slight cause often makes them reckless and abusive," wrote Henry Beeson, himself an early emigrant. "The majority of the first Emigrations to Oregon were from Missouri, and among them it was customary to speak of the Indian man as a Buck; of the woman as a Squaw; until at length, in general acceptance of these terms they ceased to recognize the rights of Humanity in those to whom they were so applied. By a very natural and easy transition, from being spoken of as brutes, they came to be thought of as game to be shot, or vermin to be destroyed." Beeson even claimed that some emigrants "think it would be a great achievement to kill an Indian" and "are heard to declare their determination to shoot the first Indian they see."[224]

As the emigrants crossed the southern plateau, they stole Indian horses, pillaged native food caches, abused individual natives, and generally disrupted the carefully wrought peace that had existed on the plateau since the 1820s. The Cayuse chief Tauwat-wai pleaded with Indian agent Elijah White to understand that "the whites were much more to blame than the Indians for recent conflicts. . . . [T]hree-fourths of them, though they taught the purest doctrines, practiced the greatest abominations."[225] White tended to agree and complained of the early emigrants' predilections toward violence and drunkenness. "Never were a people more illy prepared for self government," he reflected.[226]

Some Indians turned to the HBC for help. In 1843 the Walla Walla chief Peopeomoxmox traveled to Fort Vancouver to tell John Mc-Loughlin his fear "that the whites would come in the summer, and kill them all off." McLoughlin answered that although he did not believe the Americans were planning for war, if war did come the Indians could not look to the HBC for help.[227] In 1847, when a number of violent incidents occurred between emigrants and Indians, McLoughlin took the opportunity to write to the American secretary of war to plead the Indians' case. "In Justice to the Indians I must say I have known Many and Many a White Man as ready to impose on the Indians when in their power," McLoughlin wrote, "as Indians in a Similar situation to impose on Whites."[228]

Forced to choose between a small band of seemingly ungrateful Cayuses on the one hand and a flood of American emigrants on the other, the Whitmans abandoned the Cayuses to their fate. "I have no doubt our greatest work is to be to aid the white settlement of this country," Marcus Whitman wrote to his in-laws in 1844.[229] By 1845 the Whitmans had converted their mission station into a truck farm, growing as much produce as possible to sell to the hungry emigrants. And what would happen to the Cayuses as Oregon filled up with settlers? "The Indians have in no case obeyed the command to multiply and replenish the earth," Whitman intoned, "and they cannot stand in the way of others in doing so."[230] Whitman believed that the Indians were "an inferior race" doomed to extinction, according to one fellow missionary, and he much preferred to invest his energies in promoting the white immigration that would soon displace the vanishing Indians.[231]

The Cayuses would not vanish quietly. On November 29, 1847, they acted to remove the most immediate cause of their mortality and declining status: Marcus and Narcissa Whitman. Measles was taking a dreadful toll in the Cayuse camp, and worried natives held councils late into the night to determine how to fight the white shamans' magic. Finally it was decided to kill the Whitmans and their associates. Two men, Tomahas and Tiloukaikt, entered the Whitman house with a request for medicine. While Marcus Whitman talked with Tiloukaikt, Tomahas maneuvered behind the missionary and tomahawked him in the head. He delivered another blow as Whitman fell to the floor, then the two "chopped the doctor's face so badly that his features could not be recognized." Then the Indians fell on the other members of the mission, killing Narcissa Whitman, ten men, and two children. Others were taken captive and would be released weeks later only when the HBC paid a ransom for their lives.[232]

The Whitman massacre was an extreme example of a judgment that many Plateau Indians were making concerning Christianity at roughly the same time. The white man's religion had not proven useful to most Indians and a revival of traditional faith was under way. No more would Indians turn to whites for spiritual power. A new set of native prophets would arise in the middle of the nineteenth century, men like Smohalla of the Wanapams and Skolaskin of the Sanpoils. These "Dreamers" (as their faith was called) taught resistance to American encroachments and promised a future free of white people. As one Indian agent described the new message: "They believe that if they will continue faithful to the old habits and beliefs of the ancestors, that the Great Spirit will in the near future suddenly bring to life all Indians who have died for the last thousand years or more, and will enable the Indians to at once expel or exterminate all the whites and have the whole country to themselves the same as before the white man came."[233] A religious journey that had commenced in the protohistoric era, when trade networks brought rumors of a new kind of man to the east, had ended.

Conclusion

Spokane Garry lived a long life—as did his father, Illim-Spokanee. Together, father and son experienced the gamut of religious change: from the protohistoric era, to the fur trade, to the acceptance and rejection of the Christian missionaries and the revival of traditional faith, to the slow Christianization of the reservation era. The lives of Illim-Spokanee and Spokane Garry illuminate the history of the religious change on the Columbia Plateau.

Illim-Spokanee was a Spokan chief, born during the tumultuous protohistoric era. Illim-Spokanee was a child when horses were still a novelty on much of the plateau. Along with the rest of his people, he wondered at the metal knives, glass beads, and other strange goods that began to arrive via the expanding trade networks of the mid-1700s. The Spokans, like other Plateau peoples, were intrigued and alarmed by the stories that arrived with the goods, tales of the white people to the east. The volcanic eruptions of 1790 that blanketed the Spokan country with ash only increased the Indians' anxiety.[1] Illim-Spokanee survived the smallpox epidemics that destroyed so many of his friends and relatives during the protohistoric era. He probably took part in the Prophet Dance of the late 1700s, as his people searched for a spiritual answer to the challenges of new era.

Garry was born in 1811, the same year the fur traders arrived on the plateau to establish permanent outposts. His father welcomed the representatives of the American and Northwest fur companies who built trading posts along the Spokane River. Illim-Spokanee and his son were frequent visitors to the posts, whose proprietors considered the chief a "harmless old man."[2] The Spokans and the traders shared horse races and festivals and were soon bound by ties of marriage. On one occasion the fur traders amused themselves by getting their friend drunk, noting that Illim-Spokanee "seemed to relish" the taste of trade whiskey.[3] But if the chief and his followers welcomed the whiskey, tobacco, and trade goods of the whites, they were just as eager for spiritual knowledge.

Garry grew up in fur trade society and shared the religious curiosity of his people. As the son of a chief, he was probably more familiar with white ways than many children of his age. When George Simpson asked for Spokan boys to attend the Red River school in 1825, Illim-Spokanee was quick to volunteer his son. The Spokans placed their hope for the future with Garry and another teenager named Berens. These two boys, too young even to have traveled to the buffalo country, were to learn how to access the spirit power of the whites. Then they were to bring that knowledge home.

Garry proved an apt pupil at Red River, and when he returned home to stay in 1830, eager Indians flocked to the school he established along the Spokane River. The return of Garry and the other Red River boys sparked a new religious movement, the Columbian Religion. This syncretized faith swept the Plateau in the 1830s. Garry taught his people that there was a single supreme god, to pray directly to this god, and some simple songs and prayers. The people prayed, smallpox temporarily retreated, and the Columbian Religion grew stronger. Indians wanted to learn more of the white men's faith.

The Spokans, like many Plateau Indians, greeted the first missionaries with enthusiasm in the late 1830s. But the creed of these white shamans proved more difficult and less useful than any had imagined. These shamans demanded that Indians give up their old ceremonies, have only one wife, and pray in very specific ways. They took land from the Indians with little or no compensation. They did not share manufactured goods with the Indians as the fur traders had. And the white shamans argued among themselves, disparaging one another's teachings. Disease returned to the plateau as the shamans arrived, and to some there seemed a connection. Clearly the white religion was less useful than hoped.

Garry's own status declined precipitously in the era of the missions, as did the status of many native religious leaders. When Elkanah and Mary Walker established their Tshimakain mission in 1838, Garry looked upon them more as rivals than allies. The strict teachings of the Walkers conflicted with the more flexible instructions of Garry, himself a polygamist. And the Walkers directly contradicted much that Garry had been teaching. They found the syncretic faith of the Spokans more an impediment to Christianizing the tribe than if they had been absolute pagans. Walker complained of the difficulty of convincing a Spokan man of his "wicked heart" when "he has been thinking for ten or twelve years that he was on the road to heaven."[4] Garry gave up his own preaching soon after the Walkers arrived, later explaining that the other Indians "jawed him so much about it."[5]

Like so many others, Garry came to reject much of the missionaries' teachings. He cast aside the white clothing he had worn since his return from Red River and put on beaded moccasins and leggings. His overcoat was replaced with a blanket or buffalo robe. Garry abandoned his school and farm and went with his people to the buffalo country; he gambled assiduously and soon lost most of his possessions. In 1841 George Simpson encountered Garry on a hunting trip. Garry and some friends were playing with a deck of cards they had purchased from some traders. Garry refused to shake hands with Simpson. "A more melancholy exemplification of the influence of civilization on barbarism could hardly be imagined than the apparently scientific eagerness with which these naked and hungry savages thumbed and turned the black and greasy pasteboard," Simpson fumed. Garry, he concluded, had "relapsed to his original barbarism."[6]

The rejection of Christianity and the execution of the Whitmans plunged Plateau peoples into a generation of war. In 1848 the Oregon militia swarmed up the Columbia to extract vengeance in what became known as the Cayuse War. They destroyed most of the Cayuses' horses, cattle, and cached food. Measles struck the malnourished Cayuses that winter, carrying away still more of the rapidly diminishing tribe.[7] By 1849 the once-powerful Cayuses were broken and scattered. Under pressure from the Nez Perces and other tribes, the Cayuses surrendered the Whitman murderers to the whites in 1850.[8]

The defeat of the Cayuses encouraged further American emigration and settlement. The 1850s saw a boisterous stream of settlers crossing the plateau on their way to the Willamette Valley. More ominously from the native point of view, some whites began to settle east of the Cascades and farming communities sprung up at Walla Walla and the Dalles. Perhaps the Cayuses had been right after all, perhaps the whites were coming to take away the Indians' land.

The worst fears of the natives were confirmed in 1853 by the arrival of Isaac Ingalls Stevens, first governor of the Washington Territory. Ambitious and impatient, Stevens sought a quick solution to the "Indian Problem" by confining the natives to a series of reservations. In 1855 Stevens met with leaders of the major Plateau tribes in a grand council at Walla Walla. The Indians had previously agreed among themselves not to sign any treaties that surrendered land. But with bribes and bluster Stevens broke the unity of the tribes and persuaded many to sign a treaty that confined the Plateau Indians to three major reservations. It was, Stevens reported, a "most satisfactory" council.[9]

War erupted almost immediately. The Yakima leader Kamiakin led a two-year fight against the Americans. At one point Kamiakin had the loyalty of every tribe east of the Cascades, with the exception of the Nez Perces. But Indian resistance was crushed in 1858 by a combination of federal and militia troops, and the Indians were confined to their reservations. The Nez Perces finally revolted in 1877 with Chief Joseph's famous flight to Canada. But this too failed, and the natives of the plateau settled down to life on the reservation, determined to make the best of a bad lot.

Garry lived to see all these changes. In the disintegrating world of the Plateau Indians, Garry proved a survivor. The Walkers withdrew from the Spokan country after the Whitman murders, and Garry was able to regain some of his old influence. He planted crops along the Spokane River and carried his wheat to Fort Colville to be ground. When the Yakima War began in 1856, Garry tried and failed to keep his people on the sidelines. Though white people often denominated him "head chief" of the Spokans, his influence generally declined after the 1850s. In the 1860s and 1870s he saw his people overwhelmed by an influx of white miners and settlers. In 1881 a reservation was created for the Spokans, but the reservation was near the Canadian border, far from their ancestral homelands, and few Spokans agreed to live there. The American city of Spokane Falls grew up where Garry had established his first school and the Spokans were slowly pressed out of their homes. Garry himself established a small farm on the east edge of town, but he was defrauded of his land by a white farmer in 1888.[10]

In the aboriginal world of the Spokans and other Plateau peoples, religion was the key to survival. The traditional faith of the Spokans was integrated with their environment and way of life. The major rituals of the Indians were organized with the seasonal round. The guardian spirits of the Plateau people—bear, blue jay, moon—were drawn from their physical world. The religious tales told around Plateau campfires, stories of Coyote and Raccoon and the other animal-people, all took place on the plateau and explained the origins of prominent geographic features. And the healing rituals and practices, the herbal medicines and sweats that Plateau shamans prescribed, were effective remedies to the few maladies known to Plateau Indians before white contact. The traditional faith of the Plateau had developed over thousands of years and offered effective strategies of survival to the men and women who practiced it.[11]

The arrival of the whites drastically reordered the Plateau way of life, and the old religion no longer answered people's needs. During the protohistoric era, natives scrambled to make the old beliefs conform to the new realities. Some new realities could be integrated into the existing belief system with minimal disruption. The Yakimas began telling stories of the mythological origins of horses, for example. The disquieting news of the approaching whites triggered a wave of prophecy on the Plateau.

But as the Plateau world changed, the ground shifted under some of the old beliefs and they became unstable. The waves of epidemic disease were especially corrosive to a religion whose leaders were supposed to excel at healing. The Prophet Dance of the late protohistoric era was a last attempt to revive traditional beliefs in their pristine form. When smallpox returned to the plateau in 1800, it became clear that a simple revival of faith would not meet the new challenges. Indians began to look beyond their own belief system for the religious answers they needed.

The whites who arrived on the plateau in the 1810s and 1820s seemed to hold the key to the spiritual needs of Plateau Indians. They clearly had an abundance of spirit power and did not suffer from the same problems the natives did. Indians quickly found that they could manage the fur trade and traders pretty well. As they established friendly trading relationships, the Indians tried to peer more deeply into the religious beliefs of the traders. The fur trade era on the plateau was a time of close observation and questioning, as Indian tried to learn more about white religious beliefs and to adapt some of those ideas to the Indian reality.

The result was the first syncretic faith of the Plateau—the Columbian Religion. From Christianity the natives took the belief in a supreme being, a tradition of holy days, and other elements. These were mixed with Indian beliefs and ceremonies into a new faith that spread throughout the Plateau in the 1820s and 1830s. But this faith by itself was not enough. Smallpox swept the Plateau once more, and other white diseases began to degrade the health of the Indians as well. The Columbian Religion was at best a partial answer. Indians needed to know more about Christianity. They needed to meet some of the shamans of the white people, the missionaries. And when the missionaries did not arrive, the Indians went looking for them.

Plateau Indians were overjoyed to welcome the first missionaries to the plateau in the 1830s. Indian hands helped erect homes and churches for the missionaries and Indians hearts and ears were opened to the messages of the white shamans. The ways of Christianity were hard—Indians would have to give up their multiple wives, stop gambling and, according to the Protestants, abandon the hunt in favor of the plow. But the rewards also seemed great. The missionaries were rich both in spirit power and material goods. And they seemed not to sicken and die as often as the Indians. Here at last was the answer to the frightful erosion of status and population that Indians had been suffering for two generations.

As Indians tried to adopt Christianity, their status continued to decline. New diseases, including measles, struck the plateau. Farming was a useful supplement to the seasonal round but was not a replacement for it. Monogamy was too great an adjustment for many. And the white shamans proved stingy with the trade goods. Christianity did little or nothing to improve the existence of Plateau Indians, and the missionaries themselves were bad and dangerous neighbors. For most mission stations, Catholic and Protestant, the initial honeymoon period was brief, no more than two years. By the late 1840s, most Plateau Indians had given up on Christianity.

The Prophet Dance, the Columbian Religion, and Christianity all failed to improve the lives of the Plateau Indians. None was integrated with the plateau environment as their traditional faith had been. The new faiths fell short of the aboriginal standard, set in the precontact era.

Christianity began to make sense to Plateau Indians only in the 1870s. By the late nineteenth century, the surviving natives were living on reservations. Many of the resources on which they had previously depended—salmon, camas, buffalo, deer—had been depleted by commercial hunting and fishing and the grazing of livestock. Now that the seasonal round was no longer possible, the Indians turned to subsistence farming. At about the same time, the long population decline of Plateau Indians began to slow, partly because of large numbers of disease-experienced individuals. Indians found themselves subject to white laws and local governments, and any possibility of forcible resistance had long since been abandoned. As Indians began to live like whites, the religion of the whites proved more palatable than before, and Christianity became a potential source of strength rather than an alien oppressor. The late nineteenth century saw a growth of Christian churches on many Plateau reservations.[12]

In 1870 Spokane Garry again found himself drawn toward the Christianity of his youth. Missionaries had begun returning to the plateau, and some of the Spokans allowed themselves to be baptized by the Catholic priests who were administering to the nearby Coeur d'Alenes. Perhaps it was the anti-Catholicism Garry had learned as a youth that impelled him to action. In 1871 Garry again established a school for Spokan children, where he taught the ABC song along with

Episcopalian hymns. The next year he initiated a Protestant revival among the Spokans. He even wrote to his old rival Henry Spalding to come and baptize and marry the Spokans in the proper fashion.[13]

Garry ended his days in a canvas teepee pitched on the land of a friendly white farmer. His remaining wife was blind, and the two were supported by their daughter, who took in laundry from surrounding white families. The elderly Garry was often seen riding his horse along the streets of Spokane. White boys looking for amusement would roll rocks down on his teepee from the hillside above. He died in 1892 and was buried in a pauper's grave. The Bible and Book of Common Prayer that he had brought back from Red River some sixty years before were placed beside him. His Christian burial marked the end of the religious journey of many Plateau Indians.

Notes

Introduction

1. My description of Joe Meek and the hanging of the Cayuse men is taken from Victor, *The River of the West*; Drury, *Marcus and Narcissa Whitman*, 2:321–32; Ruby and Brown, *The Cayuse Indians*, 162–71; and Lansing, *Juggernaut*, 91–98.

2. Drury, *Marcus and Narcissa Whitman*, 2:327. The actual guilt or innocence of the five was and is controversial, but Drury, the most exacting scholar of the Oregon missions, judged that at least four of the five men had participated in the killings. See Drury, *Marcus and Narcissa Whitman*, 2:327–30.

3. Drury, *Marcus and Narcissa Whitman*, 2:330–31. It is not clear why the Cayuse men submitted to baptism, but their example was not followed by many of their tribesmen.

4. Victor, *The River of the West*, 494.

5. Campbell, *Autobiography*, 243.

6. Victor, *The River of the West*, 496.

7. Some recent studies have begun to rectify this situation. See Chance, *Influences of the Hudson's Bay Company*; Stern, *Chiefs and Chief Traders*; and especially Boyd, *People of the Dalles*.

8. See, for example, Cox, *The Columbia River*; Ross, *Adventures of the First Settlers*; and Ross, *The Fur Hunters of the Far West*. The unpublished records of the Hudson's Bay Company are found at the Hudson's Bay Company Archives.

9. Drury's best works are *Marcus and Narcissa Whitman* and *Chief Lawyer of the Nez Perces*. Peterson's *Sacred Encounters* is a fine introduction to the Jesuit missions and the native response. See also Burns, *The Jesuits and the Indian Wars*.

10. See Prucha, "Two Roads to Conversion," 130–37.

1. A World of Spirits

1. These paragraphs are a composite of some of the creation myths of different Plateau tribes, which differ only in minor details. For some typical examples see: Boas, *Kutenai Tales*; Teit, *Traditions of the Thompson River Indians*; Boas, *Folk Tales of Salishan and Sahaptin Tribes*; Slickpoo, *Nu Mee Poom Tit Wah Tit*; Phinney, *Nez Perce Texts*; Mourning Dove, *Coyote Tales*.

2. In a few creation stories the Earth is a woman, but this became part of the aboriginal belief system only after contact with Europeans. See Gill, *Mother Earth*, 40–68.

3. Boas, *Folk Tales of Salishan and Sahaptin Tribes*, 81.

4. In some tales Coyote precedes the first humans to make the earth ready for their arrival. See Phinney, *Nez Perce Texts*, 24–29.

5. Phinney, *Nez Perce Texts*, 27.

6. Boas, *Folk Tales of Salishan and Sahaptin Tribes*, 4.

7. *History of the Pacific Northwest*, 2:62.

8. Boas, *Folk Tales of Salishan and Sahaptin Tribes*, 12.

9. United States Army Corps of Engineers, *Washington*, 5–11; Meinig, *The Great Columbia Plain*, 1–17; Weis, *The Channeled Scablands*, 1–23.

10. Walker, *Mutual Crossutilization*, 39–40; Brunton, "Ceremonial Integration"; Ray, *Cultural Relations*, 9.

11. Boas, *Folk Tales of Salishan and Sahaptin Tribes*, 12; Wilkes, *Narrative of the United States Exploring Expedition*, 4:466–67.

12. Anastasio, "Intergroup Relations in the Southern Plateau," 16, 107; Boyd, "Introduction of Infectious Diseases," 136.

13. Boyd, "Introduction of Infectious Diseases," 324–413.

14. For skeptical evaluations of pre-Columbian population estimates in general, see Daniels, "The Indian Population of North America in 1492"; McArthur, "The Demography of Primitive Populations"; Henige, "Their Numbers Become Thick."

15. Ross and Brauner, "The Northwest as Prehistoric Region"; Cressman, *Prehistory of the Far West*, 73, 174.

16. Franchère, *Journal of a Voyage to the Northwest Coast*, 149.

17. Cox, *The Columbia River*, 92.

18. "Report of Chief Trader Samuel Black, 1829," Hudson's Bay Company Archives, B146/e/2.

19. Thwaites, *Journals of the Lewis and Clark Expedition*, 4:369.

20. W. G. Rae to James Hargrave, March 20 1836, Fort Nez Perces, in Glazebrook, *Hargrave Correspondence*, 234.

21. Thwaites, *Journals of the Lewis and Clark Expedition*, 4:369.

22. Older interpretations of the plateau as a land of plenty are contradicted by widespread accounts of famine, both in the literature of exploration and the fur trade and also in traditional native myths and stories. For an example of the former, see Cox, *The Columbia River*, 261. For an example of the latter, see "Bobcat and Magpie" in Weisel, "Ten Animal Myths of the Flathead Indians," 2–5. For the plateau as land of milk and honey, see Miller, *Prophetic Worlds*.

23. Meinig, *The Great Columbia Plain*, 19–22.

24. Hewes, "Aboriginal Use of Fishery Resources," 24.

25. Stuart, *On the Oregon Trail*, 58.

26. Pambrun, *Sixty Years on the Frontier*, 32.

27. The infallibility of the salmon runs is usually presented as a given by Plateau anthropologists; see, for example, Walker, *Mutual Crossutilization*, 11. However, some Indian myths point toward years of few salmon, and David Chance has shown that the salmon runs at Kettle Falls were "far from regular." See Chance, *Influences of the Hudson's Bay Company*, 20–22. The failure of similar runs of salmon on the northern plateau's Fraser River have also been documented; see Gibson, *Farming the Frontier*, 24; Cox, *The Columbia River*, 371; McLean, *John McLean's Notes*, 152.

28. Seltice, *Saga of the Coeur d'Alene Indians*, 16.

29. Ray, *Sanpoil and Nespelem*, 69–71.

30. Ogden, *Traits of American Indian Life*, 37.

31. Boas, *Folk Tales of Salishan and Sahaptin Tribes*, 47.

32. "Report of Chief Trader Samuel Black, 1829," Hudson's Bay Company Archives, B146/e/2.

33. Liljeblad, "The Religious Attitude of the Shoshoni Indians," 34–35.

34. "Report of Chief Trader Samuel Black, 1829," Hudson's Bay Company Archives, B146/e/2.

35. Walker, "Plateau: Nez Perce," 116–17.

36. Spinden, *The Nez Perce Indians*, 247–48.

37. Walker, *Conflict and Schism*, 20–25.

38. Ray, *Sanpoil and Nespelem*, 184.

39. Clark, *Indian Legends*, 181–82.

40. Malouf and White, "Recollections of Lasso Stasso," 2–3.

41. Walker, "Plateau: Nez Perce," 115–17.

42. Ray, *Sanpoil and Nespelem*, 132.

43. Walker, "Plateau: Nez Perce," 116.

44. Walker, "Plateau: Nez Perce," 116–17.

45. Ray, *Cultural Relations*, 68–76.

46. Point, *Wilderness Kingdom*, 17.

47. Ray, *Sanpoil and Nespelem*, 182–89.

48. Grim, "Cosmogony and the Winter Dance," 399.

49. Bouchard and Kennedy, *Indian History and Knowledge*, 34.

50. Ray, *Sanpoil and Nespelem*, 182–89.

51. Ray, *Cultural Relations*, 69

52. Hill-Tout, "Report of the Ethnology of the Okanaken," 153–54.

53. Ray, *Cultural Relations*, 69, 72.

54. Ray, *Cultural Relations*, 92.

55. Spinden, *The Nez Perce Indians*, 256.

56. Walker, *Conflict and Schism*, 27, 28.

57. Ray, *Cultural Relations*, 95–102.

58. "Report of Chief Trader Samuel Black, 1829," Hudson's Bay Company Archives, B146/e/2.

59. Ross, *Adventures of the First Settlers*, 290.

60. De Smet, *Indian Sketches*, 34.

61. Ross, *Adventures of the First Settlers*, 286–87.

62. Mourning Dove, *Autobiography*, 34.

63. "Report of Chief Trader Samuel Black, 1829," Hudson's Bay Company Archives, B146/e/2.

64. Murdock, "The Tenino Indians," 138–39.

65. In the discussion that follows I use Lillian Ackerman's definition of sexual equality: "Equal access, or different but balanced access, of both sexes to power, authority, and autonomy in economic, domestic, political, religious, and other social spheres" ("Sexual Equality," 2).

66. Moulton, *Journals of the Lewis and Clark Expedition*, 7:294.

67. Wilkes, *Narrative of the United States Exploring Expedition*, 4:465.

68. Bonvillain, "Gender Relations," 21–25.

69. McLean, *John McLean's Notes*, 180.

70. Cox, *The Columbia River*, 266. Cox's observation is reinforced by Lillian Ackerman's conclusion that on the Plateau good providers had authority and were listened to in village councils, whether they were male or female ("Sexual Equality," 49).

71. Wilkes, *Narrative of the United States Exploring Expedition*, 4:457.

72. *Journals of Alexander Henry*, 2:901.

73. Ray, *Sanpoil and Nespelem*, 137.

74. Parker, *Journal of an Exploring Tour*, 197.

75. Ackerman, "Sexual Equality," 52.

76. Rev. Joseph Joset, S.J., quoted in Raufer, *Black Robes and Indians*, 26.

77. Mourning Dove, *Autobiography*, 61.

78. John Work, quoted in Chance, *Influences of the Hudson's Bay Company*, 100.

79. Turney-High, *Ethnography of the Kutenai*, 52. For women and food ownership, see also Ruby and Brown, *The Spokane Indians*, 22; Wilkes, *Narrative of the United States Exploring Expedition*, 4:449; Armstrong, *Oregon*, 133.

80. Ross, *Adventures of the First Settlers*, 310.

81. Ackerman, "Sexual Equality," 69–71.

82. Ackerman, "Sexual Equality," 78–80; Ray, *Sanpoil and Nespelem*, 134.

83. Spier, *The Sinkaietk*, 159.

84. Boas, *Folk Tales of Salishan and Sahaptin Tribes*, 207–9.

85. Ackerman, "Sexual Equality," 78–80; Ray, *Cultural Relations*, 93.

86. Moulton, *Journals of the Lewis and Clark Expedition*, 7:187.

87. So dangerous was this menstrual blood that a malign shaman could kill an already wounded man by placing a rag dipped in menstrual blood in his bed. See Curtis, *The North American Indian*, 7:68.

88. Interestingly enough, these prohibitions may have some basis in fact. Modern research shows that many animals shy away from the scent of human menstrual blood. See March, "Deer, Bears, and Blood."

89. Ray, *Sanpoil and Nespelem*, 70–71, 135.

90. Thwaites, *Journals of the Lewis and Clark Expedition*, 4:355.

91. Drury, *First White Women*, 1:139.

92. Thwaites, *Journals of the Lewis and Clark Expedition*, 2:371.

93. Mourning Dove, *Autobiography*, 11; Ray, *Sanpoil and Nespelem*, 131.

94. Franchère, *Journal of a Voyage to the Northwest Coast*, 105.

95. Ray, *Cultural Relations*, 6–8.

96. De Smet, *Life, Letters, and Travels*, 3:1004–5.

97. Francis Heron, quoted in Glazebrook, *Hargrave Correspondence*, 71–72.

98. Ray, *Cultural Relations*, 19–20.

99. Ross, *Adventures of the First Settlers*, 300.

100. Turney-High, *Ethnography of the Kutenai*, 154–55.

101. Turney-High, *Ethnography of the Kutenai*, 155; Spier and Sapir, *Wishram Ethnography*, 213–15.

102. Ray, *Cultural Relations*, 8–10.

103. Turney-High, *Ethnography of the Kutenai*, 42–43, 52, 152–54.

104. Kane, *Paul Kane's Frontier*, 123.

105. Thompson, *Narrative*, 335.

106. Ruby and Brown, *The Spokane Indians*, 17–19; Kane, *Paul Kane's Frontier*, 125–26; Ray, *Sanpoil and Nespelem*, 69–75.

107. Ross, *Adventures of the First Settlers*, 300.

108. Ross, *Adventures of the First Settlers*, 300.

109. Ray, *Cultural Relations*, 10–15.

110. Walker, *Conflict and Schism*, 13.

111. Brunton, "Ceremonial Integration," 1–28; Ray, *Cultural Relations*, 6–8, 10–15.

112. Ray, *Sanpoil and Nespelem*, 27.

113. Ray, *Sanpoil and Nespelem*, 27–28.

114. "Report of Chief Trader Samuel Black, 1829," Hudson's Bay Company Archives, B146/e/2.

115. Ackerman, "Sexual Equality," 88.

116. Ray, *Sanpoil and Nespelem*, 44.

117. Stevens, *Reports of Explorations and Surveys*, 5:199.

118. Thwaites, *Journals of the Lewis and Clark Expedition*, 4:354.

119. Moulton, *Journals of the Lewis and Clark Expedition*, 8:21.

120. Ruby and Brown, *The Spokane Indians*, 22.

121. Minto, "Reminiscences of Experiences," 224.

122. Ross, *Adventures of the First Settlers*, 297.

123. Walker, *Mutual Crossutilization*, 19.

124. Kane, *Paul Kane's Frontier*, 125.

125. Mrs. Elkanah Walker, in Drury, *First White Women*, 2:158.

126. Ray, *Sanpoil and Nespelem*, 28.

127. Kane, *Paul Kane's Frontier*, 122.

128. Turney-High, *Ethnography of the Kutenai*, 95.

129. Allison, "Account of the Similkameen Indians" 306.

130. Turney-High, *Ethnography of the Kutenai*, 97.

131. Ray, *Sanpoil and Nespelem*, 28–29.

132. Ray, *Sanpoil and Nespelem*, 151.

133. Slickpoo, *Noon Nee-Me-Poo*, 189–200.

134. Grim, "Cosmology and the Winter Dance," 402–5; Boas and Teit, *Coeur d'Alene, Flathead, and Okanagon Indians*, 150–51.

135. Thompson, *Narrative*, 387.

136. Simpson, *Journal of Occurrences*, 236.

137. Gass, *Gass's Journal*, 211.

138. Simpson, *Fur Trade and Empire*, 94.

139. Franchère, *Journal of a Voyage to the Northwest Coast*, 155. Franchère noted that "this happens fairly frequently among these Indians" when "the hunting is not good." In an important article concerning the Canadian fur trade, Mary Black-Rodgers suggests that

many accounts of Indian "starvation" might actually reflect a negotiating ploy by the Indians, a plea for the fur traders' generosity. Following Black-Rogers, Elizabeth Vibert all but dismisses fur trade-era accounts of plateau starvation, arguing that these reflect only the biases of the fur traders against eating salmon instead of red meat. But Vibert's analysis is undermined by the large number of firsthand accounts of spring hunger on the plateau, as well as by the numerous Indian myths depicting this season as one of extreme hunger. See Black-Rogers, "Varieties of 'Starving' "; Vibert, "Traders' Tales," 180–210.

140. Cox, *The Columbia River*, 261.

141. Franchère, *Journal of a Voyage to the Northwest Coast*, 155.

142. Ray, *Sanpoil and Nespelem*, 107.

143. White, "Scarred Trees in Western Montana," 1–5.

144. Ray, *Sanpoil and Nespelem*, 199.

145. "Report of Chief Trader Samuel Black, 1829," Hudson's Bay Company Archives, B146/e/2.

146. Parker, *Journal of an Exploring Tour*, 105.

2. Change in the Protohistoric Era

1. Moulton, *Journals of the Lewis and Clark Expedition*, 4:9.

2. Swagerty, "Protohistoric Trade."

3. See, for example, Salisbury, *Manitou and Providence*; Merrell, *The Indians' New World*.

4. For the interactions between the Corps of Discovery and the native inhabitants of the plateau, see Ronda, *Lewis and Clark among the Indians*.

5. The Coeur d'Alenes recalled their tradition of the first horse to anthropologist James Teit in 1910. See Boas and Teit, *Coeur d'Alene, Flathead, and Okanagon Indians*, 59, 73–74.

6. Haines, "Where Did the Plains Indians Get Their Horses?"; Haines, "The Northward Spread of Horses"; Stern, *Chiefs and Chief Traders*, 41–49.

7. Gass, *Gass's Journal*, 228.

8. Gunkel, "Culture in Conflict," 40; Jones, " 'Women Never Used to War Dance,' " 24.

9. Thwaites, *Journals of the Lewis and Clark Expedition*, 4:369.

10. Spinden, *The Nez Perce Indians*, 206; Slickpoo, *Noon Nee-Me-Poo*, 35.

11. Vibert, "Trader's Tales," 248.

12. Vibert, "Trader's Tales," 257.

13. Lawrence Aripa, quoted in Frey, *Stories That Make the World,* 15.

14. Spinden, *The Nez Perce Indians,* 271.

15. Teit, *Salishan* Tribes, 156, 316–22; Chalfant, "Aboriginal Territories," 25–116, 36; Wilkes, *Narrative of the United States Exploring Expedition,* 4:447; Dunn, *History of the Oregon Territory,* 208.

16. Cox, *The Columbia River,* 202–3; Stern, *Chiefs and Chief Traders,* 41–46.

17. See Medicine and Albers, *The Hidden Half;* Weist, "Plains Indian Women"; Liberty, "Hell Came with Horses"; Holder, *The Hoe and the Horse.*

18. Jones, " 'Women Never Used to War Dance,' " 27–28.

19. "Report of Chief Trader Samuel Black, 1829," Hudson's Bay Company Archives, B146/e/2.

20. Walker, *Conflict and Schism,* 14–19.

21. Turney-High, *Ethnography of the Kutenai,* 33.

22. Boas and Teit, *Coeur d'Alene, Flathead, and Okanagon Indians,* 73–75.

23. Cox, *The Columbia River,* 244.

24. Teit, "The Coeur d'Alenes," in Boas and Teit, *Coeur d'Alene, Flathead, and Okanagon Indians.*

25. Gass, *Gass's Journal,* 140.

26. Gass, *Gass's Journal,* 150.

27. Gass, *Gass's Journal,* 233.

28. Moulton, *Journals of the Lewis and Clark Expedition,* 5:318.

29. Moulton, *Journals of the Lewis and Clark Expedition,* 5:318.

30. Chatters and Zweifel, *The Cemetery at Sntl'exwenewixwtn,* 1.

31. Earlier interpretations of the "pacifism" of the prehistoric Plateau have been overturned by recent archeological excavations, which have revealed large numbers of skeletons showing signs of death by violence. See Chatters, "Pacifism and the Organization of Conflict"; Chatters and Zweifel, *The Cemetery at Sntl'exwenewixwtn;* Kent, "Pacifism—a Myth of the Plateau."

32. Miller, *Prophetic Worlds,* 18–37.

33. Hyde, *Indians of the High Plains,* 116–45.

34. Secoy, *Changing Military Patterns,* 45–64; Hyde, *Indians of the High Plains,* 117–45; Thompson, *Narrative,* 215.

35. Josephy, *The Nez Perce Indians,* 33.

36. Rich, *Cumberland House Journals,* 1:262–63.

37. Gass, *Gass's Journal,* 127.

38. Chalfant, "Aboriginal Territories," 25–116; Teit, *Salishan Tribes,* 303–18.

39. Malouf, "Cultural Connections," 301.

40. Thompson, *Narrative*, 380.

41. Secoy, *Changing Military Patterns*, 58.

42. Bailey, *Indian Slave Trade*, 58; Ruby and Brown, *Indian Slavery*, 230.

43. Ruby and Brown, *The Cayuse Indians*, 17.

44. Chatters, "Pacifism and the Organization of Conflict," 128; *Journals of Alexander Henry*, 2:853; Cox, *The Columbia River*, 233.

45. Clark, *History of the Willamette Valley*, 1:56. For a comprehensive treatment of the subject, see Ruby and Brown, *Indian Slavery*, ch. 9, "The Klamath Slave Cluster."

46. Ruby and Brown, *The Spokane Indians*, 15.

47. Ross, *The Fur Hunters of the Far West*, 155.

48. Moulton, *Journals of the Lewis and Clark Expedition*, 5:222, 309, 346–47; 7:224, 247, 253, 341; Thwaites, *Journals of the Lewis and Clark Expedition*, 7:106, 170, 173, 176, 177.

49. "Report of Chief Trader Samuel Black, 1829," Hudson's Bay Company Archives, B146/e/2.

50. Swagerty, "Protohistoric Trade," 352–57.

51. Swagerty, "Protohistoric Trade," 353; Stern, *Chiefs and Chief Traders*, 34.

52. "Report of Chief Trader Samuel Black, 1829," Hudson's Bay Company Archives, B146/e/2.

53. Griswold, "Aboriginal Patterns of Trade."

54. Turney-High, *The Flathead Indians of Montana*, 137–38.

55. Ross, *Adventures of the First Settlers*, 291–92.

56. Chance, *Influences of the Hudson's Bay Company*, 23.

57. Butler, "Prehistory of the Dice Game."

58. Griswold, "Aboriginal Patterns of Trade," 150.

59. Griswold, "Aboriginal Patterns of Trade," 150; Swagerty, "Protohistoric Trade," 353; Wood, "Plains Trade in Prehistoric and Protohistoric Intertribal Relations."

60. Teit, *Salishan Tribes*, 77–78.

61. Fahey, *The Flathead Indians*, 10.

62. Moulton, *Journals of the Lewis and Clark Expedition*, 7:242.

63. *Journal of François Larocque*, 78, 85.

64. Swagerty, "Protohistoric Trade," 352–55.

65. "Spokane House Report for 1822–23," Hudson's Bay Company Archives, B208/e/1; Griswold, "Aboriginal Patterns of Trade," 115.

66. Layton, "Traders and Raiders."

67. Sapir, *Wishram Texts*, 104.

68. Gunkel, "Culture in Conflict," 34–40; Swagerty, "Protohistoric Trade," 355; Layton, "Traders and Raiders," 127.

69. For the coastal trade, see Gibson, *Otter Skins, Boston Ships, and China Goods.*

70. Moulton, *Journals of the Lewis and Clark Expedition,* 6:187.

71. Moulton, *Journals of the Lewis and Clark Expedition,* 6:199.

72. Stern, *Chiefs and Chief Traders,* 19.

73. White, " 'Firsts' among the Flathead Lake Kutenai."

74. Stapp, "Copper Artifacts," 365–85, 381–82; Strong, *Stone Age on the Columbia River,* 230; Moulton, *Journals of the Lewis and Clark Expedition,* 5:359, 361.

75. Moulton, *Journals of the Lewis and Clark Expedition,* 7:64–65.

76. Moulton, *Journals of the Lewis and Clark Expedition,* 6:285. Though Lewis's remarks were primarily directed at the Clatsops, his reference to deserted villages "on the river" would indicate he was including the plateau as well.

77. Dobyns, "Native American Trade Centers as Contagious Disease Foci."

78. See Crosby, "Virgin Soil Epidemics"; Thornton, *American Indian Holocaust and Survival;* Ramenofsky, *Vectors of Death.*

79. Sarah K. Campbell argues for a sixteenth-century epidemic based on "discontinuities" in the archeological record at selected sites. The small size of the sample and the tentativeness of the evidence, however, makes her case less than convincing. See Campbell, *PostColumbian Culture History;* Boyd, "Smallpox in the Northwest." Boyd calls Campbell's thesis "still hypothetical" (27).

80. Boyd, "Introduction of Infectious Diseases," 73–111; Boyd, "Smallpox in the Northwest," 19–26.

81. Boas, *Kutenai Tales,* 268–71.

82. Dixon, *Smallpox,* 5–42.

83. Clark, *Indian Legends,* 103.

84. Dixon, *Smallpox,* 297–306.

85. Drury, *Diaries and Letters of Spalding and Smith,* 136–37; Boas and Teit, *Coeur d'Alene, Flathead, and Okanagon Indians,* 315–16.

86. Boyd, "Introduction of Infectious Diseases," 82; Dixon, *Smallpox,* 297–317.

87. Curtis, *The North American Indian,* 7:119; Turney-High, *Ethnography of the Kutenai,* 87.

88. Mengarini, *Recollections of the Flathead Mission,* 193–94; Grabert, "Early Fort Okanogon," 11.

89. Crosby, "Virgin Soil Epidemics," 44; Dixon, *Smallpox,* 325.

90. Teit, *Salishan Tribes,* 211–12, 315; Vibert, " 'The Natives Were

Strong to Live,' " 209. Though Vibert calls it "almost inconceivable" that smallpox did not strike the northern plateau, there is abundant evidence from other parts of native America that protohistoric epidemics were not universal within a culture area. See Snow, "Disease and Population Decline in the Northeast"; Thornton, Warren, and Miller, "Depopulation in the Southeast after 1492"; Walker and Johnson, "The Decline of the Chumash Indian Population"; Blakely and Detweiler-Blakely, "The Impact of European Diseases in the Sixteenth-Century Southeast."

91. Dixon, *Smallpox*, 14–19.

92. Mengarini, *Recollections of the Flathead Mission*, 194.

93. Drury, *Diaries and Letters of Spalding and Smith*, 137.

94. Curtis, *The North American Indian*, 7:119.

95. Dixon, *Smallpox*, 325; Ross, *Adventures of the First Settlers*, 286.

96. Mourning Dove, *Autobiography*, 15–16.

97. Cox, *The Columbia River*, 169; Boyd, "Introduction of Infectious Diseases," 138–39; Ray, *Sanpoil and Nespelem*, 215.

98. Walker, "Plateau: Nez Perce," 117.

99. Mourning Dove, *Autobiography*, 16.

100. Sprague, "Aboriginal Burial Practices."

101. Ray, *Sanpoil and Nespelem*, 143–50, 163.

102. Murdock, "The Tenino Indians," 138–39.

103. Ray, *Sanpoil and Nespelem*, 146–49.

104. Moulton, *Journals of the Lewis and Clark Expedition*, 7:65.

105. Thornton, Miller, and Warren, "American Indian Population Recovery following Smallpox Epidemics."

106. Boyd, "Introduction of Infectious Diseases," 328–30.

107. "Report of Chief Trader Samuel Black, 1829," Hudson's Bay Company Archives, B146/e/2.

108. Moulton, *Journals of the Lewis and Clark Expedition*, 5:81, 88–90.

109. Moulton, *Journals of the Lewis and Clark Expedition*, 8:40–43.

110. Moulton, *Journals of the Lewis and Clark Expedition*, 6:213.

111. Moulton, *Journals of the Lewis and Clark Expedition*, 7:181. Many prophecies are collected in Spier, *The Prophet Dance*.

112. Moulton, *Journals of the Lewis and Clark Expedition*, 5:81, 230, 256, 327; 7:108–9, 165–66.

113. Thompson, *Narrative*, 346.

114. Thompson, *Narrative*, 348.

115. Moulton, *Journals of the Lewis and Clark Expedition*, 7:242.

116. Moulton, *Journals of the Lewis and Clark Expedition*, 5:112, 6:199, 233; 7:57–58.

117. Miller and Hammell, "A New Perspective on Indian-White Contact"; White, "Encounters with Spirits"; Axtell, "Imagining the Other."

118. Thompson, *Narrative*, 347.

119. Gunkel, "Culture in Conflict," 43–46.

120. Moulton, *Journals of the Lewis and Clark Expedition*, 5:88–90, 197, 226, 235, 328, 346–47; Thwaites, *Journals of the Lewis and Clark Expedition*, 7:173, 184; Quaife, *Journals of Lewis and Ordway*, 281, 299.

121. Layton, "Traders and Raiders," 130; Fahey, *The Flathead Indians*, 11.

122. Moulton, *Journals of the Lewis and Clark Expedition*, 6:111.

123. Clark, "Watkuese and Lewis and Clark"; Moulton, *Journals of the Lewis and Clark Expedition*, 5:225 n.2; Ronda, *Lewis and Clark among the Indians*, 159.

124. Franchère, *Journal of a Voyage to the Northwest Coast*, 151.

125. Moulton, *Journals of the Lewis and Clark Expedition*, 6:147–48; Coues, *New Light on the Early Northwest*, 2:768.

126. Franchère, *Journal of a Voyage to the Northwest Coast*, 83; Coues, *New Light on the Early Northwest*, 2:799.

127. In Lewis's journal these people are called the "sho-toes," but the map of the area shows their village labeled "Choteaus Tribe," implying that the name is that of an individual. See Moulton, *Journals of the Lewis and Clark Expedition*, 1:plate 79; 7:33.

128. Thwaites, *Journals of the Lewis and Clark Expedition*, 7:180.

129. Gass, *Gass's Journal*, 221.

130. Du Pratz, *History of Louisiana*, 185–90.

131. Moodie, "Indian Maps," plate 59.

132. Karamanski, "Iroquois and the Fur Trade."

133. Mackenzie, *Journals and Letters*, 411.

134. Thompson, *Narrative*, 302.

135. Spry, "Routes through the Rockies"; Karamanski, "Iroquois and the Fur Trade," 9.

136. Ross, *The Fur Hunters of the Far West*, 194.

137. Nicks, "Iroquois and the Fur Trade."

138. For the date of the eruption, see Hunn, *Nch'i-Wana*.

139. Gwydir, "Prehistoric Spokane."

140. Teit, *Salishan Tribes*, 291; Ray, *Sanpoil and Nespelem*, 108.

141. Teit, *Salishan Tribes*, 291–92.

142. Spier, *The Prophet Dance*, 7, 9, 10, 55.

143. The most extensive collection of prophetic narratives is Spier, *The Prophet Dance*, 55–63.

144. Ray, *Sanpoil and Nespelem*, 149–55.

145. Dixon, *Smallpox*, 14–19.

146. Boas, *Folk Tales of Salishan and Sahaptin Tribes*, 83.

147. Wilkes, *Narrative of the United States Exploring Expedition*, 4:439.

148. Spier, *The Prophet Dance*, 16–17. Of course, both of these apparently contradictory prophecies were true.

149. Spier, *The Prophet Dance*, 3–8.

150. Movements resembling the dance have been recorded for the Nez Perces, Spokans, Yakimas, Colvilles, Okanagons, Kutenais, Sanpoils, Nespelems, Coeur d'Alenes, Flatheads, Pend d'Oreilles, Thompson, and Shushwap groups. See Spier, *The Prophet Dance*, 3–12, 55–64.

151. Two major nineteenth-century Indian prophets, Skolaskin and Smohalla, were sometimes traveling preachers. See Ruby and Brown, *Dreamer-Prophets*.

152. Curtis, *The North American Indian*, 7:77–78.

153. Spier, *The Prophet Dance*, 10.

154. Spier, *The Prophet Dance*, 7–8.

155. Spier, *The Prophet Dance*, 13–16. Yet at another point (p. 1), he calls the dance a "renewal" movement, prompting the question, a renewal of what?

156. Spier, *The Prophet Dance*, 13–16.

157. Vibert, " 'The Natives Were Strong to Live,' " 119, 221. The most persuasive argument for the link between prophecy and smallpox is Walker, "New Light on the Prophet Dance." See also Aberle, "Prophet Dance and Reactions to White Contact"; Spier, Herskovits, and Suttles, "Comment on Aberle's Thesis of Deprivation"; Miller, *Prophetic Worlds*.

158. Hunn, *Nch'i-Wana*, 270.

159. Boyd, "Introduction of Infectious Diseases," 99–111.

160. Walker, "New Light on the Prophet Dance," 247–48, 252.

161. Spier, *The Prophet Dance*, 7, 9, 10, 55.

162. Spier, *The Prophet Dance*, 58–59.

163. Cox, *The Columbia River*, 169–70.

164. See, for example, Walker, *Conflict and Schism*, 36.

165. Wilkes, *Narrative of the United States Exploring Expedition*, 4:439. Wilkes himself dated the prophecy to 1790.

166. For accounts following Spier's interpretation, see Trafzer and Sheuerman, *Renegade Tribe*, 1–9; Miller, *Prophetic Worlds*, 37–50.

167. Wilkes, *Narrative of the United States Exploring Expedition*, 4:439; Miller, *Prophetic Worlds*, 45.

168. Jones, "'Women Never Used to War Dance,'" 96–99. Jones specifically cites the dance the Nez Perces used to greet Lewis and Clark on October 16, 1805, as a traditional *telikliin* dance.

169. Cited in Chance, *Influences of the Hudson's Bay Company*, 71.

170. Ross, *Adventures of the First Settlers*, 137.

171. "Journal of the Spokane House, 1822–23," Hudson's Bay Company Archives, B208/a/1.

3. First Encounters, 1800–1825

1. Townsend, *Narrative of a Journey*, 117.

2. Townsend, *Narrative of a Journey*, 116–18.

3. The term *Columbian Religion* comes from the journal of a fur trader, John McLean, who witnessed the spread of the faith to the northern plateau in 1836. The religious movement was called the "Christianized form of the Prophet Dance" by anthropologist Leslie Spier in 1935. Because my interpretation is so different than Spier's, I have reverted to McLean's term. See McLean, *John McLean's Notes*, 152; Spier, *The Prophet Dance*.

4. For the concept of disease pools and their influence on history, see McNeill, *Plagues and Peoples*.

5. Boas, *Folk Tales of Salishan and Sahaptin Tribes*, 64.

6. *Letters and Journals of Simon Fraser*, 119.

7. Moulton, *Journals of the Lewis and Clark Expedition*, 5:256.

8. Moulton, *Journals of the Lewis and Clark Expedition*, 5:255.

9. Ross, *Adventures of the First Settlers*, 151.

10. Teit, "Mythology of the Thompson Indians," 415.

11. Wilkes, *Narrative of the United States Exploring Expedition*, 4:460.

12. Cox, *The Columbia River*, 190.

13. Thompson, *Narrative*, 346.

14. Thompson, *Narrative*, 340–41.

15. Ross, *Adventures of the First Settlers*, 148.

16. *Letters and Journals of Simon Fraser*, 119.

17. Thwaites, *Journals of the Lewis and Clark Expedition*, 4:333–34.

18. Thwaites, *Journals of the Lewis and Clark Expedition*, 4:358.

19. Ross, *Adventures of the First Settlers*, 143.

20. Ross, *Adventures of the First Settlers*, 143.

21. Thwaites, *Journals of the Lewis and Clark Expedition*, 7:144.

22. Thompson, *Narrative*, 316.

23. Ross, *Adventures of the First Settlers*, 287.

24. Ross, *Adventures of the First Settlers*, 275.

25. *Letters and Journals of Simon Fraser*, 88.

26. Ray, *Sanpoil and Nespelem*, 85–86, 96.

27. Anastasio, "Intergroup Relations in the Southern Plateau," 60.

28. *The Journal of Duncan M'Gillivray*, 56.

29. Carlos, *The North American Fur Trade*, 139–42.

30. Ross, *Adventures of the First Settlers*, 141.

31. Ross, *Adventures of the First Settlers*, 141.

32. Thompson, *Narrative*, 297.

33. Thompson, *Narrative*, 351.

34. *Journals of Alexander Henry*, 2:827.

35. Ross, *Adventures of the First Settlers*, 304.

36. Cox, *The Columbia River*, 260–61.

37. Cox, *The Columbia River*, 116.

38. Thompson, *Narrative*, 385.

39. Simpson, *Journal of Occurrences*, 67.

40. Simpson, *Part of a Dispatch*, 382–83.

41. "Report of Chief Trader Samuel Black, 1829," Hudson's Bay Company Archives, B146/e/1.

42. "Fort Nez Perces Post Journal," Hudson's Bay Company Archives, B/146/a/1.

43. Simpson, *Fur Trade and Empire*, 42–43.

44. Chance, *Influences of the Hudson's Bay Company*, 46.

45. Turney-High, *Ethnography of the Kutenai*, 41.

46. Ross, *Adventures of the First Settlers*, 215.

47. Ray, *Sanpoil and Nespelem*, 77; Dickason, "Historical Reconstruction."

48. Dickason, "Historical Reconstruction," 49.

49. "Fort Nez Perces Post Journal," Hudson's Bay Company Archives, B146/a/1.

50. "Report on the Spokane District, 1822–23," Hudson's Bay Company Archives, B208/e/1.

51. Simpson, *Fur Trade and Empire*, 94–95.

52. Grabert, "Early Fort Okanagon"; see also Grabert, "Prehistoric Cultural Stability."

53. "Report on Districts," Hudson's Bay Company Archives, B/223/e/1.

54. "Spokane House Report for 1822–23," Hudson's Bay Company Archives, B208/e/1.

55. Ray, *Sanpoil and Nespelem*, 77–82. For a comparative study of the relative efficiencies of nineteenth-century guns and native weapons, see Townsend, "Firearms against Native Arms."

56. Simpson, *Fur Trade and Empire*, 42.

57. McLoughlin, *Letters of John McLoughlin*, 76.

58. Wilkes, *Narrative of the United States Exploring Expedition*, 4:457.

59. Simpson, *Fur Trade and Empire*, 95.

60. Quaife, *Journals of Lewis and Ordway*, 41.

61. Stuart, *Robert Stuart's Narrative*, 62.

62. Cox, *The Columbia River*, 259.

63. Thompson, *Narrative*, 382.

64. Cox, *The Columbia River*, 114; "Spokane House Report for 1822–23," Hudson's Bay Company Archives, B208/e/1.

65. Simpson, *Fur Trade and Empire*, xix.

66. "Fort Kamloops Post Journal," Hudson's Bay Company Archives, B97/a/1; Work, *Journal of John Work*, 159, 161, 162, 169, 175, 177.

67. Wilkes, *Narrative of the United States Exploring Expedition*, 4:427, 466.

68. "Fort Kamloops Post Journal," Hudson's Bay Company Archives, B97/a/3. For a survey of the effects of trapping on plateau beaver populations, see Johnson and Chance, "Presettlement Overharvest."

69. Chance, *Influences of the Hudson's Bay Company*, 60–61, 63, 65.

70. "Fort Colvile Report on District," Hudson's Bay Company Archives, B45/e/3; Chance, *Influences of the Hudson's Bay Company*, 60–61.

71. McLean, *John McLean's Notes*, 152.

72. "Fort James Report on District," Hudson's Bay Company Archives, B188/e/2.

73. "Fort Kamloops Post Journal," Hudson's Bay Company Archives, B97/a/1.

74. Gibson, *Farming the Frontier*, 25.

75. Gibson, *Farming the Frontier*, 24–27; "Fort Kamloops Post Journal," Hudson's Bay Company Archives, B97/a/2; B97/a/1.

76. "Fort Kamloops Post Journal," Hudson's Bay Company Archives, B97/a/2.

77. Douglas, *Journal Kept by David Douglas*, 200.

78. Stern, *Chiefs and Chief Traders*, 136.

79. Simpson, *Fur Trade and Empire*, 128.

80. "Spokane House Report for 1822–23," Hudson's Bay Company Archives, B208/e/1.

81. Chance, *Influences of the Hudson's Bay Company*, 70.

82. Chance, *Influences of the Hudson's Bay Company*, 70.

83. Chance, *Influences of the Hudson's Bay Company*, 67–69; Ross, *The Fur Hunters of the Far West*, 195.

84. Quoted in Chance, *Influences of the Hudson's Bay Company*, 67.

85. Skeels, "Style in the Unwritten Literature of the Nez Perce Indians," 157–58.

86. "Fort Nez Perces Post Journal," Hudson's Bay Company Archives, B146/a/1.

87. Cox, *The Columbia River*, 184.

88. Simpson, *Fur Trade and Empire*, 42; Parker, *Journal of an Exploring Tour*, 274.

89. Gunkel, "Culture in Conflict," 75; Chance, *Influences of the Hudson's Bay Company*, 91.

90. "Spokane House Report for 1822–23," Hudson's Bay Company Archives, B208/e/1.

91. "Fort Nez Perces Post Journal," Hudson's Bay Company Archives, B146/a/1.

92. "Fort Nez Perces Post Journal," Hudson's Bay Company Archives, B146/a/1.

93. See White, "Fear of Pillaging."

94. "Fort Nez Perces Post Journal," Hudson's Bay Company Archives, B146/a/1.

95. Ross, *The Fur Hunters of the Far West*, 22–29.

96. Ross, *The Fur Hunters of the Far West*, 42–43.

97. Work, "Journal of John Work," 91.

98. Pambrun, *Sixty Years on the Frontier*, 38.

99. Pambrun, *Sixty Years on the Frontier*, 38; Gunkel, "Culture in Conflict," 125; Allen, *Ten Years in Oregon*, 175; Ruby and Brown, *The Cayuse Indians*, 58.

100. For examples of this anxiety, see Ogden, *Traits of American Indian Life*, 10; Morice, *History of the Northern Interior*, 181–85; "Fort Nez Perces Post Journal," Hudson's Bay Company Archives, B146/a/1; Ross, *The Fur Hunters of the Far West*, 20–29, 154–55.

101. Morice, *History of the Northern Interior*, 181.

102. Ross, *The Fur Hunters of the Far West*, 195.

103. "Report on Districts," Hudson's Bay Company Archives, B223/e/3.

104. Work, "Journal of John Work," 34–35.

105. McLean, *John McLean's Notes,* 182–83.

106. Townsend, *Narrative of a Journey,* 249.

107. Russell, *Messages from the President,* 55.

108. McLean, *John McLean's Notes,* 183.

109. Wilkes, *Narrative of the United States Exploring Expedition,* 4:333.

110. *Overland Diary of Wilson Price Hunt,* 69.

111. "Fort George Report on District," Hudson's Bay Company Archives, B76/e/1.

112. De Smet, *Life, Letters, and Travels,* 3:959.

113. Allison, "Account of the Similkameen Indians," 307.

114. Chance, *Kootenay Fur Trade,* 14.

115. Chance, *Influences of the Hudson's Bay Company,* 100–101; Mourning Dove, *Autobiography,* 12.

116. See Van Kirk, *Many Tender Ties;* Brown, *Strangers in Blood.*

117. Simpson, *Journal of Occurrences,* 396.

118. Ross, *The Fur Hunters of the Far West,* 195.

119. Ross, *The Fur Hunters of the Far West,* 195.

120. Simpson, *Fur Trade and Empire,* 58.

121. Boyd, *People of the Dalles,* 157.

122. Pambrun, *Sixty Years on the Frontier,* 35–36; Parker, *Journal of an Exploring Tour,* 255–56; Ross, *The Fur Hunters of the Far West,* 118–23.

123. Ross, *The Fur Hunters of the Far West,* 96.

124. Ray, *Sanpoil and Nespelem,* 189.

125. For the relationship of knowledge and technology in nonsedentary societies, see Riddington, "Technology, World View, and Adaptive Strategy."

126. Moulton, *Journals of the Lewis and Clark Expedition,* 6:233.

127. "Report of Chief Trader Samuel Black, 1829," Hudson's Bay Company Archives, B146/e/2.

128. McLean, *John McLean's Notes,* 171. For other instances of white traders rendering medical assistance to Plateau Indians, see Chance, *Influences of the Hudson's Bay Company,* 32, 43; Ross, *The Fur Hunters of the Far West,* 160–61; "Fort Colvile Post Journal," Hudson's Bay Company Archives, B45/a/1; "Fort Nez Perces Post Journal," B146/a/2; "Journal of the Spokane House," B208/a/1.

129. Chance, *Influences of the Hudson's Bay Company,* 31.

130. Cox, *The Columbia River,* 170.

131. Pambrun, *Sixty Years on the Frontier,* 38.

132. McLean, *John McLean's Notes,* 177.

133. McLean, *John McLean's Notes,* 177.

134. Chance, *Influences of the Hudson's Bay Company*, 74.

135. Cox, *The Columbia River*, 180. Cox does not specify the tribe, but such *berdaches* were known to most Plateau groups. See Roscoe, "Bibliography of Berdache and Alternative Gender Roles"; Williams, *The Spirit and the Flesh*.

136. Cox, *The Columbia River*, 191–92.

137. Gray, *History of Oregon*.

138. *Reports and Letters of Herbert Beaver*, 2.

139. David Chance describes the "gentleman class of traders" as believers in eighteenth-century Deism, and the "lower orders" as "orthodox Catholics." See Chance, *Kootenay Fur Trade*, 85.

140. Bigsby, *Shoe and the Canoe*, 2:205–6.

141. Ross, *Adventures of the First Settlers*, 155.

142. McLean, *John McLean's Notes*, 244.

143. Payne and Thomas, "Literacy, Literature, and Libraries."

144. West, *Substance of a Journal*, 72.

145. Scalberg, "Perception of *Coureur de Bois* Religious Life"; for French Canadian settlers seeking a priest, see Bischoff, *Jesuits*, 2–3.

146. Fleming, *Minutes of the Council*, 60.

147. Blanchet, *Historical Sketches of the Catholic Church*, 83.

148. Vera Kathrin Fast, "The Protestant Missionary and Fur Trade Society: Initial Contact in the Hudson's Bay Territory, 1820–1850" (Ph.D. diss., History Dept., Univ. of Manitoba, 1984), 36.

149. Fleming, *Minutes of the Council*, 60.

150. Stern, *Chiefs and Chief Traders*, 54.

151. Simpson, *Fur Trade and Empire*, 102.

152. Palladino, *Indian and White*, 8–9.

153. Blanchet, *Historical Sketches of the Catholic Church*, 1:9–149, 94–95; Palladino, "Historical Notes on the Flatheads."

154. Simpson, *Fur Trade and Empire*, 127.

155. Boyd, "Introduction of Infectious Diseases," 338–44.

156. Splawn, *Ka-mi-akin*, 426.

157. Splawn, *Ka-mi-akin*, 393.

158. Townsend, *Narrative of a Journey*, 197.

159. For identification of the intermittent fever as malaria, see Boyd, *People of the Dalles*, 141–42.

160. *Diary of Philip Leget Edwards*, 41.

161. Boyd, *People of the Dalles*, 140–44.

162. Barker, *McLoughlin Letters*, 132, 140, 212, 289.

163. Barker, *McLoughlin Letters*, 163–64.

164. Barker, *McLoughlin Letters*, 175.

165. Boyd, "Introduction of Infectious Diseases," 112–44, 267–323.

166. *Journal of Captain Wyeth's Expeditions*, 128.

167. Boyd, *Peoples of the Dalles*, 94.

168. "Fort Nez Perces Post Journal," Hudson's Bay Company Archives, B146/a/1.

169. For the following discussion of winter illness I am indebted to Boyd, "Introduction of Infectious Diseases," 342–45.

170. Boyd, "Introduction of Infectious Diseases," 342–45.

171. Boyd, "Introduction of Infectious Diseases," 383–89.

172. Simpson, *Fur Trade and Empire*, 132

173. Simpson, *Fur Trade and Empire*, 135.

174. Simpson, *Fur Trade and Empire*, 136.

175. Oliphant, "George Simpson and Oregon Missions," 224.

176. Ross, *The Fur Traders of the Far West*, 2:160.

177. An exception was Angus MacDonald, an early trader who considered Indian religion at least as legitimate as Christianity. "The wild red man is a man," wrote MacDonald, "and his simple yet profound faith compares with anything of that kind we yet had from Paris or Rome" (MacDonald, Reminiscence, William S. Lewis Collection, Eastern Washington Historical Society Archives).

178. "Report of Chief Trader Samuel Black, 1829," Hudson's Bay Company Archives, B146/e/2.

179. "Report of Chief Trader Samuel Black, 1829," Hudson's Bay Company Archives, B146/e/2.

180. DuBois, *Feather Cult*, 10.

181. DuBois, *Feather Cult*, 11.

182. DuBois, *Feather Cult*, 9.

183. "Report of Chief Trader Samuel Black, 1829," Hudson's Bay Company Archives, B146/e/2.

184. "Fort Nez Perces Post Journal," Hudson's Bay Company Archives, B/146/a/1.

185. Chance, *Influences of the Hudson's Bay Company*, 90.

186. "Fort Nez Perces Post Journal," Hudson's Bay Company Archives, B/146/a/1.

187. Stern, *Chiefs and Chief Traders*, 6.

188. "Fort Nez Perces Post Journal," Hudson's Bay Company Archives, B/146/a/1.

189. Irving, *Adventures of Bonneville*, 259.

190. Pambrun, *Sixty Years on the Frontier*, 34–35.

191. Pambrun, *Sixty Years on the Frontier*, 34.

192. Chance, *Influences of the Hudson's Bay Company*, 79.

193. Chance, *Influences of the Hudson's Bay Company*, 80.

194. Hudson's Bay Company Archives, D4/125/31a.

195. Glazebrook, *Hargrave Correspondence*, 70–71.

196. Chance, *Influences of the Hudson's Bay Company*, 75.

197. "Sir George Simpson Correspondence Inward," Hudson's Bay Company Archives, E12/3.

198. Parker, *Journal of an Exploring Tour*, 85. The story of Indians being sold decks of cards and told they were the Bible was a popular one in missionary literature of the time, but was probably apocryphal. When the missionary Asa Smith asked the Nez Perce chief Lawyer about the story, the chief responded that "he had never known of any such instance—altho' he has been in the mountains & knows what has been done there by the Americans as well as any other man" (Drury, *Diaries and Letters of Spalding and Smith*, 128).

4. The Columbian Religion, 1825–1840

1. Jessett, *Chief Spokane Garry*, 37. Clifford Drury includes another boy among the scholars, San Poils Harrison. See Drury, *Marcus and Narcissa Whitman*, 1:35.

2. Fast, "The Protestant Missionary and Fur Trade Society," 64 n.10.

3. West, *Substance of a Journal*, 90–191.

4. Jessett, *Chief Spokane Garry*, 29.

5. Jessett, *Chief Spokane Garry*, 28–32.

6. Tucker, *Rainbow of the North*, 70–71.

7. McDonald, *Peace River*, 34.

8. Jessett, *Chief Spokane Garry*, 38.

9. Jessett, *Chief Spokane Garry*, 45. David Chance estimates that perhaps 50 percent of all Indian boys sent to Red River eventually died there. Chance, *Kootenay Fur Trade*, 47.

10. Jessett, *Chief Spokane Garry*, 35.

11. Stern, *Chiefs and Change*, 12.

12. Stern, *Chiefs and Change*, 13.

13. Tucker, *Rainbow of the North*, 73.

14. Stern, *Chiefs and Change*, 14.

15. Josephy, *The Nez Perce Indians*, 90.

16. Jessett, *Chief Spokane Garry*, 46.

17. Jessett, *Chief Spokane Garry*, 33. Jessett is quoting a contemporary of Garry's. Italics in the original.

18. Jessett, *Chief Spokane Garry*, 42.

19. Tucker, *Rainbow of the North*, 70–71.

20. Lewis, *The Case of Spokane Garry*, 14.

21. Gray, *Journal*, 75.

22. Jessett, *Chief Spokane Garry*, 34–38; Spier, *The Prophet Dance*, 38.

23. McLean, *John McLean's Notes*, 159.

24. McLean, *John McLean's Notes*, 159.

25. David Thompson journal notebooks, manuscript, Special Collections, Provincial Archives of Ontario. I thank Jack Nisbet, author of *Sources of the River: Tracking David Thompson Across North America*, for making his notes from Thompson's journals available to me.

26. "Fort Colvile Report on District," Hudson's Bay Company Archives, B/45/e/2.

27. Boyd, *People of the Dalles*, 72–73.

28. Simpson, *Fur Trade and Empire*, 102.

29. "Report of Chief Trader Samuel Black, 1829," Hudson's Bay Company Archives, B146/e/2.

30. McLean, *John McLean's Notes*, 160.

31. Boyd, *People of the Dalles*, 177–78.

32. Irving, *Adventures of Bonneville*, 343.

33. Chance, *Influences of the Hudson's Bay Company*, 77.

34. Drury, *Diaries and Letters of Spalding and Smith*, 107.

35. Ross, *Adventures of the First Settlers*, 304.

36. Dubois, *Feather Cult*, 10.

37. Chance, *Influences of the Hudson's Bay Company*, 83.

38. Irving, *Adventures of Bonneville*, 83.

39. "Diary of Jason Lee," 255.

40. Wilson, "Report on the Indian Tribes," 305.

41. Irving, *Adventures of Bonneville*, 384.

42. Irving, *Adventures of Bonneville*, 80–83.

43. Wyeth, *Oregon*, 21:75.

44. Townsend, *Narrative of a Journey*, 240.

45. Parker, *Journal of an Exploring Tour*, 102–3.

46. *Correspondence and Journals of Captain Wyeth*, 202–3.

47. Irving, *Adventures of Bonneville*, 344.

48. Parker, *Journal of an Exploring Tour*, 258. Missionary Samuel Perkins got the same story from the Indians of the Dalles, who said the traders had taught them to worship by dancing. See Boyd, *People of the Dalles*, 179.

49. Parker, *Journal of an Exploring Tour*, 258 n.1.

50. Irving, *Adventures of Bonneville*, 345.

51. Chance, *Influences of the Hudson's Bay Company*, 77.

52. *Correspondence and Journals of Captain Wyeth*, 247–48. 53. *Correspondence and Journals of Captain Wyeth*, 190.

54. Irving, *Adventures of Bonneville*, 343.

55. Spier, *The Prophet Dance*, 30–39.
56. Nicolay, *Oregon Territory*, 107–8.
57. Gairdner, "Geography of the Columbia River," 257.
58. Gairdner, "Geography of the Columbia River," 257.
59. Parker, *Journal of an Exploring Tour*, 235.
60. Irving, *Adventures of Bonneville*, 88. The Nez Perces expressed similar sentiments; see Irving, *Adventures of Bonneville*, 106.
61. Irving, *Adventures of Bonneville*, 88–89.
62. Irving, *Adventures of Bonneville*, 101–2.
63. *Correspondence and Journals of Captain Wyeth*, 100–102.
64. Irving, *Adventures of Bonneville*, 355–56.
65. Drury, *Diaries and Letters of Spalding and Smith*, 107.
66. Irving, *Adventures of Bonneville*, 83–84.
67. Boyd, *People of the Dalles*, 184.
68. Drury, *Chief Lawyer of the Nez Perces*, 31; Drury, *Diaries and Letters of Spalding and Smith*, 106.
69. For Clark's son, see Ronda, *Lewis and Clark among the Indians*, 233.
70. For the best retelling of the famous journey to St. Louis, see Josephy, *The Nez Perce Indians*, 91–103, 666–669.

5. The Rejection of Christianity, 1836–1850

1. Drury, *Nine Years*, 39.
2. For the mental world of the members of the Oregon mission, see McCoy, "Sanctifying the Self."
3. Hall, *Conversion of the World*, 1, 68.
4. For Brainerd's influence on nineteenth-century Protestant missionaries, see Conforti, "Jonathan Edwards's Most Popular Work."
5. McCoy, "Women of the ABCFM Oregon Mission," 73, 76. McCoy describes Newell and Boardman as "pious but practical failures."
6. Phillips, *Protestant America and the Pagan World*, 1–32.
7. Hutchison, *Errand to the World*, 15.
8. Phillips, *Protestant America and the Pagan World*, 57.
9. Phillips, *Protestant America and the Pagan World*, 58.
10. *Account of Baptist Missions*, 50–51.
11. Cocks, "Selfish Savage," 32.
12. Cocks, "Selfish Savage," 39.
13. Hutchison, *Errand to the World*, 64.
14. Cocks, "Selfish Savage," 44.
15. Hutchison, *Errand to the World*, 64–65.
16. *Account of Baptist Missions*, 13–14.

17. Cocks, "Selfish Savage," 59.
18. Green, *Journal of a Tour.*
19. Cocks, "Selfish Savage," 44.
20. Cocks, "Selfish Savage," 47.
21. Josephy, *The Nez Perce Indians,* 99. Josephy suggests that Walker actually visited William Clark after the Nez Perces had departed, and that the drawing Walker provided of an Indian with a flattened head was copied from Clark's drawing of a Chinook Indian. Clifford Drury offers a more friendly but unconvincing appraisal of Walker's story in "The Nez Perce 'Delegation' of 1831."
22. Walker's letter appeared in the *Christian Advocate and Journal and Zion's Herald* on Friday, March 1, 1833. It is reprinted, but without Walker's drawing of a "Flathead," in Chittenden, *Fur Trade of the Far West,* 2:912–25.
23. Chittenden, *Fur Trade of the Far West,* 2:919–20.
24. Garraghan, *Jesuits,* 2:244–45.
25. Chittenden, *Fur Trade of the Far West,* 2:919–20.
26. Miller, *Prophetic Worlds,* 78; Josephy, *The Nez Perce Indians,* 120–29.
27. "Diary of Jason Lee," 139.
28. Hulbert, *Oregon Crusade,* 168.
29. Josephy, *The Nez Perce Indians,* 126.
30. Josephy, *The Nez Perce Indians,* 123, 126.
31. Brosnan, *Jason Lee,* 71.
32. "Diary of Jason Lee," 264.
33. Williams, *Narrative of a Tour,* 39.
34. Ruby and Brown, *The Cayuse Indians,* 68–69.
35. Phillips, *Protestant America and the Pagan World,* 82.
36. Parker, *Journal of an Exploring Tour,* 81–82.
37. Parker, *Journal of an Exploring Tour,* 102.
38. Cocks, "Selfish Savage," 110.
39. Josephy, *The Nez Perce Indians,* 145.
40. Drury, *Where Wagons Could Go,* 194–95.
41. The most thorough examinations of the Protestant missions are the works of Clifford Merrill Drury, especially *Marcus and Narcissa Whitman.* Drury wrote between the 1930s and the 1970s and, like most historians of that era, he was far more interested in the lives of the missionaries than he was in those of the Indians. The best examination of the Indian perspective on a Protestant mission is Josephy's *The Nez Perce Indians.* But Josephy considers only the experience of the Nez Perces. Christopher Miller devotes considerable attention to

the native view of the Protestant missions in his *Prophetic Worlds*, but his interpretation is dubious. Miller places a great deal of faith in a supposed protohistoric prophecy that the arrival of the whites would mean the end of the native world, and argues that this prophecy continued to govern native actions throughout the fur trade and mission eras. See Miller, *Prophetic Worlds*, 37–50, 89, 106.

42. A good introduction to the topic is Burns, *The Jesuits and the Indians Wars*, 31–60. Burns's approach is dated by a condescending view of Indian religions (described as the "weakest element" in their culture and a "theological vacuum") and too great an emphasis on the differences between Catholics and Protestants.

43. Garraghan, *Jesuits*, 2:246.

44. Bagley, ed., *Early Catholic Missions in Old Oregon*, 19.

45. Garraghan, *Jesuits*, 2:250.

46. Garraghan, *Jesuits*, 2:237–38.

47. Garraghan, *Jesuits*, 2:246–47.

48. Garraghan, *Jesuits*, 2:248–49.

49. Davis, "Peter John De Smet," 40.

50. De Smet, *Life, Letters, and Travels*, 1:227.

51. De Smet, *Life, Letters, and Travels*, 1:226.

52. De Smet, *Life, Letters, and Travels*, 1:233–34.

53. De Smet, *Life, Letters, and Travels*, 1:316.

54. De Smet, *Life, Letters, and Travels*, 1:317.

55. De Smet, *Life, Letters, and Travels*, 1:339.

56. The belief that Indians would have to adopt agriculture and a sedentary way of life to be saved is an old one, dating almost to the initial encounters of natives and missionaries in the colonial era. See Axtell, *Invasion Within*, 162–67; Simmons, *Spirit of the New England Tribes*; Bowden, *American Indians and Christian Missions*.

57. De Smet, *Life, Letters, and Travels*, 125.

58. Mengarini, *Recollections of the Flathead Mission*, 207.

59. Point, *Wilderness Kingdom*, 43.

60. Drury, *Diaries and Letters of Spalding and Smith*, 121.

61. Drury, *Nine Years*, 94–95.

62. Tolan, *Shining from the Mountains*, 34.

63. Raufer, *Black Robes and Indians*, 26.

64. Drury, *Nine Years*, 85, 87.

65. Hulbert, *Oregon Crusade*, 312–15.

66. Boyd, *People of the Dalles*, 150.

67. Boyd, *People of the Dalles*, 148.

68. Drury, *Diaries and Letters of Spalding and Smith*, 149.

69. Drury, *Diaries and Letters of Spalding and Smith*, 134–35.

70. Boyd, *People of the Dalles,* 148–49.

71. For native farming, see the chapter "Indian Agriculture" in Gibson, *Farming the Frontier.*

72. Stevens, *Report of Exploration,* 141.

73. Wilkes, *Narrative of the United States Exploring Expedition,* 4:461–62.

74. Drury, *Diaries and Letters of Spalding and Smith,* 157.

75. Point, *Wilderness Kingdom,* 43.

76. *New York Daily Tribune,* March 29, 1843, 7.

77. Eliza Spalding, Spalding Collection, s-202A 5.

78. Parker, *Journal of an Exploring Tour,* 55.

79. Wilkes, *Narrative of the United States Exploring Expedition,* 4:467.

80. Cox, *The Columbia River,* 255.

81. Drury, *Nine Years,* 72.

82. Drury, *Nine Years,* 81.

83. Drury, *Nine Years,* 88.

84. Drury, *Nine Years,* 87–88.

85. Drury, *Nine Years,* 88, 111.

86. Drury, *Nine Years,* 124.

87. Drury, *Nine Years,* 131.

88. Drury, *Diaries and Letters of Spalding and Smith,* 139.

89. Drury, *Diaries and Letters of Spalding and Smith,* 172.

90. Howay, *Origin of the Chinook Jargon;* Jacobs, *Texts in Chinook Jargon.*

91. *Journals of William Fraser Tolmie,* 221–22.

92. McKevitt, "Jesuit Missionary Linguistics," 290.

93. Williams, *Narrative of a Tour,* 52.

94. Ruby and Brown, *The Cayuse Indians,* 68–69; Ramsey, "The Bible in Western Indian Mythology," 446.

95. Drury, *Nine Years,* 72.

96. Drury, *Diaries and Letters of Spalding and Smith,* 123. The alleged unsuitability of native languages to communicate Christian beliefs was a common complaint by nineteenth-century American missionaries. See Bowden, *American Indians and Christian Missions,* 80–81.

97. Drury, *Nine Years,* 112.

98. *Letters of Narcissa Whitman,* 65.

99. McKevitt, "Jesuit Missionary Linguistics," 288.

100. Drury, *Diaries and Letters of Spalding and Smith,* 106.

101. Cocks, "Selfish Savage," 205–6.

102. Drury, *Diaries and Letters of Spalding and Smith,* 106.

103. Drury, *Diaries and Letters of Spalding and Smith*, 106.

104. Blanchet, *Historical Sketches of the Catholic Church*, 46.

105. Carriker, *Father Peter John De Smet*, 5–6. See also Hanzeli, *Missionary Linguistics in New France*, 32–44.

106. De Smet, *Life, Letters, and Travels*, 163, 226, 254, 261, 338, 381.

107. Fahey, *The Flathead Indians*, 75.

108. De Smet, *Indian Sketches*, 65.

109. De Smet, *Indian Sketches*, 51.

110. De Smet, *Indian Sketches*, 65.

111. De Smet, *Indian Sketches*, 65–66.

112. Mourning Dove, *Autobiography*, 25.

113. Point, *Wilderness Kingdom*, 12.

114. Point, *Wilderness Kingdom*, 12.

115. Eliza Spalding, Diary, Spalding Collection, s-202 H 1.

116. Drury, *Nine Years*, 88.

117. Point, *Wilderness Kingdom*, 25, 85, 88. For more of Point's drawings with some insightful commentary by the author, see Peterson, *Sacred Encounters*.

118. Drury, *Diaries and Letters of Spalding and Smith*, 128.

119. Again, this is an old story in the history of missionary efforts to the Indians. See Axtell, "Power of Print in the Eastern Woodlands."

120. Hines, *Voyage around the World*, 177.

121. De Smet, *Indian Sketches*, 30.

122. Drury, *Marcus and Narcissa Whitman*, 1:250.

123. Drury, *Marcus and Narcissa Whitman*, 1:250–51.

124. Raufer, *Black Robes and Indians*, 33.

125. Williams, *Narrative of a Tour*, 81.

126. De Smet, *Indian Sketches*, 30–33.

127. Point, *Wilderness Kingdom*, 74–75.

128. Eliza Spalding, Spalding Collection, s-202A 5.

129. Drury, *Nine Years*, 210–18.

130. De Smet, *Life, Letters, and Travels*, 2:1147.

131. Point, *Wilderness Kingdom*, 59, 70–71.

132. Point, *Wilderness Kingdom*, 75. Disposal of native "medicine bags" was considered an essential proof of converts' sincerity by the missionaries. Natives too considered it a turning point. The Pend d'Oreilles recall that one of the early missionaries to that tribe dug a hole in the ground and commanded the whole tribe to line up and throw their medicine bags in the hole. After they had done so, the priest erected a cross over the hole to symbolize the victory of Christianity. "From that time on," the Pend d'Oreilles remembered, "the

tribe slackened and died away." See Dusenberry, "Visions among the Pend d'Oreille Indians," 55.

133. Josephy, *The Nez Perce Indians*, 140–41.

134. Ackerman, "Effect of Missionary Ideals," 67.

135. Drury, *Diaries and Letters of Spalding and Smith*, 137.

136. Raufer, *Black Robes and Indians*, 112.

137. Raufer, *Black Robes and Indians*, 94, 112, 223, 225, 229, 233, 235.

138. Point, *Wilderness Kingdom*, 70.

139. Drury, *Marcus and Narcissa Whitman*, 2:107–8.

140. Boyd, *People of the Dalles*, 102–3.

141. Billington, *Protestant Crusade*, 67.

142. Billington, *Protestant Crusade*, 120.

143. Drury, *Marcus and Narcissa Whitman*, 2:376.

144. Drury, *Where Wagons Could Go*, 44–45. Eliza Spalding noted that the missionary party left before the mass was over due to the "unpleasant sensations we experienced on witnessing their heartless forms and ceremonies" (186).

145. Drury, *Diaries and Letters of Spalding and Smith*, 110.

146. Drury, *Nine Years*, 98.

147. Josephy, *The Nez Perce Indians*, 673.

148. Garraghan, *Jesuits*, 2:286.

149. Drury, *Diaries and Letters of Spalding and Smith*, 110.

150. Drury, *Nine Years*, 148.

151. Drury, *Diaries and Letters of Spalding and Smith*, 177.

152. Hines, *Voyage around the World*, 185.

153. Garraghan, *Jesuits*, 2:267.

154. Lyman, "Reminiscences of James Jory," 281.

155. Hines, *Voyage around the World*, 169–70.

156. Drury, *Nine Years*, 189.

157. Hanley, *Catholic Ladder*, 25.

158. Blanchet, *Notices & Voyages*, 45.

159. For a detailed analysis of the De Smet ladder, see Hanley, *Catholic Ladder*, 95–106. For a painting of some Flatheads using the ladder to share instruction, see Point, *Wilderness Kingdom*, 85.

160. The best printed reproduction of both the Catholic and Protestant ladders is found in Peterson, *Sacred Encounters*, 110–11.

161. Hanley, *Catholic Ladder*, 107.

162. Hanley, *Catholic Ladder*, 108.

163. Hanley, *Catholic Ladder*, 112–13.

164. Hanley, *Catholic Ladder*, 113.

165. Hanley, *Catholic Ladder*, 113.

166. Ross, *Adventures of the First Settlers*, 311, 317–18.

167. John Rowand to James Hargrave, December 29, 1840, in Glaze-brook, *Hargrave Correspondence*, 175.

168. Hines, *Voyage around the World*, 175.

169. Josephy, *The Nez Perce Indians*, 123.

170. Gray, *Journal*, 20.

171. Cebula, " 'They think us much beholden to them.' "

172. Gray, *Journal*, 25.

173. Blanchet, *Notices & Voyages*, 80, 82–83.

174. Ruby and Brown, *Indians of the Pacific Northwest*, 71.

175. Drury, *Diaries and Letters of Spalding and Smith*, 107.

176. Drury, *Nine Years*, 111.

177. Wilkes, *Narrative of the United States Exploring Expedition*, 4:455.

178. Drury, *Diaries and Letters of Spalding and Smith*, 176.

179. Drury, *Nine Years*, 111.

180. Drury, *Nine Years*, 127.

181. Cocks, "Selfish Savage," 151.

182. Drury, *Diaries and Letters of Spalding and Smith*, 151.

183. Boyd, *People of the Dalles*, 151.

184. David Greene, Spalding Collection, s-2 LG 2.

185. Drury, *Marcus and Narcissa Whitman*, 1:405.

186. Drury, *Nine Years*, 80.

187. Cocks, "Selfish Savage," 148.

188. Boyd, "Introduction of Infectious Diseases," 349–50.

189. Drury, *Nine Years*, 143–44.

190. Beeson, *Plea for the Indians*, 120.

191. Drury, *Nine Years*, 136.

192. Drury, *Nine Years*, 441.

193. Sprague, "Plateau Shamanism and Marcus Whitman."

194. Walker, "Plateau: Nez Perce," 117–21.

195. Boyd, *People of the Dalles*, 81.

196. Chance, *Influences of the Hudson's Bay Company*, 76.

197. Peterson, *Sacred Encounters*, 24.

198. Drury, *Diaries and Letters of Spalding and Smith*, 124.

199. Cocks, "Selfish Savage," 91.

200. Mengarini, *Recollections of the Flathead Mission*, 102.

201. Olsen, "Power of Song," 8.

202. Eels, *Father Eels*, 95, 103, 110.

203. Cocks, "Selfish Savage," 152.

204. Drury, *Nine Years*, 124.

205. Boyd, *People of the Dalles*, 81; Ogden, *Traits of American Indian Life*, 85.

206. This pattern of initial enthusiasm followed by a falling off of interest has been described for other missions as well. In her study of Protestant missions around Hudson Bay, Vera Kathryn Fast offers a model of four stages for native interest in missions: (1) initial enthusiasm; (2) a period of variable response; (3) increasing native disillusionment: and (4) falling away. But even after the fourth stage, "a remnant remained; a core of active and faithful believers." See Fast, "Protestant Missionary and Fur Trade Society," 218.

207. Drury, *Henry Harmon Spalding*, 216.

208. Drury, *Diaries and Letters of Spalding and Smith*, 259–61.

209. Eliza Spalding, Spalding Collection, s-202A 10.

210. Drury, *Diaries and Letters of Spalding and Smith*, 194–97, 201–2.

211. Fahey, *The Flathead Indians*, 83–84.

212. Fahey, *The Flathead Indians*, 84–88.

213. Williams, *Narrative of a Tour*, 40.

214. Drury, *Diaries and Letters of Spalding and Smith*, 174.

215. Henry Spalding, Spalding Collection, s-2A 7.

216. Hulbert, *Oregon Crusade*, 207.

217. Henry Spalding, Spalding Collection, s-2A 7.

218. Drury, *First White Women*, 1:138.

219. Drury, *Diaries and Letters of Spalding and Smith*, 137–38.

220. Ruby and Brown, *The Cayuse Indians*, 29–30.

221. Hines, *Voyage around the World*, 415–16.

222. Beeson, *Plea for the Indians*, 19.

223. Parkman, *Oregon Trail*.

224. Beeson, *Plea for the Indians*, 19, 21.

225. United States Department of the Interior, *Letter*, 13.

226. Allen, *Ten Years in Oregon*, 253.

227. Boyd, *People of the Dalles*, 163–64.

228. McLoughlin, *McLoughlin's Business Correspondence*, 69.

229. Drury, *Marcus and Narcissa Whitman*, 2:110.

230. Drury, *Marcus and Narcissa Whitman*, 2:109.

231. Drury, *Marcus and Narcissa Whitman*, 2:110.

232. The most careful reconstruction of the Whitman massacre is found in Drury, *Marcus and Narcissa Whitman*, 205–65. The term "Whitman massacre" is itself currently in disfavor with some scholars. A 1997 symposium held at Whitman College to mark the 150th anniversary of the event was titled "The Whitman Tragedy."

233. Ruby and Brown, *Dreamer-Prophets*, 30.

Conclusion

1. Spier, *The Prophet Dance*, 57–58.
2. Cox, *The Columbia River*, 114.
3. Cox, *The Columbia River*, 266.
4. Jessett, *Chief Spokane Garry*, 77.
5. Simpson, *Narrative of a Journey*, 2:145.
6. Simpson, *Narrative of a Journey*, 2:145–46.
7. Ruby and Brown, *The Cayuse Indians*, 128–43.
8. Josephy, *The Nez Perce Indians*, 283–84.
9. The best treatment of the Walla Walla Council is Josephy, *The Nez Perce Indians*, 285–332.
10. Jessett, *Chief Spokane Garry*, 202.
11. For the integration of native American religions with the environment, see Hulkrantz, *Belief and Worship*, 70–78.
12. See, for example, Fahey, *The Flathead Indians*, 187–226; Ruby and Brown, *The Cayuse Indians*, 282–296; Raufer, *Black Robes and Indians*, 204–21.
13. Jessett, *Chief Spokane Garry*, 170–76.

Bibliography

Archival Materials

Eastern Washington Historical Society Archives. Cheney-Cowles Museum. Spokane WA.

Hudson's Bay Company Archives. Manitoba Provincial Archives. Winnipeg, Manitoba.

Missouri Provincial Archives. Society of Jesus. St. Louis MO.

Provincial Archives of Ontario. Toronto, Ontario.

Spalding Collection. Penrose Memorial Library. Whitman College. Walla Walla WA.

Books, Articles, and Dissertations

Aberle, David F. "The Prophet Dance and Reactions to White Contact." *Southwestern Journal of Archeology* 15:1 (spring 1959): 74–83.

Account of Baptist Missions within the Indian Territory, for the Year Ending December 31, 1836. Westport CT: N.p., 1837.

Ackerman, Lillian. "The Effect of Missionary Ideals on Family Structure and Women's Roles in Plateau Indian Culture." *Idaho Yesterdays* (spring—summer 1987): 64–73.

———. "Sexual Equality in the Plateau Culture Area." Ph.D. diss., Washington State University, 1982.

Allen, A. J. *Ten Years in Oregon*. Ithaca NY: Mack, Andrus., 1848.

Allison, Susan. "Account of the Similkameen Indians of British Columbia." *Journal of the Anthropological Institute of Great Britain and Ireland* 21 (1892): 305–18.

Anastasio, Angelo. "Intergroup Relations in the Southern Plateau." Ph.D. diss., University of Chicago, 1955.

Armstrong, A. N. *Oregon: Comprising a Brief History and Full Description of the Territories of Oregon and Washington* Chicago: C. Scott, 1857.

Axtell, James. "Imagining the Other: First Encounters in North America." In *Beyond 1492: Encounters in Colonial North America*, 25–74. New York: Oxford University Press, 1992.

———. *The Invasion Within: The Contest of Cultures in Colonial North America*. New York: Oxford University Press, 1985.

———. "The Power of Print in the Eastern Woodlands." *William and Mary Quarterly* 44:2 (April 1987): 300–309.

Bagley, Clarence, ed. *Early Catholic Missions in Oregon*. Seattle: Lowman & Hanford, 1932.

Bailey, Lynn Robison, *Indian Slave Trade in the Southwest: A Study of Slavetaking and the Traffic of Indian Captives*. Los Angeles: Westernlore, 1966.

Barker, Burt Brown, ed. *Letters of Dr. John McLoughlin Written at Fort Vancouver, 1829–1832*. Portland OR: Binfords & Mort, 1948.

Beaver, Herbert. *Reports and Letters of Herbert Beaver, 1836–1838*. Edited by Thomas E. Jessett. Portland OR: Champoeg Press, 1959.

Beeson, John. *A Plea for the Indians*. Fairfield WA: Ye Galleon Press, 1982.

Bigsby, John J. *The Shoe and the Canoe; or, Pictures of Travels in the Canadas*. 2 vols. London: Chapman & Hall, 1850.

Billington, Ray Allen. *Protestant Crusade, 1800–1860: A Study of the Origins of American Nativism*. Chicago: Quadrangle, 1964.

Bischoff, William N. *The Jesuits in Old Oregon, 1840–1940*. Caldwell ID: Caxton, 1945.

Black-Rogers, Mary. "Varieties of 'Starving': Semantics and Survival in the Subarctic Fur Trade, 1750–1850." *Ethnohistory* 33:4 (fall 1986): 353–83.

Blakely, Robert L., and Bettina Detweiler-Blakely. "The Impact of European Diseases in the Sixteenth-Century Southeast: A Case Study." *Midcontinental Journal of Archeology* 14:1 (1989): 62–89.

Blanchet, Francis Norbert. *Historical Sketches of the Catholic Church in Oregon*. Edited by Edward J. Kowrach. Fairfield WA: Ye Galleon Press, 1983.

———. *Notices & Voyages of the Famed Quebec Mission to the Pacific Northwest*. Portland OR: Champoeg Press, 1956.

Boas, Franz. *Folk Tales of Salishan and Sahaptin Tribes*, Memoirs of the American Folk-Lore Society, vol. 11 (1917).

———. *Kutenai Tales*. Washington DC: Bureau of American Ethnology, 1918.

Boas, Franz, and James Teit. *Coeur d'Alene, Flathead, and Okanagon Indians*. Fairfield WA: Ye Galleon Press, 1985.

Bonvillain, Nancy. "Gender Relations in Native North America." *American Indian Culture and Research Journal* 13:2 (1989): 1–28.

Bouchard, Randy, and Dorthy Kennedy. *Indian History and Knowledge of the Lower Similkameen River—Lake Palmer Area.* Victoria BC: Indian Languages Project, 1984.

Bowden, Henry Warner. *American Indians and Christian Missions: Studies in Cultural Conflict.* Chicago: University of Chicago Press, 1981.

Boyd, Robert C. "The Introduction of Infectious Diseases among the Indians of the Pacific Northwest, 1774–1874." Ph.D. diss., University of Washington, 1985.

———. *People of the Dalles: The Indians of the Wascopam Mission.* Lincoln: University of Nebraska Press, 1996.

———. "Smallpox in the Northwest: The First Epidemics." *BC Studies* 101:1 (spring 1994): 5–40.

Brosnan, Cornelius J. *Jason Lee: Prophet of the New Oregon.* New York: MacMillan, 1932.

Brown, Jennifer. *Strangers in Blood: Fur Trade Company Families in Indian Country.* Norman: University of Oklahoma Press, 1996.

Brunton, Bill B. "Ceremonial Integration in the Plateau of Northwestern North America." *Northwest Anthropological Research Notes* 2:1 (spring 1968): 1–28.

Burns, Robert Ignatius. *The Jesuits and the Indian Wars of the Northwest.* New Haven CT: Yale University Press, 1966.

Butler, Robert B. "The Prehistory of the Dice Game in the Southern Plateau." *Tebiwa: The Journal of the Idaho State College Museum* 2:1 (winter 1958): 65–71.

Campbell, Samuel L. *Autobiography of Samuel L. Campbell, 1824–1902: Frontiersman and Oregon Pioneer.* Portland OR: Rowena Campbell Grant, 1986.

Campbell, Sarah K. *PostColumbian Culture History in the Northern Columbia Plateau, A.D. 1500–1900.* New York: Garland, 1990.

Carlos, Ann M. *The North American Fur Trade, 1804–1821: A Study in the Life-Cycle of a Duopoly.* New York: Garland, 1986.

Carriker, Robert C. *Father Peter John De Smet: Jesuit in the West.* Norman: University of Oklahoma Press, 1995.

Cebula, Larry, ed. " 'They think us much beholden to them': Spokane House Report for 1822–1823." *Pacific Northwest Forum* 9:1–2 (fall–winter 1996): 52–61.

Chalfant, Stuart A. "Aboriginal Territories." In *Interior Salish and Eastern Washington Indians II,* edited by David Agee Horr. New York: Garland, 1974.

Chance, David. *Influences of the Hudson's Bay Company on the Native Cultures of the Colvile District.* Moscow: Idaho State University Press, 1973.

———. *The Kootenay Fur Trade and Its Establishments, 1795–1871.* Seattle: United States Army Corps of Engineers, 1981.

Chatters, James C. "Pacifism and the Organization of Conflict on the Plateau of Northwestern North America." In *Cultures in Conflict: Current Archaeological Perspectives,* edited by D. C. Tkuczuk and B. Vivian. Calgary: University of Calgary Press, 1989.

Chatters, James C., and Matthew W. Zweifel. *The Cemetery at Sntl'exwenewixwtn, Okanagon County, Washington.* Ellensberg: Central Washington University Press, 1987.

Chittenden, Hiram Martin. *The American Fur Trade of the Far West.* 2 vols. Stanford CA: Academic Reprints, 1954.

Clark, Ella E. *Indian Legends of the Pacific Northwest.* Berkeley: University of California Press, 1953.

———. "Watkuese and Lewis and Clark." *Western Folklore* 12 (1953): 175–78.

Clark, Robert Carlton. *History of the Willamette Valley, Oregon.* 3 vols. Chicago: S. J. Clarke, 1927.

Cocks, James Fraser. "The Selfish Savage: Protestant Missionaries and Nez Perce and Cayuse Indians, 1835–1847." Ph.D. diss., University of Michigan, 1975.

Conforti, Joseph A. "Jonathan Edwards's Most Popular Work: *The Life of David Brainerd* and Nineteenth-Century Evangelical Culture." *Church History* 54 (June 1985): 28–50.

Cox, Ross. *The Columbia River; or, Scenes and Adventures during a Residence of Six Years on the Western Side of the Rocky Mountains.* Edited by Edgar I. Stewart and Jane R. Stewart. Norman: University of Oklahoma Press, 1957.

Cressman, Luther Sheeleigh. *Prehistory of the Far West: Homes of Vanished Peoples.* Salt Lake City: University of Utah Press, 1977.

Crosby, Alfred. "Virgin Soil Epidemics as a Factor in the Aboriginal Depopulation of North America." *William and Mary Quarterly,* 3d ser., 33 (1976): 289–99.

Curtis, Edward S. *The North American Indian.* 12 vols. Norwood MA: Plimpton Press, 1911.

Daniels, John D. "The Indian Population of North America in 1492." *William and Mary Quarterly,* 3d ser., 49:2 (April 1992): 298–320.

Davis, W. L. "Peter John De Smet: The Journey of 1840." *Pacific Northwest Quarterly* 25:1 (spring 1944): 29–43, 121–42.

De Smet, Pierre Jean. *Life, Letters, and Travels of Father Pierre-Jean*

De Smet, S.J., 1801–1873. 4 vols. Edited by Hiram Martin Chitten-den and Alfred Talbot Richardson. New York: F. P. Harper, 1905.

———. *New Indian Sketches*. Fairfield WA: Ye Galleon Press, 1985.

Dickason, Olive Patricia. "A Historical Reconstruction for the North-western Plains." In *The Prairie West: Historical Readings*, edited by R. Douglas Francis and Howard Palmer, 39–57. Edmonton: University of Alberta Press, 1985.

Dixon, C. W. *Smallpox*. London: J. & A. Churchill, 1962.

Dobyns, Henry F. "Native American Trade Centers as Contagious Disease Foci." In *Disease and Demography in the Americas*, edited by John W. Verano and Douglas H. Ubelaker, 215–22. Washington DC: Smithsonian Institution Press, 1992.

Douglas, David. *Journal Kept by David Douglas during His Travels in North America, 1823–27*. London: W. Wesley & Son, 1914.

Drury, Clifford Merrill. *Chief Lawyer of the Nez Perces*. Glendale CA: Arthur H. Clark, 1979.

———. *Henry Harmon Spalding*. Caldwell ID: Caxton, 1936.

———. *Marcus and Narcissa Whitman and the Opening of Old Oregon*. 2 vols. Seattle: Pacific Northwest Parks & Forests Association, 1986.

———. "The Nez Perce 'Delegation' of 1831." *Oregon Historical Quarterly* 40 (1939): 283–87.

———. *Where Wagons Could Go: Narcissa Whitman and Eliza Spalding*. Lincoln: University of Nebraska Press, 1997.

———, ed. *The Diaries and Letters of Henry H. Spalding and Asa Bowen Smith relating to the Nez Perce Mission, 1838–1842*. Glendale CA: Arthur H. Clark, 1958.

———, ed. *First White Women over the Rockies: Diaries, Letters, and Biographical Sketches of the Six Women of the Oregon Mission Who Made the Overland Journey in 1836 and 1838*. 3 vols. Glendale CA: Arthur H. Clark, 1963–66.

———, ed. *Nine Years with the Spokane Indians: The Diary of Elkanah Walker*. Glendale CA: Arthur H. Clark, 1976.

DuBois, Cora. *The Feather Cult of the Middle Columbia*. Menasha WI: General Series in Anthropology, 1938.

Dunn, John. *History of the Oregon Territory and the British North American Fur Trade*. Philadelphia: G. B. Zieber, 1845.

Du Pratz, Antoine Le Page. *The History of Louisiana*. New Orleans: Pelican Press, 1947.

Dusenberry, Verne. "Visions among the Pend d'Oreille Indians." *Ethnos* 1–2:24 (1962): 52–57.

Edwards, Jonathan. *The Life of David Brainerd*. New Haven CT: Yale University Press, 1985.

Edwards, Philip Leget. *The Diary of Philip Leget Edwards*. Fairfield WA: Ye Galleon Press, 1989.

Eels, Myron. *Father Eels; or, The Results of Fifty-five Years of Missionary Labors in Washington and Oregon*. Boston: Congregational Sunday School, 1894.

Fahey, John. *The Flathead Indians*. Norman: University of Oklahoma Press, 1974.

Fast, Vera Kathrin. "The Protestant Missionary and Fur Trade Society: Initial Contact in the Hudson's Bay Territory, 1820–1850." Ph.D. diss., University Of Manitoba, 1984.

Fleming, R. Harvey, ed., *Minutes of the Council, Northern Department of Rupert Land, 1821–31*. Toronto: Champlain Society, 1940.

Foxe, John. *Fox's Book of Martyrs*. New York: W. Borradaile, 1829.

Franchère, Gabriel. *Journal of a Voyage to the Northwest Coast of North America during the Years 1811, 1812, 1813, and 1814*. Edited by W. Kaye Lamb. Toronto: Champlain Society, 1969.

Fraser, Simon. *The Letters and Journals of Simon Fraser, 1806–1808*. Edited by W. Kaye Lamb. Toronto: Pioneer, 1960.

Frey, Rodney, ed. *Stories That Make the World: Oral Literature of the Indian Peoples of the Inland Northwest*. Norman: University of Oklahoma Press, 1995.

Gairdner, Meredith. "Notes of the Geography of the Columbia River." *Journal of the Royal Geographical Society* 11 (1841): 250–57.

Garraghan, Gilbert J. *The Jesuits of the Middle United States*. 3 vols. New York: America Press, 1938.

Gass, Patrick. *Gass's Journal of the Lewis and Clark Expedition*. Chicago: A. C. McClurg, 1904.

Gibson, James R. *Farming the Frontier: The Agricultural Opening of the Oregon Country, 1786–1848*. Seattle: University of Washington Press, 1985.

———. *Otter Skins, Boston Ships, and China Goods: The Maritime Fur Trade of the Northwest Coast, 1785–1841*. Montreal: McGill-Queen's University Press, 1992.

Gill, Sam. *Mother Earth: An American Story*. Chicago: University of Chicago Press, 1987.

Glazebrook, G. P. T., ed. *The Hargrave Correspondence, 1821–1843*. Toronto: Champlain Society, 1938.

Grabert, Garland F. "Early Fort Okanagon: Euro-American Impact on the Historic Okanagon Indians." In *Historical Archaeology in*

Northwestern North America, edited by Ronald M. Getty and Knut R. Fladmark, 109–25. Calgary: University of Calgary Press, 1973.

———. "Prehistoric Cultural Stability in the Okanagon Valley of Washington and British Columbia." Ph.D. diss., University of Washington, 1970.

Gray, William H. *A History of Oregon, 1792–1849.* Portland OR: Harris & Holman, 1870.

———. *William H. Gray: Journal of His Journey East, 1836–37.* Fairfield WA: Ye Galleon Press, 1980.

Green, Jonathan S. *Journal of a Tour of the North West Coast of America in the Year of 1829.* New York: C. F. Heartman, 1915.

Grim, John A. "Cosmogony and the Winter Dance." *Journal of Religious Ethics* 20:2 (fall 1992): 389–413.

Griswold, Gillette. "Aboriginal Patterns of Trade between the Columbia Basin and the Northern Plains." M.A. thesis, Montana State University, 1954.

Gunkel, Alexander. "Culture in Conflict: A Study of Contrasted Interrelations and Reactions between Euroamericans and the Wallawalla Indians of Washington State." Ph.D. diss., Southern Illinois University, 1978.

Gwydir, R. D. "Prehistoric Spokane—An Indian Legend." *Washington Historical Quarterly* 1:2 (January 1907): 136–37.

Haines, Francis. "The Northward Spread of Horses among the Plains Indians." *American Anthropologist* 40:3 (July–September 1938): 429–37.

———. "Where Did the Plains Indians Get Their Horses?" *American Anthropologist* 40:1 (January–March 1938): 112–17.

Hall, Gordon. *The Conversion of the World; or, The Claims of Six Hundred Millions and the Ability and the Duty of the Churches respecting Them.* Andover MA: Flagg & Gould, 1818.

Hanley, Philip M. *History of the Catholic Ladder.* Fairfield WA: Ye Galleon Press, 1993.

Hanzeli, Victor Egon. *Missionary Linguistics in New France: A Study of Seventeenth- and Eighteenth-Century Descriptions of American Indian Languages.* Janua Linguarum, Series Major 29. The Hague, 1969.

Henige, David. "Their Numbers Become Thick: Native American Historical Demography as Expiation." In *The Invented Indian: Cultural Fictions and Government Policies*, edited by James A. Clifton, 169–92. New Brunswick NJ: Transaction, 1990.

Henry, Alexander. *New Light on the Early History of the Greater*

Northwest: The Manuscript Journals of Alexander Henry. 3 vols. Edited by Elliot Coues. New York: Francis P. Harper, 1897.

Hewes, Gordon Winant. "Aboriginal Use of Fishery Resources in Northwestern North America." Ph.D. diss., University of California, 1947.

Hill-Tout, Charles. "Report of the Ethnology of the Okanaken of British Columbia." *Journal of the Royal Anthropological Institute* (London) 41 (January–June, 1911): 130–61.

Hines, Gustavus. *A Voyage around the World: With a History of the Oregon Mission.* Buffalo: G. H. Derby, 1850.

History of the Pacific Northwest: Oregon and Washington. 2 vols. Portland OR: North Pacific History, 1889.

Holder, Preston. *The Hoe and the Horse on the Plains: A Study of Cultural Development among North American Indians.* Lincoln: University of Nebraska Press, 1970.

Howay, Frederic William. *Origin of the Chinook Jargon on the Northwest Coast.* Portland OR: Oregon Historical Quarterly, 1943.

Hulbert, Archer Butler, ed. *The Oregon Crusade: Across Land and Sea to Oregon.* Denver: Denver Public Library, 1935.

Hulkrantz, Ake. *Belief and Worship in Native North America.* Syracuse NY: Syracuse University Press, 1981.

Hunn, Eugene S. *Nch'i-Wana, "The Big River": Mid-Columbia Indians and Their Land.* Seattle: University of Washington Press, 1990.

Hunt, Wilson Price. *Overland Diary of Wilson Price Hunt.* Edited by C. Hoyt. Portland OR: Oregon Book Society, 1973.

Hutchison, William R. *Errand to the World: American Protestant Thought and Foreign Missions.* Chicago: University of Chicago Press, 1987.

Hyde, George. *Indians of the High Plains: From the Prehistoric Period to the Coming of the Europeans.* Norman: University of Oklahoma Press, 1959.

Irving, Washington. *The Adventures of Captain Bonneville, U.S.A., in the Rocky Mountains and the Far West.* Edited by Edgeley W. Todd. Norman: University of Oklahoma Press, 1986.

Jacobs, Melville. *Texts in Chinook Jargon.* Seattle: University of Washington Press, 1936.

Jessett, Thomas E. *Chief Spokane Garry, 1811–1892: Christian, Statesman, and Friend of the White Man.* Minneapolis: T. S. Denison, 1960.

Johnson, Donald R., and David H. Chance. "Presettlement Overharvest of Upper Columbia River Beaver Populations." *Canadian Journal of Zoology* 52:12 (December 1974): 1519–21.

Jones, Judith Ann. " 'Women Never Used to War Dance': Gender and Music in Nez Perce Culture Change." Ph.D. diss., Washington State University, 1995.

Josephy, Alvin M. *The Nez Perce Indians and the Opening of the Northwest.* New Haven CT: Yale University Press, 1965.

Kane, Paul. *Paul Kane's Frontier: Including Wanderings of an Artist among the Indians of North America.* Edited by J. Russell Harper. Toronto: University of Toronto Press, 1971.

Karamanski, Theodore J. "The Iroquois and the Fur Trade of the Far West." *Beaver* 312:4 (spring 1982): 4–13.

Kent, Susan. "Pacifism—a Myth of the Plateau." *Northwest Anthropological Research Notes* 14 (1980): 125–34.

Lansing, Ronald B. *Juggernaut: The Whitman Massacre Trial.* Sacramento: Ninth Judicial Circuit Historical Society, 1993.

Larocque, François. *The Journal of François Larocque.* Fairfield WA: Ye Galleon Press, 1981.

Layton, Thomas N. "Traders and Raiders: Aspects of Trans-basin and California Plateau Commerce, 1800–1830." *Journal of California and Great Basin Anthropology* 3:1 (1981): 127–37.

Lee, Jason. "The Diary of Jason Lee." *Oregon Historical Quarterly* 17 (1916): 116–46, 240–66, 397–430.

Lewis, William S. *The Case of Spokane Garry: Being a Brief Statement of the Principal Facts Connected with His Career.* Spokane WA: Cole, 1917.

Liberty, Margot. "Hell Came with Horses: Plains Indian Women in the Equestrian Era." *Montana: The Magazine of Western History* 32:3 (summer 1982): 10–19.

Liljeblad, Sven. "The Religious Attitude of the Shoshoni Indians." *Rendezvous: Idaho State Journal of Arts and Letters* 25:2 (spring 1990): 32–46.

Lyman, H. S. "Reminiscences of James Jory." *Quarterly of the Oregon Historical Society* 3:2 (June 1902): 271–86.

Mackenzie, Alexander. *The Journals and Letters of Sir Alexander Mackenzie.* Edited by W. Kaye Lamb. Cambridge: Cambridge University Press, 1970.

Malouf, Carling. "The Cultural Connections between the Prehistoric Inhabitants of the Upper Missouri and Columbia River Systems." Ph.D. diss., Columbia University, 1956.

Malouf, Carling, and Thain White. "Recollections of Lasso Stasso." In *Anthropology and Sociology Papers,* vol. 12, edited by Carling Malouf, 2–3. Missoula: Montana State University, 1952.

March, Kathryn. "Deer, Bears, and Blood: A Note on Nonhuman Ani-

mal Response to Menstrual Odor." *American Anthropologist* 82:1
(March 1980): 125–27.

McArthur, Norma. "The Demography of Primitive Populations." *Science* 167 (February 1970): 1097–1101.

McCoy, Genevieve. "Sanctifying the Self and Saving the Savage: The Failure of the ABCFM Oregon Mission and the Conflicted Language of Calvinism." Ph.D. diss., University of Washington, 1991.

———. "The Women of the ABCFM Oregon Mission and the Conflicted Language of Calvinism." *Church History* 64:1 (March 1995): 109–25.

McDonald, Archibald. *Peace River: A Canoe Voyage from Hudson's Bay to Pacific by George Simpson in 1828.* Edited by Malcolm McLeod. Rutland VT: Charles E. Tuttle, 1971.

McKevitt, Gerald. "Jesuit Missionary Linguistics in the Pacific Northwest: A Comparative Study." *Western Historical Quarterly* 21:3 (August 1990): 281–304.

McLean, John. *John McLean's Notes of a Twenty-Five Years' Service in the Hudson's Bay Territory.* Edited by W. S. Wallace. Toronto: Champlain Society, 1932.

McLoughlin, John. *John McLoughlin's Business Correspondence, 1847–48.* Edited by William R. Sampson. Seattle: University of Washington Press, 1973.

———. *The Letters of John McLoughlin from Fort Vancouver to the Governor and Committee: First Series, 1825–38.* Edited by E. E. Rich. Toronto: Champlain Society, 1941.

McNeill, William H. *Plagues and Peoples.* New York: Doubleday, 1976.

Medicine, Bea, and Pat Albers. *The Hidden Half: Studies of Plains Indian Women.* Washington DC: University Press of America, 1983.

Meinig, D. W. *The Great Columbia Plain: A Historical Geography, 1805–1910.* Seattle: University of Washington Press, 1968.

Mengarini, Gregory. *Recollections of the Flathead Mission.* Glendale CA: Arthur H. Clark, 1977.

Merrell, James H. *The Indians' New World: Catawbas and Their Neighbors from European Contact through the Era of Removal.* New York: W. W. Norton, 1989.

M'Gillivray, Duncan. *The Journal of Duncan M'Gillivray of the Northwest Company at Fort George on the Saskatchewan, 1794–5.* Fairfield WA: Ye Galleon Press, 1989.

Miller, Christopher. " 'After That the World Will Fall to Pieces': An Ethnohistorical Analysis of Indian-White Contact on the Pacific Northwest Frontier." Ph.D. diss., University of California, 1981.

———. *Prophetic Worlds: Indians and Whites on the Columbia Plateau.* New Brunswick NJ: Rutgers University Press, 1985.

Miller, Christopher, and George R. Hammell. "A New Perspective on Indian-White Contact: Cultural Symbols and Colonial Trade." *Journal of American History* 73 (1986): 311–28.

Minto, John. "Reminiscences of Experiences on the Oregon Trail in 1844." *Quarterly of the Oregon Historical Society* 2:2–3 (1901): 117–67, 209–54.

Moodie, D. Wayne. "Indian Maps." In *Historical Atlas of Canada.* Vol. 1, *From the Beginning to 1800,* edited by R. Cole Harris, plate 59. Toronto: University of Toronto Press, 1987.

Morgan, Lewis Henry. "Indian Migrations." *North American Review* 109:2 (1869):33–82.

Morice, A. G. *The History of the Northern Interior of British Columbia.* Toronto: W. Briggs, 1904.

Moulton, Gary E., ed. *The Journals of the Lewis and Clark Expedition.* 8 vols. Lincoln: University of Nebraska Press, 1983.

Mourning Dove. *Coyote Tales.* Caldwell ID: Caxton, 1933.

———. *Mourning Dove: A Salishan Autobiography.* Edited by Jay Miller. Lincoln: University of Nebraska Press, 1990.

Murdock, George Peter. "The Tenino Indians." *Ethnology: An International Journal of Cultural and Social Anthropology* 19:2 (April 1980): 129–50.

New York Daily Tribune, March 29, 1843.

Nicks, Trudy. "The Iroquois and the Fur Trade in Western Canada." In *Old Trails and New Directions: Papers of the Third North American Fur Trade Conference,* edited by Carol M. Judd and Arthur J. Ray, 85–101. Toronto: University of Toronto Press, 1980.

Nicolay, C. G. *The Oregon Territory: A Geographical and Physical Account.* London: Charles Knight, 1846.

Nisbet, Jack. *Sources of the River: Tracking David Thompson across Western North America.* Seattle: Sasquatch, 1994.

Ogden, Peter Skene. *Traits of American Indian Life and Character, by a Fur Trader.* San Francisco: Grabhorn Press, 1933.

Oliphant, J. Orin. "George Simpson and Oregon Missions." *Pacific Historical Review* 6 (1937): 213–48.

Olsen, Loran. "The Power of Song: Native Music in the Northwest." *Idaho Yesterdays* 39:2 (summer 1995): 3–11.

Ought I Become a Missionary to the Heathen? Missionary Paper 15. American Board of Commissioner for Foreign Missions, 183?.

Palladino, L. B. "Historical Notes on the Flatheads." *Indian Sentinel* (October 1919).

———. *Indian and White in the Northwest: A History of Catholicity in Montana, 1831–91.* Lancaster PA: Wickersham, 1922.

Pambrun, Andrew Dominique. *Sixty Years on the Frontier in the Pacific Northwest.* Fairfield WA: Ye Galleon Press, 1978.

Parker, Samuel. *Journal of an Exploring Tour beyond the Rocky Mountains.* Moscow: University of Idaho Press, 1990.

Parkman, Francis. *The Oregon Trail,* ftp://uiarchive.cso.uiuc.edu/pub/etext/gutenberg/etext97/ortrl10.txt (August 1997).

Payne, Michael, and Gregory Thomas. "Literacy, Literature, and Libraries in the Fur Trade." *Beaver* 313:4 (1983): 44–54.

Peterson, Jacqueline. *Sacred Encounters: Father De Smet and the Indians of the Rocky Mountain West.* Norman: University of Oklahoma Press, 1993.

Phillips, Clifton Jackson. *Protestant America and the Pagan World: The First Half Century of the American Board of Commissioners for Foreign Missions, 1810–1860.* Cambridge MA: Harvard University Press, 1969.

Phinney, Archie. *Nez Perce Texts.* New York: Columbia University Press, 1934.

Point, Nicolas. *Wilderness Kingdom: Indian Life in the Rocky Mountains, 1840–1847.* Translated by Joseph P. Donnelly. New York: Holt, Rinehart, & Wilson, 1967.

Prucha, Francis Paul. "Two Roads to Conversion: Protestant and Catholic Missionaries in the Pacific Northwest." *Pacific Northwest Quarterly* 79:4 (October 1988): 130–37.

Quaife, Milton Milo, ed. *The Journals of Captain Meriwether Lewis and Sergeant John Ordway, Kept on the Expedition of Western Exploration.* Madison: State Historical Society of Wisconsin, 1965.

Ramenofsky, Ann F. *Vectors of Death: The Archaeology of European Contact.* Albuquerque: University of New Mexico Press, 1987.

Ramsey, Jarold. "The Bible in Western Indian Mythology." *Journal of American Folklore* (October—December 1977): 442–54.

Raufer, Maria Ilma. *Black Robes and Indians on the Last Frontier: A Study of Heroism.* Milwaukee: Bruce, 1966.

Ray, Verne F. *Cultural Relations in the Plateau of Northwestern America.* Los Angeles: Southwestern Museum, 1939.

———. *Sanpoil and Nespelem: Salishan Peoples of Northeastern Washington.* New Haven CT: Human Relations Area Files, 1954.

Rich, E. E., ed. *Cumberland House Journals and Inland Journal, 1775–82.* 2 vols. London: Hudson's Bay Company Record Society, 1951–52.

Riddington, Robin. "Technology, World View, and Adaptive Strategy in a Northern Hunting Society." *Canadian Review of Sociology and Anthropology* 19:4 (November 1982): 469–81.

Ronda, James P. *Lewis and Clark among the Indians.* Lincoln: University of Nebraska Press, 1984.

Roscoe, Will. "Bibliography of Berdache and Alternative Gender Roles among North American Indians." *Journal of Homosexuality* 14:3–4 (1987): 81–171.

Ross, Alexander. *Adventures of the First Settlers on the Oregon or Columbia River, 1810–1813.* Lincoln: University of Nebraska Press, 1986.

———. *The Fur Hunters of the Far West.* Edited by Kenneth Spalding. Norman: University of Oklahoma Press, 1956.

Ross, Richard E., and David Brauner. "The Northwest as Prehistoric Region." In *Regionalism and the Pacific Northwest,* edited by William Robbins, 99–108. Corvallis: Oregon State University Press, 1983.

Ruby, Robert H. and John A. Brown. *The Cayuse Indians: Imperial Tribesmen of Old Oregon.* Norman: University of Oklahoma Press, 1972.

———. *Dreamer-Prophets of the Columbia Plateau: Smohalla and Skolaskin.* Norman: University of Oklahoma Press, 1989.

———. *Indian Slavery in the Pacific Northwest.* Spokane: Arthur H. Clark, 1993.

———. *Indians of the Pacific Northwest: A History.* Norman: University of Oklahoma Press, 1981.

———. *The Spokane Indians: Children of the Sun.* Norman: University of Oklahoma Press, 1970.

Russell, Terry, ed. *Messages from the President on the State of the Fur Trade, 1824–32.* Fairfield WA: Ye Galleon Press, 1985.

Salisbury, Neal. *Manitou and Providence: Indians, Europeans, and the Making of New England, 1500–1643.* New York: Oxford University Press, 1982.

Sapir, Edward. *Wishram Texts: Together with Wasco Tales and Myths.* Leyden PA: American Ethnological Society, 1909.

Scalberg, Daniel A. "Seventeenth and Early Eighteenth-Century Perception of *Coureur de Bois* Religious Life." *Proceedings of the Annual Meeting of the Western Society for French History* 17 (1990): 82–91.

Secoy, Frank Reymond. *Changing Military Patterns on the Great Plains.* Locust Valley NY: J. J. Augustin, 1953.

Seltice, Joseph. *Saga of the Coeur d'Alene Indians.* Edited by Edward J.

Kowrach and Thomas E. Connolly. Fairfield wa: Ye Galleon Press, 1990.

Simmons, William S. *Spirit of the New England Tribes: Indian History and Folklore, 1620–1984.* Hanover nh: University Presses of New England, 1986.

Simpson, George. *Fur Trade and Empire: George Simpson's Journal Entitled "Remarks Connected with the Fur Trade in the Course of a Voyage from York Factory to Fort George and Back to York Factory, 1824–25".* Edited by Frederick Merk. Cambridge ma: Harvard University Press, 1968.

———. *Journal of Occurrences in the Athabasca Department by George Simpson, 1820–1821, and Report.* Edited by E. E. Rich. Toronto: Champlain Society, 1938.

———. *Narrative of a Journey Round the World.* 2 vols. London: H. Colburn, 1847.

———. *Part of a Dispatch from Sir George Simpson, Esquire, Governor of Rupert's Land to the Governor and Committee of the Hudson's Bay Company in London.* Edited by E. E. Rich and W. Steward Wallace. Toronto: Champlain Society, 1947.

Skeels, Dell Roy. "Style in the Unwritten Literature of the Nez Perce Indians." Ph.D. diss., University of Washington, 1949.

Slickpoo, Allen P. *Noon Nee-Me-Poo (We, the Nez Perces): Culture and History of the Nez Perces.* Lapwai id: Nez Perce Tribe, 1973.

———. *Nu Mee Poom Tit Wah Tit (Nez Perce Legends).* Lapwai id: Nez Perce Tribe, 1972.

Snow, Dean R. "Disease and Population Decline in the Northeast." In *Disease and Demography in the Americas,* edited by John W. Verano and Douglas H. Ubelaker, 177–86. Washington dc: Smithsonian Institution Press, 1992.

Spier, Leslie. *The Prophet Dance of the Northwest and Its Derivatives.* Menasha wi: George Banta, 1935.

———. *The Sinkaietk or Southern Okanagon of Washington.* Menasha wi: American Anthropological Association, 1938.

Spier, Leslie, and Edward Sapir. *Wishram Ethnography.* Seattle: University of Washington Press, 1930.

Spier, Leslie, Melville J. Herskovits, and Wayne Suttles. "Comment on Aberle's Thesis of Deprivation." *Southwestern Journal of Anthropology* 15:1 (spring 1959): 84–88.

Spinden, Herbert Joseph. *The Nez Perce Indians.* Lancaster pa: New Era, 1908.

Splawn, A. J. *Ka-mi-akin: The Last Hero of the Yakimas.* Portland wa: Kilham, 1917.

Sprague, Roderick. "Aboriginal Burial Practices on the Plateau Region of North America." Ph.D. diss., University of Arizona, 1967.

———. "Plateau Shamanism and Marcus Whitman." *Idaho Yesterdays* (spring—summer 1987): 55–56.

Spry, Irene. "Routes through the Rockies." *Beaver* 294:3 (autumn 1963): 26–39.

Stapp, Darby. "Copper Artifacts from the Upper Columbia River Region, Northeast Washington." In *Kettle Falls 1978: Further Archeological Excavations in Lake Roosevelt*, edited by David H. Chance and Jennifer V. Chance, 365–85. Moscow: University of Idaho Press, 1985.

Stern, Theodore. *Chiefs and Change in the Oregon Country.* Corvallis: Oregon State University Press, 1996.

———. *Chiefs and Chief Traders: Indian Relations at Fort Nez Perces, 1818–1855.* Corvallis: Oregon State University Press, 1993.

Stevens, Isaac Ingalls. *Report of Exploration of a Route for the Pacific Railroad.* Washington DC: United States Government, 1855.

———. *Reports of Explorations and Surveys, to Ascertain the Most Practicable and Economical Route for a Railroad from the Mississippi River to the Pacific Ocean.* 12 vols. Washington DC: Thomas A. Ford, 1860.

Strong, Emory M. *Stone Age on the Columbia River.* Portland OR: Binfords & Mort, 1959.

Stuart, Robert. *The Discovery of the Oregon Trail: Robert Stuart's Narrative of His Overland Trip Eastward from Astoria in 1812–13.* Edited by Philip Aston Rollins. New York: Edward Eberstadt & Sons, 1935.

———. *On the Oregon Trail: Robert Stuart's Journey of Discovery.* Edited by Kenneth A. Spaulding. Norman: University of Oklahoma Press, 1953.

Swagerty, William R. "Protohistoric Trade in Western North America: Archaeological and Ethnohistorical Considerations." In *Columbian Consequences: The Spanish Borderlands in Pan-American Perspective*, edited by David Hurst Thomas, 471–99. Washington DC: Smithsonian Institution Press, 1989.

Teit, James A. "The Coeur d' Alenes." In *Coeur d'Alene, Flathead, and Okanagon Indians*, by Franz Boas and James Teit. Fairfield WA: Ye Galleon Press, 1985.

———. "Mythology of the Thompson Indians." *Memoirs of the American Museum of Natural History* 12 (1919): 199–416.

———. *Salishan Tribes of the Western Plateaus.* Washington DC: Government Printing Office, 1928.

————. *Traditions of the Thompson River Indians of British Colum-bia.* Lancaster PA: American Folk-Lore Society, 1898.

Thompson, David. *Narrative, 1784–1812.* Edited by Richard Glover. Toronto: Champlain Society, 1962.

Thornton, Russell. *American Indian Holocaust and Survival: A Pop-ulation History since 1492.* Norman: University of Oklahoma Press, 1987.

Thornton, Russell, Jonathan Warren, and Tim Miller. "Depopulation in the Southeast after 1492." In *Disease and Demography in the Americas,* edited by John W. Verano and Douglas H. Ubelaker, 187–95. Washington DC: Smithsonian Institution Press, 1992.

Thornton, Russell, Tim Miller, and Jonathan Warren. "American In-dian Population Recovery Following Smallpox Epidemics." *American Anthropologist* 93:1 (March 1991): 28–45.

Thwaites, Reuben Gold, ed. *The Original Journals of the Lewis and Clark Expedition, 1804–1806.* 8 vols. New York: Dodd, Mead, & Co., 1904–5.

Tolan, Providencia. *A Shining from the Mountains.* Montreal: Sisters of Providence, 1980.

Tolmie, William Fraser. *The Journals of William Fraser Tolmie, Physi-cian and Fur Trader.* Vancouver: Mitchell Press, 1963.

Townsend, Joan B. "Firearms against Native Arms: A Study in Com-parative Efficiencies with an Alaskan Example." *Arctic Anthropol-ogy* 20:2 (1983): 1–33.

Townsend, John Kirk. *Narrative of a Journey across the Rocky Moun-tains to the Columbia River.* Lincoln: University of Nebraska Press, 1978.

Trafzer, Clifford E., and Richard D. Sheuerman. *Renegade Tribe: The Palouse Indians and the Invasion of the Inland Pacific Northwest.* Pullman: Washington State University Press, 1986.

Tucker, Sarah. *Rainbow of the North: A Short Account of the Estab-lishment of Christianity in Rupert's Land.* London: James Nisbet, 1853.

Turney-High, Harry Holbert. *Ethnography of the Kutenai.* Menasha WI: American Anthropological Association, 1941.

————. *The Flathead Indians of Montana.* Menasha WI: American Anthropological Association, 1937.

United States Army Corps of Engineers. *Washington: An Environ-mental Atlas.* Washington DC: Government Printing Office, 1975.

United States Department of the Interior. *Letter from the Secretary of the Interior . . . in relation to the Early Labors of the Missionaries.* Fairfield WA: Ye Galleon Press, 1988.

Van Kirk, Sylvia. *Many Tender Ties: Women in Fur Trade Society, 1670–1870.* Norman: University of Oklahoma Press, 1983.

Vibert, Elizabeth. " 'The Natives Were Strong to Live': Reinterpreting Early-Nineteenth-Century Prophetic Movements in the Columbia Plateau." *Ethnohistory* 42:2 (spring 1995): 197–229.

———. "Trader's Tales: British Fur Traders' Narratives of the Encounter with Plateau Peoples, 1807–1846." Ph.D. diss., University of Oxford, 1993.

Victor, Francis Fuller. *The River of the West: Life and Adventure in the Rocky Mountains and Oregon.* Hartford CT: Columbian, 1870.

Walker, Deward E. *Conflict and Schism in Nez Perce Acculturation: A Study of Religion and Politics.* Moscow: University of Idaho Press, 1985.

———. *Mutual Crossutilization of Economic Resources in the Plateau: An Example from Aboriginal Nez Perce Fishing Practices.* Pullman: Washington State University Press, 1967.

———. "New Light on the Prophet Dance Controversy." *Ethnohistory* 16:3 (1969): 245–55.

———. "Plateau: Nez Perce." In *Witchcraft and Sorcery of the Native American Peoples,* edited by Deward Walker, 113–40. Moscow: University of Idaho Press, 1989.

Walker, Philip, and John Johnson, "The Decline of the Chumash Indian Population." In *In the Wake of Contact: Biological Responses to Conquest,* edited by Clark Spencer Larsen and George R. Milner, 109–20. New York: Wiley-Liss, 1994.

Weis, Paul L. *The Channeled Scablands of Eastern Washington: The Geological Story of the Spokane Flood.* Cheney WA: Eastern Washington University Press, 1989.

Weisel, George F. "Ten Animal Myths of the Flathead Indians." In *Anthropology and Sociology Papers,* vol. 18, edited by Carling Malouf, 2–5. Missoula: Montana State University, 1954.

Weist, Katherine. "Plains Indian Women: An Assessment." In *Anthropology on the Great Plains,* edited by Raymond Wood and Margot Liberty, 255–71. Lincoln: University of Nebraska Press, 1980.

West, John. *The Substance of a Journal during a Residence at the Red River Colony, British North America.* London: L. B. Seely & Son, 1827.

White, Bruce M. "Encounters with Spirits: Ojibwa and Dakota Theories about the French and Their Merchandise." *Ethnohistory* 41:3 (summer 1994): 369–406.

———. "The Fear of Pillaging: Economic Folktales of the Great Lakes Fur Trade." In *The Fur Trade Revisited: Selected Papers of the Sixth*

North American Fur Trade Conference, 199–216. Edited by Jennifer S. H. Brown, W. J. Eccles, and Donald P. Heldman. Lansing: Michigan State University Press, 1991.

White, Thain. " 'Firsts' among the Flathead Lake Kutenai, as Told to Thain White." In *Anthropology and Sociology Papers*, vol. 8, edited by Carling Malouf, 2–4. Missoula: Montana State University, 1952.

———. "Scarred Trees in Western Montana." In *Anthropology and Sociology Papers*, vol. 17, edited by Carling Malouf, 1–5. Missoula: Montana State University, 1954.

Whitman, Narcissa. *The Letters of Narcissa Whitman*. Fairfield WA: Ye Galleon Press, 1986.

Wilkes, Charles. *Narrative of the United States Exploring Expedition during the Years 1838, 1839, 1840, 1841, 1842*. 5 vols. Philadelphia: Lee & Blanchard, 1845.

Williams, Joseph. *Narrative of a Tour from the State of Indiana to the Oregon Territory in the Years 1841–1842*. Cincinnati: J. B. Wilson, 1843.

Williams, Walter L. *The Spirit and the Flesh: Sexual Diversity in American Indian Culture*. Boston: Beacon Press, 1986.

Wilson, Charles. "Report on the Indian Tribes Inhabiting the Country in the Vicinity of the 49th Parallel of North Latitude." *Transactions of the Ethnological Society of London* 4 (1866): 275–322.

Wood, W. Raymond. "Plains Trade in Prehistoric and Protohistoric Intertribal Relations." In *Anthropology on the Great Plains*, edited by W. Raymond Wood and Margot Liberty, 98–109. Lincoln: University of Nebraska Press, 1980.

Work, John. *The Journal of John Work: A Chief Trader of the Hudson's Bay Company during His Expedition from Vancouver to the Flatheads and Blackfeet of the Pacific Northwest*. Edited by William S. Lewis and Paul C. Phillips. Cleveland: Arthur C. Clark, 1923.

———. "The Journal of John Work: July 5—September 15, 1826." Edited by T. C. Eliot. *Washington Historical Quarterly* 6:1 January 1915): 26–49.

Wyeth, John B. *Oregon; or, A Short History of a Long Journey*. Edited by Reuben Gold Thwaites. New York: A.M.S. Press, 1966.

Wyeth, Nathaniel Jarvis. *The Correspondence and Journals of Captain Nathaniel J. Wyeth, 1831–1836*. Edited by F. G. Young. Eugene: Oregon University Press, 1899.

———. *Journal of Captain Nathaniel J. Wyeth's Expeditions to the Oregon Country*. Fairfield WA: Ye Galleon Press, 1984.

Index

Early view of Kettle Falls. Thousands of Indians gathered at the falls each summer to capture the salmon that were the staple of plateau life. Reproduced from Stevens, *Report of Exploration of a Route for the Pacific Railroad.* Courtesy of Eastern Washington University.

On the Columbia Plateau, hunting and gathering food were communal affairs, organized by a leader known to have the appropriate spirit power for the task. Here a duck chief leads a hunt. Courtesy of Midwest Jesuit Archives (RMS IX C9-41).

Fort Walla Walla in the 1840s. Note the protective palisade around the fort and the close proximity of the Indian dwellings. Trading posts like this one offered the Indians more than trinkets and tobacco; they were windows into the spiritual world of the whites. Reproduced from Stevens, *Report of Exploration of a Route for the Pacific Railroad.* Courtesy of Eastern Washington University.

Plateau Indians teach one another the gospel in this idealized painting of a Catholic mission. Adults study pictures of biblical events, while a group of children reviews a Catholic ladder that shows the steps to heaven. The sacred heart of Jesus illuminates the scene. Painting by Père Nicolas Point, S.J. Courtesy of Archives de la Compagnie de Jésus Province du Canada-français (ASJCF), Saint-Jérôme.

A Jesuit missionary consecrates some Indians' weapons before a hunt. Plateau natives expected that the spirit power of the whites would work in ways analogous to their traditional faith—but would be more effective. Courtesy of Midwest Jesuit Archives (RMS IX C9–82).